Meet the Boone boys: Bob, Bret, Ray, and Aaron (left to right) on Family Day at Philadelphia's Veterans Stadium in the '70s.

HOME GAME

☆ ☆ ☆

Big-League Stories from

My Life in Baseball's

First Family

Bret Boone and Kevin Cook

CROWN
ARCHETYPE
NEW YORK

Photography credits appear on page 253.

Library of Congress Cataloging-in-Publication Data
Names: Boone, Bret, 1969– | Cook, Kevin, 1956–
Title: Home game : [Big-League stories from my life in baseball's First Family] /
Bret Boone and Kevin Cook.
Description: First Edition. | New York : Crown Archetype, [2016]
Identifiers: LCCN 2015046664 | ISBN 9781101904909 | ISBN 9781101904916
(Ebook)
Subjects: LCSH: Boone, Bret, 1969– | Baseball players—United States—
Biography. | Baseball players—Family relationships—United States.
Classification: LCC GV865.B67 A3 2016 | DDC 796.357092—dc23 LC record
available at http://lccn.loc.gov/2015046664

ISBN 978-1-101-90490-9
eBook ISBN 978-1-101-90491-6

Printed in the United States of America

Jacket design by Elena Giavaldi

10 9 8 7 6 5 4 3 2 1

First Edition

THIS BOOK IS ABOUT FAMILY. IT'S DEDICATED TO MY FAMILY, STARTING WITH PATRIARCH RAY BOONE AND HIS WIFE, OUR MATRIARCH, PATSY BOONE. IT'S ALSO FOR MY PARENTS, BOB AND SUE, MY BROTHER AARON AND HIS FAMILY, MY BROTHER MATT, AND ALL OF MY CHILDREN: SAVANNAH, JACOB, ISAIAH, AND JUDAH.

CONTENTS

WARM-UP: *He's Got the Look*   1

1   *Meet the Boones*   5

2   *My First Parade*   17

3   *Growing Up Boone*   33

4   *The Littlest Phillie*   45

5   *The Education of a Ballplayer*   59

6   *The Old College Try*   75

7   *You Fight Your Way Up*   87

8   *The Rookie*   101

9   *Red Alert*   113

10   *An Intervention*   131

11   *Trade Bait*   147

Contents

12   *The Boone Goes Boom*   159

13   *A Blast in the Bronx*   177

14   *Aaron, A-Rod, 'Roid Wrongs,
and Goodbyes*   193

15   *Comebacker*   211

16   *Game Changer*   223

Extra Inning: *Kid in a Cage*   243

Boone Family Stats   247

Acknowledgments   251

Photography Credits   253

Index   254

HOME GAME

HE'S GOT THE LOOK

There I was at third base, keeping an eye on the runner at second. Yelling at him.

"Jake, keep your head up!"

I was dressed in my usual dad uniform: shorts, a T-shirt, and flip-flops. I've been retired from the big leagues since 2005, so I wasn't playing that day—just helping out with my thirteen-year-old son's youth-league team, the Titans. I was coaching third base, and my buddy Trevor Hoffman—a seven-time All-Star closer for the Padres and Brewers—was across the diamond, coaching first. He had a son on the team, too. How many travel teams can say their base coaches had a total of thirty-two years in the big leagues?

Not that the kids cared about our has-been status. To them we were just Bret and Trevor, a couple of regular dads. That's the kind of team we had—no feuds, no fights, no egos. And no high-pressure parents. Baseball's hard enough without pain-in-the-ass parents making everybody miserable. So Trevor and I kept things loose. We made sure the Titans had fun on the field.

But still . . . there's such a thing as fundamentals. Once you take the field, you play to win. You play the game the right way.

That's why I was yelling at Jake. Just *reminding* him that there's a right way to run the bases, and there's a knucklehead way. The way he was wandering off second like a pee-wee leaguer wasn't the right way.

"Jake! Be aware out there! Where are the middle infielders?"

Too late. The catcher threw behind him. Picked him off easy.

Except that by the time the ball got to second, Jake was sliding into third. He'd outsmarted the catcher, decoyed him. Gained a base without hardly trying.

He dusted himself off and smiled at me. "Hi, Dad."

I admit I was impressed. I'd never taught him that move. I asked him, "How'd you know how to do that?"

He just shrugged. "Dad, isn't it obvious? They had nobody covering third."

Good instincts. You couldn't teach that if you tried.

That was a couple of years ago. Jake's fifteen now. He's a hell of a high school player for a freshman. Maybe he'll make the big leagues someday. If he does, Jake Boone will be the first fourth-generation player in major-league history.

Of course I'll love my son just as much if he winds up as a doctor or a lawyer or a Walmart greeter. But right now he wants to be a ballplayer, and I'm helping as much as I can, advising him on training, nutrition, motivation—everything. Sometimes he listens, and sometimes he just pretends to listen because he's a good kid who thinks his dad is the biggest baseball nerd in San Diego County, and maybe he's not so wrong about that.

Getting older, having a son who wants to play the game you love—that stuff makes you stop and think. It's so fun to see him on the field, and to see my dad in him, and my brother. I was always the fiery one, the one who wore his emotions on his sleeve. Jake's more like his grandpa Bob and his uncle Aaron. Smoother. Calmer. But he's still a Boone.

I don't have to tell Jake how special our family is. He's well aware of our lineage. It's the same thing I soaked up from my dad, who was still playing in the majors while I played high school and college ball. But my father never once pushed me to play the game he played. Now I'm trying to bring my kids up the same way. Whether or not Jake makes the big leagues, there are two things he knows for sure: he'll get no pressure from me, and I'll always be there for him, no matter what.

But there's something I can and do share with him—a love of the game that has been passed down in our family since his great-grandfather was growing up in the 1920s and '30s. Our family's story is a baseball story, one of the best in the game's long history, but it's about more than the national pastime. It's our family history, full of home runs and disappointments, big seasons and season-ending injuries, behind-the-scenes moments and across-the-dinner-table arguments. It's also packed with million-dollar mistakes, famous teammates, clubhouse traditions, and a hundred other things that are part of your life when big-league baseball's in your blood. Jake knows some, but nowhere near all, of the stories I'm about to tell—the adventures of his dad, a guy who loves the game his family has lived and breathed for more than eighty years. Now he'll hear the rest—and you will, too.

1
MEET THE BOONES

You could say I've got baseball in my blood.

My grandpa was a major-league player. He was also an All-Star. So was my dad. So was my brother. So was I. We're the baseball Boones, the first family ever to send three generations of ballplayers to the major leagues. The *only* family with three generations of All-Stars.

Not that I cared about that stuff when I became the first third-generation player in baseball history. I was more about me in those days. Do I have regrets? Sure. Was I intense? A little headstrong? Well, you don't hit .331 with 37 homers and 141 RBIs, like I did in 2001, if you're racked with self-doubt. So don't expect apologies. As you'll find out in this book, that's not something you're going to get from me.

A little wisdom, maybe—I like to think I've gained some of that. Injuries, age, a personal crisis or two, and the sheer, brutal difficulty of hitting in the big leagues—that'll humble any man who's paying attention, and smarten him up. In 1996 I batted .233 with only 12 homers, and I wasn't even hurt, just scuffling.

But you know what? I'm still headstrong. Opinionated for sure.

Today, coaching minor leaguers for the Oakland A's, I keep an eye out for young players who remind me of me. Kids who think they're *unstoppable*. Sure, they're naïve. For every hundred nineteen-year-old studs who think they're future Hall of Famers, ninety-nine end up with a ticket home to Bakersfield or Macon or Santo Domingo. Of course, I was just as cocky when I was nineteen. And without some of the screw-you watch-me attitude that got me to the big leagues, they've got no chance. In a game as demanding as pro baseball, you've gotta visualize. In the same way you picture the perfect swing before you hit the ball out of the park, you have to believe you're a star if you ever want to be one.

That's part of what this book is about: the mental and even spiritual side of baseball at the highest level. I've been there and done it. My whole family has. Big-league baseball is the Boone family business.

But it's a tough, tough business, and it gets tougher every year. That's another topic I'll hit in these pages—how the game keeps evolving, getting harder, getting better. (Don't tell my dad I said this, but if the stars of Gramps's era played today, they'd be average.) With help from my family and friends, old rivals and teammates, and some of today's top baseball minds, I'll delve into every level of the sport: hitting and fielding, coaching, scouting, training. How to win with grace and lose with class. How to be the right kind of baseball parent. How to help a son max out his talent. And we're just getting started.

Above all, this is a fan's book. If you're a baseball fan—and I'm guessing you are, since you picked up this book—I can help you enjoy the game even more. How? By helping you see a ballgame the way the pros do. Starting with three generations' worth of know-how. Let me introduce you to the baseball Boones.

Ray Boone, my grandfather, broke in with the Indians in 1948. A two-time All-Star, he led the American League with 116 RBIs—eight more than Yogi Berra—in 1955. His son Bob—my dad—outdid Gramps by making four All-Star teams in the 1970s and '80s. Dad used to catch Steve Carlton. He won a World Series in 1980, helping anchor a Philadelphia Phillies team starring Carlton, Mike Schmidt, and Pete Rose, and went on to manage the Royals and Reds.

In their time, Gramps and Dad were the best father-son duo in baseball history. (Some guys you may have heard of one-upped them after Dad retired, a couple of outfielders named Bonds and a couple more named Griffey.) Next came me and my brother Aaron, growing up in a house where baseball was practically all we talked about. And Aaron and I lived up to our name. We both made the Show. I had four or five of the best years any Boone ever had, and Aaron hit a home run no Yankees or Red Sox fan will ever forget. To this day, plenty of people in Boston think my little brother's full name is Aaron (fill in the blank)ing Boone.

All told, the Boones you'll meet in this book account for 58 big-league seasons, 10 All-Star appearances, 634 home runs, 3,139 RBIs, and 11 Gold Gloves. But stats don't tell the story. There are millions of memories, too, and we're still making them. Today, Dad's a vice president of the Washington Nationals. I'm a special advisor for the Oakland A's. Aaron's in the broadcast booth for ESPN, and our brother Matt, who played seven seasons in the minors before a back injury forced him to retire, runs Boone Action Turf, the family's artificial-turf company.

Home Game is about growing up with RBIs in your DNA. It's about how easy major-league baseball is, at least when you're hot. But it's also about how brutal the game can be when you're struggling. You're going to find out about the lessons I learned from my grandpa, my dad, and my brother, plus some things I learned from players who were better than me. Here's one: greatness is a lot subtler and more interesting than it looks.

I want to tell you some of the game's secrets. You're going to hear about famous names, games, and personalities. There will be bush-league bus trips, big-league luxury, and clubhouse feuds, as well as dugout and mound scenes to make *Bull Durham* look tame, postseason pressure, injuries, comebacks, and off-the-field crises. Drawing on eighty years of family history, I'll give you behind-the-scenes looks at Ted Williams, Dad's teammates Mike Schmidt, Steve Carlton, and Pete Rose, as well as Griffey, Jeter, Bonds, Maddux, Glavine, and Smoltz, and other stars and scrubs, including today's players. I'll also share some great Boone moments, like the night I was in the Fox TV booth at Yankee Stadium, calling the 2003 American League Championship Series (ALCS), when Aaron beat Boston with his historic homer.

This is inside baseball like you've never seen it before. I'll address the biggest issues in the game: money, metrics, injuries, awards, replays, new rules, and more. This might be the only book I ever write, so I want it to be the best one I *can* write.

It starts first thing in the morning.

☆ ☆ ☆

When I was a toddler, my dad was catching for the Phillies, trying to help them win the first World Series in franchise history. Mom went to the park to see him play. So who was going to babysit Bret?

Gramps.

I used to knock around my grandfather's house, watching ballgames with him. I remember the Phillies' red-pinstriped uniforms on the TV screen, and the weird green of the Veterans Stadium Astroturf. And how Gramps would doze off in his easy chair. He needed his sleep, because I was gonna wake him up at five in the morning.

"Ball, ball!"

That was my first word, *ball*. Hitting or throwing a baseball or Wiffle ball—that was about all I wanted to do from the time I was in diapers. You might say I was precocious. Adventurous. Okay, maybe obnoxious. As soon as I could walk, I invented a new game—chasing the lawnmower, trying to tackle it. Dad and Gramps forgave me because I was also smacking Wiffle balls over the house at the age of two.

"*Ball,* Grampa!"

Gramps would drag himself out of bed and we'd go for a catch while the sun came up. My six-foot grandfather seemed super-tall to me. He seemed super-old, too, at least one hundred years old if not two hundred, with his graying hair and creaky knees. He was actually young for a grandfather, not even fifty when I was a toddler. (The Boones tend to marry young and have kids early.) But he was a patriarch. That's what Dad called him, *the patriarch.* I had no idea what that meant. I was doing pretty good to remember *ball.* Was a patriarch a kindly old man who snoozed through the ten o'clock news? A gimpy-kneed senior citizen who liked vanilla ice cream?

Later I found out that he was a lot more than that. Our patriarch was a hell of a player in his time, a time that began in San Diego almost one hundred years ago.

Raymond Otis Boone was born in 1923. He was the son of a woodworker who built walls on construction sites. According to family lore, he was a descendant of Daniel Boone, which makes me one, too.

San Diego was a small town in the 1920s. Electric streetcars rolled down Broadway, clanging past Model-T Fords and a few men on horseback. The new San Diego & Arizona Railway, an engineering miracle called "the Impossible Railroad," with its wooden bridges across desert gulleys and canyons, had connected the city to the rest of America in 1919. Four years later, the year Gramps was born, a local businessman gave a speech. "What is the matter with San Diego?" he asked. "Why is it not the metropolis and seaport that its geography and other advantages entitle it to be? Why does San Diego always just miss the train, somehow?" Maybe because people thought the city 120 miles up the coast was bigger and better. San Diego was growing—from a population of 74,000 in 1920 to 148,000 in 1930—but that didn't seem like much when Los Angeles had 1.2 million.

Gramps grew up in the Great Depression. He learned carpentry, his father's trade. But once he got his hands on a piece of lumber, all he really wanted to do was swing it at a ball. The major leagues were thousands of miles away—they wouldn't reach California until the Brooklyn Dodgers and New York Giants moved west in 1958. During his boyhood the nearest big-league teams were in St. Louis, the majors' far western outpost. But even if nobody knew it, San Diego was starting to be a baseball town. The weather was perfect year-round, and Ray had a local hero to follow, a kid who could outhit any of the American League's St. Louis Browns, and maybe even the St. Louis Cardinals' great Stan Musial.

His name was Ted Williams.

My grandpa loved and respected his father, but Ted Williams was the only man he ever put on a pedestal. A rangy left-handed-hitting outfielder, five years older than Gramps, he was the best ballplayer San Diego ever produced, maybe the best hitter ever. Ted Williams graduated from San Diego's Hoover High School in 1937, the year before Gramps's freshman year there. By then Williams, the "Splendid Splinter," was already a legend. Gramps and his friends used to ride their bikes to see Williams play high school games. In his junior year at Hoover, he batted .583. The New York Yankees offered him $200 a month to turn pro, but his mother didn't want her son to play so far from home, so he signed with a local semipro outfit for $3 a week. Two years later he signed with the Red Sox, who shipped the nineteen-year-old Splinter to the minor-league Minneapolis Millers. But you couldn't keep Ted Williams in the minors for long. The Millers' only teenager batted .366 with 43 homers. A year later, as a twenty-one-year-old rookie with the 1939 Red Sox, he hit .327 with 31 homers and 145 RBIs.

By then Gramps was a sophomore at Hoover High. He made the varsity team as a catcher and wound up signing a pro contract with a scout for the Cleveland Indians. It was 1942. The Indians sent him to Wisconsin to catch for the Class-C Wausau Timberjacks. This was the low minors. The *low* low minors. It wasn't a glamorous job. At the time, playing pro baseball was like being a circus performer: exciting, maybe, but the pay was lousy and respectable people thought the players were a little shady. Nice girls didn't date baseball players. Gramps was lonely so far from home, but he still batted .306 in his first pro season. He rode the Impossible Railroad back home and made a few dollars doing carpentry with his dad in the offseason. Then came World War II. In 1943, he enlisted in the navy. Like his hero Ted Williams, a fighter pilot who later served as wingman for future astronaut John Glenn, Gramps lost three baseball seasons to the war. Finally, in 1948, he reached the big leagues. And all he did was hit .400 in his rookie year.

Okay, it was a small sample—he had a single and a double in five at-bats at the end of the 1948 season—but that average sure looks good in the record books.

Gramps batted once in that year's World Series, facing the Boston Braves' future Hall of Famer Warren Spahn. He struck out. But Cleveland went on to win its first Series since 1920, and he soon settled in as the Indians' shortstop. Teammates called him "Ike" for his resemblance to an Ike Boone who played in the 1920s and '30s. Gramps hit just enough—a .301 average in 1950, .233 with 12 homers in 1951—to make fans forgive his erratic fielding. Remember, this was a catcher playing shortstop in the majors. But then, when the Indians finished two games behind the Yankees in 1952, some fans and sportswriters blamed his league-leading 33 errors.

"Many people in Cleveland think we ought to get rid of him," Indians general manager Hank Greenberg said. "Well, it's easy to say a player had a bad season. It isn't so easy to find a fellow who is certain to do better."

There's nothing like a GM's vote of confidence to make a player start packing his bags. Halfway through the next season, Greenberg traded Gramps to Detroit.

Ray Boone was a family man by then. He'd married Patsy Brown, his high school sweetheart, after his 1946 season with the minor-league Wilkes-Barre Barons. He was twenty-three. Patsy was twenty-two. A year later she gave birth to a boy, Robert. My dad.

Dad tells me he was at the 1948 World Series, but he might have fallen asleep by the time Gramps struck out against Spahn. "I don't remember the game too well," he says. "I was eight months old."

We Boones are a pretty athletic bunch. Patsy, my grandmother, and her twin sister, Martha, were synchronized swimmers who swam with Esther Williams in the movies. Martha went on to be a golf pro. My great-aunt Betty was one of the best softball pitchers San Diego ever produced. My dad's sister Terry was a champion swimmer, and his brother Rod was a college baseball star who played Triple-A ball in the Astros and Royals organizations. And Dad's uncle George played guard for Navy and made the College Football Hall of Fame. The NFL wasn't much more than a minor league at the time, so George Brown went to medical school and became a doctor of some distinction. For one thing, he served as team physician for San Diego State University's sports teams. For another, he delivered me.

But we're not there yet. Twenty-some years before that, pre-schooler Bob Boone was going to work with his father, my Gramps. Dad remembers riding shotgun while Gramps drove down cobblestone streets toward Cleveland Municipal Stadium, and watching a man use giant tongs to pull a chunk of ice the size of a TV set off the back of his truck. People still had iceboxes in those days, the original fridges.

Gramps would park near the stadium, right on the street. His son didn't know much about his job yet—Dad was only four or five—but he could tell there was something special about it. They'd walk past fans who wanted to shake his dad's hand. These strangers would say, "Hiya Ray," or "Have a good game, Ray," and hand him programs or baseballs. He would write his name and they'd slap him on the back and say thanks like he was giving them a gift. And you know what? That's just what he was giving them—a moment with a guy who had the greatest job in the world.

That's how he thought of it, too. Gramps used to tell Dad how special it was to be a ballplayer, and Dad told his sons the same thing. "Never forget you're playing the best game in the world." That's something none of us ever forgot.

Gramps got traded to Detroit, and then to Kansas City, and then to the Chicago White Sox. Each trade uprooted him and his family, but they didn't complain. "It's all we knew. I figured everybody's dad might get traded," Dad says. "I got to see different cities and see all the greats up close. Ted Williams, Yogi Berra, Mickey Mantle. I was eleven when my father got traded to the Kansas City Athletics, and they let me work out with them. Roger Maris played right field for that team. Whitey Herzog was a substitute. Then Dad got traded to the White Sox, and I worked out at Comiskey Park. They gave me one of Nellie Fox's uniforms. It was big on me but not too big because Fox was a little guy. The 'Mighty Mite,' they called him."

The White Sox won the American League pennant that year. Early Wynn won 22 games and the Cy Young Award—and threw batting practice to my eleven-year-old dad.

In the mid-1950s, Gramps hit 20 or more home runs four seasons in a row. His fielding troubles disappeared after the Tigers moved him to third base. He drove in 114 runs in '53 and homered off Robin Roberts in the 1954 All-Star Game. He led the league with 116 RBIs in '55. Gramps earned $28,750 that year, which doesn't sound like much, but it was equal to about $200,000 today. Naturally he expected a raise after another All-Star season in '56. But when he went in to discuss his contract with Muddy Ruel, the Tigers' general manager, Ruel said, "Ray, we finished fifth last year. We could have finished fifth without you."

Like most players, Gramps didn't even have an agent. It would be another twenty years before free agency and million-dollar contracts turned .220 hitters into millionaires. In 1956, with no bargaining power and only two options—sign Ruel's contract or go home to San Diego—he signed.

How big a raise did the Tigers' All-Star third baseman get for hitting .308 with 25 homers the year before? He got a *pay cut* of $750.

His knees were almost shot by then. He batted .273 with 12 home runs in 1957, and .242 with 13 homers in '58, practically limping around the bases. A year later he was a bench player, a substitute first baseman. Managers now had someone pinch-run for him every chance they got. Gramps was hurting. When the Milwaukee Braves traded him to Boston in 1960, he pictured himself knocking doubles off the Green Monster—the left-field wall at Fenway Park. He'd always hit like hell at Fenway. But he was so broken down that he hit only one homer all year. Still, there was one thing he loved about that last season. One of his teammates on the 1960 Red Sox was Ted Williams, still playing left field at the age of forty-two—with an attitude, too.

Gramps wasn't like that, but he always respected Williams for being his own brash, supremely confident self at all times. He never forgot what Williams did back in 1941, the year he went into the last day of the season batting an even .400. Boston manager Joe Cronin wanted to give him the day off, but Ted said hell no. He played both games of a doubleheader, went 6-for-8, and finished at .406—the last player ever to bat .400. Gramps always called that the most impressive thing he ever saw in baseball. Twenty years later, he was thrilled to be Ted's teammate, even if it was near the end of the line for them both.

They did an old baseball exercise together. In those days players would drill a hole in a bat and knot a length of rope to the bat. They'd tie the other end of the rope to a ten-pound weight, then twist the bat, "reeling in" the weight till it touched the bat's barrel. "Builds up your forearms and hands," Williams said. Gramps loved spending time with his hero. He'd talk hitting with Williams while Ted went through his fan mail, and Gramps never forgot the offers Williams got for personal appearances. He'd hold up a letter and say, "Twenty-five thousand dollars to sign autographs." Then he'd wad up the letter and throw it away. "Can't do it. I'm goin' fishing." Gramps struggled to bat .205 in 1960, with that one lonesome home run at the age of thirty-seven, while Williams hit .316 with 29 homers at the age of forty-two. Then they both retired.

Gramps finished with a career batting average of .275, 151 home runs, and 737 RBIs. Not like his hero's .344, 521, and 1,839, maybe, but a damn fine career. And the Boones weren't finished. Not even close. For one thing, Ray's son Bob was already a Little League super-star.

2

MY FIRST PARADE

After his baseball career ended, Gramps couldn't imagine working a nine-to-five job. He'd been a ballplayer his whole life. After retiring in 1960 he signed on as a scout for the Red Sox, his last big-league team. At that point the job had nothing to do with radar guns, which wouldn't be invented for another fourteen years. In Ray Boone's day, scouting meant using your eyes, your experience, and your gut to tell the prospects from the suspects.

He signed some good players, but the best one grew up right there in the house where Gramps and Grandma Patsy raised their family. Their first son, Bob, was a straight-A student and multisport star at San Diego's Crawford High School. For a future pro athlete, Dad was pretty typical. Meaning great. Meaning *special*.

Do you remember the most popular guy at your high school? The student council president who excelled at every sport, throwing touchdown passes, pulling down rebounds, pitching perfect games, and dominating at the plate? The All-American hero? Well, that was my dad. I don't say that because we're family. I say it because that's the man he was and is. But you know what? The vast majority of high school heroes get weeded out long before they reach the professional ranks.

And yet, millions of parents watch their sons dominate the local Little League and assume their little guy is headed for the big leagues. They forget one thing: There aren't millions of spots on major-league rosters. There are 750. I'll come back to this topic later. For now, just bear in mind that practically everybody who plays pro ball was a total legend in high school. And you still never heard of 99 percent of them. It's *hard* to make a living playing baseball.

It's all about levels. At every level, from high school to the rookie leagues up to Double-A, Triple-A, and finally the majors, ferocious competition eliminates all but the most elite talent. By the time you reach the majors—or the NFL or the NBA or the PGA Tour—the very worst guy is a lot better than your typical high school hero.

Take Dad, for example. He starred at third base for Crawford High. He was also San Diego's best high school pitcher and the Crawford basketball team's star forward, not to mention an A student (which he likes to mention). Stanford University offered him a scholarship, but all he wanted was to play major-league baseball.

Gramps, being a Red Sox scout, asked him, "Would you sign with the Sox for thirty-five thousand dollars?" A small fortune, worth about $250,000 today.

Dad said, "Give me the paper. Where do I sign?"

But Gramps shook his head and told him to forget it—because Dad was going to college. He wanted his son to be a Stanford man. A smart man himself, he'd signed with the Indians right out of high school, and always he'd wished he'd had a college education. Gramps also knew that the odds were stacked against every high school hero who dreamed of making the majors. The smart play was taking the scholarship.

My dad pictured thirty-five thousand dollar bills scattered in the wind. *Four years of college*, he thought. *I'll be a creaky old man with gray hair by the time I get out.*

Actually, he only recently turned into a creaky old man with gray hair. But I know how he felt at that age. Impatient. Dying to prove himself in the pros. Every young ballplayer wants to start his trip to the majors today, if not sooner. But Dad listened to his father. He put his big-league dreams on hold, and headed north to Palo Alto.

At his first Stanford basketball practice, Crawford High's hoops star got a look at his college teammates. "We scrimmaged a little, and there was no doubt I was one of the worst guys on the team," Dad remembers. "I asked the coach if I could quit the team and focus on baseball. He looked relieved."

Dad had found his level in basketball. The weed whacker got him. Baseball was another story.

He played third base at Stanford for four years, and while his grades could have gotten him into medical school, he signed with the Philadelphia Phillies in 1969. "I got a twenty-five-thousand-dollar bonus," he says. Since that was ten thousand less than the Red Sox would have given him four years before, he figures, "I guess my college education cost me ten grand." He reported to the Raleigh-Durham Phillies of the Class A Carolina League in the summer of '69, the first summer when he could legally drink a beer. "The first surprise was how life in the minors was *worse* than college ball. I was making a hundred and twenty-five dollars a week, living on soup and hot dogs. My first minor-league uniform was so old and threadbare you could see my leg right through the pants. The ballpark lights were so bad you had to squint to see the pitcher. And I loved it because I was a professional baseball player."

Raleigh-Durham manager Nolan Campbell, a baseball lifer out of Weedpatch, California, took a look at the Boone kid's range at shortstop—basically one step left or right—and moved him to third base. Dad made 20 errors that year, reminding a few old-timers of Gramps in his early, error-prone days. But he also batted .300.

He was married by then. He and his high school sweetheart, Sue, not yet known as Mom, were teenagers when he popped the question after asking her father's permission. His proposal wasn't the smoothest. After a long dinner at San Diego's best restaurant, Mr. A's, he finally got up the nerve on the elevator to the parking garage.

"Here," he said, handing her an engagement ring. "Do you want to marry me?"

At her bridal shower, her friends all gave her girlie gifts: tea sets and frilly stuff. It was Grandma Patsy who gave her what Mom calls "the best gift I ever got." After twenty years married to Gramps, she knew what a ballplayer's wife would really need. "I unwrapped the box and found a thermos, a seat cushion, a stadium blanket to keep my legs warm on cold nights, a scorebook, and a box of pencils." Welcome to the life of a baseball wife and mom.

Grandma Patsy was Mom's mentor in that department. My parents were both nineteen on their wedding day in 1967. They had grown up together, but Mom had never been to a baseball game before she met Dad, so her mother-in-law showed her the ropes. She taught her how to keep score, filling in the little diamonds in her scorebook when a run scored, writing a K for strikeout if the batter swung and a ⅄ for a called third strike.

"You're going to see a lot of ballgames," Grandma Patsy said. "Keeping score keeps you interested."

She taught her daughter-in-law to pack a suitcase. "Always pack an electric fry pan," she said. "You can use it to make a meal out of anything, anywhere." She also showed Mom how to fold shirts so that Dad, who couldn't care less, looked as sharp as he could. Then the newlyweds went on the road. Call it a baseball honeymoon. They rented rooms in Durham, North Carolina, a dozen little towns in

Florida, and even in Alaska. Money was always tight, so the young wives pitched in together, cooking and babysitting for each other while their men—most of them nineteen or twenty years old—tried to prove themselves as pro ballplayers.

A little less than a year later, Mom met Dad after a long road trip. "Bob, I'm pregnant," she said. They couldn't afford a doctor, so Dad's uncle George, the college football Hall of Famer who went on to be an MD, pinch-doctored for free. He had to act fast, because Bob and Sue Boone's first baby was in a hurry to get going. Dad was at a basketball game—the 1969 NBA Finals between the Wilt Chamberlain–Jerry West–Elgin Baylor Lakers and the Bill Russell–John Havlicek Celtics—when Mom went into labor. The word went out: *Call Bob, it's happening!* He raced to the hospital, and came hustling in just in time to see his wife holding my minutes-old self.

Mom remembers the moment. "Bob came in and kissed me. He took his first look at the baby and said, 'Well, we're batting a thousand.'"

They had decided to name me Sean. But then Dad sprang a surprise. He was a huge fan of the '60s TV show *Maverick,* starring James Garner as the poker-playing cowboy Bret Maverick. So Bob Boone went all maverick on his young wife. He said, "Sue, you can name our baby whatever you want, but I'm calling him Bret." So I was Bret, not Sean—Bret with one *t* like the TV cowboy. Mom went along with the name, but she made her tardy husband promise one thing—if they ever had another child, he'd be there for the birth.

Gramps had his own view of my arrival. He always said, "Bret came out of the womb hitting." In a year or two I'd be toddling around his backyard, smacking Wiffle balls onto the roof with Gramps. Meanwhile, my dad was fighting his way to the Show—and the World Series.

☆ ☆ ☆

After serving a hitch in the Army Reserves, Dad returned to the Double-A Reading (Pennsylvania) Phillies in 1970. Still minor-league ball, but a level up from Raleigh-Durham. The pitching was tougher, the buses and motels a little more comfortable. In 1971, his first Double-A season, my dad batted .265 with just four home runs. That was the year Philadelphia drafted a skinny shortstop out of Ohio University. Gramps, still scouting for the Red Sox, kept hearing that the Phillies planned to move the new kid, Mike Schmidt, to third base. Dad's position.

Gramps spent a few days watching the two young infielders in action. Then he told his son, "You may want to think about another position. Schmidt's better than you."

"Gee, thanks, Dad."

"Can you catch?"

At that point, Dad had worn a catcher's mitt once or twice in his life. He said, "Hell yes. If that's what it takes to make the big leagues, I can catch."

Two things I can tell you about my dad. He's smart. And there's no quit in him. In my book, that's about the best thing you can say about a man.

And so, at the pivot point of his career, he switched positions. It's kind of weird—his own father started out as a catcher and wound up as a third baseman. Dad went the other way. A ballplayer does what it takes to get to the big leagues.

Mike Schmidt hit .291 and clubbed 26 home runs for the 1972 Eugene Emeralds of the Triple-A Pacific Coast League. Emeralds catcher Bob Boone hit .308 with 17 homers. The last-place Phillies gave them both a quick taste of the majors at the end of the season. Then, in 1973, Philadelphia manager Danny Ozark put the two rookies in his everyday lineup.

The '73 Phillies finished last again, but their new boys made some noise. Schmidt batted .196 but had 18 homers and 52 RBIs. Boone finished with a .261 average, 10 homers, and 61 RBIs. More important, he handled a veteran pitching staff featuring future Hall of Famer Steve Carlton, Jim Lonborg, and Ken Brett—in just his second full season as a catcher. That fall, after Reggie Jackson and the Oakland A's beat the Mets in the World Series, Dad was second runner-up (behind the Giants' Gary Matthews and the Expos' Steve Rogers) for the National League's Rookie of the Year award.

It turned out he was born to be a catcher. Despite standing six foot two and weighing 200, my dad was a ping hitter (his words, not mine). But that big brain of his came in handy. He was good at thinking two or three pitches ahead. He'd outsmart hitters by calling for fastballs on breaking-ball counts and bully a pitcher into throwing the right pitch. He'd bark at a strike-zone-squeezing umpire, or block the plate against a charging runner, or steal a strike call by "framing" a borderline pitch—snagging it in the webbing of his mitt and pulling it back an inch, making a ball look like a strike. He hit only three home runs in 1974 and just two in 1975, but his all-around game was so strong that he made the National League's All-Star team in '76, backing up Johnny Bench.

The game changed forever in those years. In 1975, with help from the players' union, pitchers Andy Messersmith and Dave McNally beat the owners in court. For the first time in history, baseball players became free agents. Now they could choose who they worked for, just like anybody else. As a result, players' pay started rising, and it hasn't stopped since. The man responsible for this happy result—more than Messersmith, McNally, or anyone else—was Marvin Miller, the longtime executive director of the Major League Baseball Players Association (MLBPA).

Miller led the players to legal victories that ended the "reserve clause," an eighty-year-old rule that tied players to their teams forever, like servants. The reserve clause had given owners all the power in salary negotiations, which meant there were no real negotiations.

It was the clause that had allowed the Tigers to cut Gramps's pay after his All-Star season in 1956. Nineteen years later, Marvin Miller and the MLBPA beat it in court. Now players could finally sell their services to the highest bidder. Some fans may not like it, but what's more American than that?

The end of the reserve clause led directly to today's multimillion-dollar salaries. I'll agree that some of those salaries sound ridiculous. Fifty million dollars for a .250 hitter? But you have to ask yourself why this is happening. Are the owners of major-league teams idiots who like throwing their money away? No, they're businessmen. Smart, ruthless businessmen who pay workers—pitchers, catchers, and hitters—what the market will bear. Modern baseball salaries are nothing but capitalism in action. Major-league talent is rare, and in an age of $200 tickets, $12 beers, and billion-dollar TV deals, baseball stars are as valuable as $20-million-a-picture movie stars. That's why I don't begrudge today's players their $100 million contracts . . . even if Robinson Cano's $240 million deal with my old team makes me wonder what I'd be worth today.

Back in 1974, my dad's third year in the majors, he considered quitting the game. "I figured I could go to med school and do a better job providing for my family." A year later, just as he was scrapping and pinging his way to All-Star status, Miller and the players' union had changed the game, and my dad's life, forever. By 1977, his salary was up to $80,000. By 1985, the California Angels would be paying him $880,000 a year.

Dad admired Miller. So do I. Dad served the union as the Phillies' player representative, and later as player rep for the whole National League. I followed his lead as an active member of the MLBPA, pushing my teammates to support the union that made so many of us multimillionaires. By the way, it's a travesty that Miller, one of the most important men in baseball history, is not in the Hall of Fame. But don't get me started on the Hall of Fame. That's another topic we'll return to a little later. For now, let's just say that there are lots of great bats and balls and plaques in Cooperstown, and some people who are going to be mad at me when they throw this book across the room.

Dad had what some baseball insiders—Peter Gammons, Aaron Boone, me—consider a Hall of Fame career. He did it with smarts and toughness as much as talent. One night, Ted Williams joined Gramps at a Phillies game. Gramps was thrilled to see his old idol and teammate again. Williams was in his sixties by then. After watching Dad catch one of Carlton's victories, blocking sliders in the dirt all night, he told Gramps, "That's the best catcher I've ever seen."

Among other things, Dad was the most durable receiver of his time. He played with torn ligaments and broken bones. Catching 140-plus games a season, the ultimate gamer helped Schmidt and his teammates turn the Phillies from doormats to pennant contenders. Dad made four All-Star teams. He batted over .270 with 60-plus RBIs year after year, winning seven Gold Gloves as the league's best-fielding catcher while bullying, babying, and whatever-it-tooking a pitching staff that featured surly ace Carlton, veterans like Jim Lonborg and Jim Kaat, and flaky closer Tug McGraw. According to Dallas Green, who replaced Ozark as Phillies manager in 1979, "Boone ran a pitching staff as well as any catcher I've ever been around." One pitcher called him a genius. Another said, "Throwing to Bob Boone is like falling in love."

But then, pitchers are weird.

I don't know about pitcher-catcher love or even genius, but I *do* know that Dad was smart enough to go against conventional wisdom. In those days, everybody said baseball players had no business lifting weights. "It'll make you muscle-bound," people said. Dad ignored them. He not only lifted weights, he lifted and worked out all winter so he could report to spring training at his fighting weight. At a time when players still smoked cigarettes in the dugout—when most guys' idea of doing curls was sitting at a bar, lifting beers—Dad worked out 364 days a year, every day but Christmas. He talked the Phillies into installing Nautilus exercise machines in their locker room—the first big-league clubhouse with a weight room. That was in 1975, after he and Carlton, another stubborn individualist, began working with fitness guru Gus Hoefling. "It was just me and Carlton for the first couple years. Then it caught on with the other guys, and changed the game," he says. "I know I couldn't have caught as many games, or lasted as long as I did, without all the time I spent in the gym."

He won bets by hitting the floor in the clubhouse and doing 1,000 sit-ups in a row. That bet was a lock for Dad, who could easily do 1,500 or even 2,000 sit-ups. As if that wasn't freaky enough, he and Carlton built strength and flexibility with a daily kung fu routine.

Picture a couple of ballplayers in the disco '70s, doing kung fu exercises while their teammates lounge around playing cards, dipping Skoal, and smoking cigarettes. Anyone but a pair of hardnosed SOBs like Carlton and Boone would have been laughed out of the ballpark. A few of the veterans teased them with lines from the hit song:

Everybody was kung fu fighting,
Those kicks were fast as lightning.

It was all very funny—until Carlton went 23-10 to win the 1977 Cy Young Award. Until Boone made another All-Star Game. Pretty soon their teammates were pumping iron and kung fu kicking, and the best was yet to come.

☆ ☆ ☆

On the first day of October 1980, the Phillies trailed the Montreal Expos by half a game. There were no wild-card playoffs yet—you had to win your division to make the postseason. And the Philadelphia Phillies had a long tradition of losing. The World Series had been going on since 1903, and they were the only one of the major leagues' original sixteen franchises that had never won a World Series. The Yankees had won 22. Even the Cubs had won 2. Philadelphia hadn't even reached the World Series since 1950, and hadn't won a single Series *game* since 1915. But 1980 kind of looked like it might be their year.

Schmidt, now the best player in the game, led the majors with 48 homers. His teammate Greg Luzinski had more sheer light-tower power, but Schmidt was a better home run hitter because he could hit the ball out to all fields. In his quiet way he was The Man in the clubhouse, sauntering through there like he knew he was going to hit a couple homers. Schmidt won his first National League MVP award that year and his fifth straight Gold Glove at third base. (I guess Gramps had been right to tell Dad to find a new position.) Carlton won his third Cy Young Award with a little help from his Gold Glove catcher. The Phillies slipped past Montreal by a single game to claim the NL East, and then edged Nolan Ryan, Joe Morgan, and the Houston Astros to win a trip to the Series against George Brett and the Kansas City Royals.

All Brett did that year was bat .390, the highest big-league average in forty years, with 24 homers and 118 RBIs. He was the American League's MVP. Outfielder Willie Wilson hit .326 and stole 79 bases. First baseman Willie Mays Aikens smacked 20 homers and drove in 98 runs.

Dad had struggled that season, batting only .229 with 9 homers, playing part of the year with a torn ligament in his knee. Then he broke his foot in a home-plate collision in the playoffs. His foot was killing him, but he found his stroke at the plate and batted .412 in the World Series, which came down to a pop-up and a cross-up.

In Game 6, with the Phillies leading the Series three games to two, Philadelphia had a chance to break the home team's age-old curse. The fans were holding their breath at Veterans Stadium, praying for one more win.

The Phillies took a 4–1 lead into the ninth inning. They had left-handed closer Tug McGraw—Tim's dad, for you country music fans—on the mound. But McGraw looked scared. He usually had perfect command of his pitches, but during his warm-ups every pitch came in high. Dad was jumping to catch them. McGraw fell behind the Royals' Amos Otis with two balls at helmet level. His catcher kept trying to figure out what was wrong. Was Tug's release point off? Was his stride too short? He couldn't figure out the problem, but he could see the scared look in his pitcher's eyes. So he went to the mound.

"Tuggles," he said, "we can't afford to walk him."

"What am I doing wrong?" McGraw asked.

Dad shrugged. "I dunno."

"Well, figure it out! What do I do?"

They stood on the mound with the whole world watching. Finally, Dad handed him the ball. *"Aim lower."*

McGraw came back to strike Otis out. Phillies fans felt pretty comfortable. One out, nobody on. Then Willie Aikens walked. John Wathan singled. Jose Cardenal singled. Suddenly the bases were loaded. Frank White, the Royals' second baseman, stepped to the plate with the tying runs on base. McGraw looked exhausted.

White popped the first pitch toward the Philadelphia dugout. Dad tossed his mask aside and took off after the ball—the second out the Phillies were dying to get. He was settling under it when Pete Rose, playing first base, came running over. "Charlie Hustle, they called him," Dad remembers. "But there I am waiting for the ball to come down, and where's Pete? Late to the play. And it's the first baseman's play. So I'm waiting for him to take charge, thinking, *Where's Rose? He'll be here any second.*"

Dad had one eye on the ball and one on Rose, arriving a step late. The ball came down. Boone expected Rose to call for it. Rose waited for Boone to catch it. At the last instant they both reached for the ball. It bounced off Dad's mitt. For a second it looked like the Phillies had blown one of the biggest outs ever. Then Rose snagged the ball out of midair—the most famous grab in modern Phillies history.

Pete Rose and Bob Boone have been friends for forty years, but they're a couple of the most competitive guys you ever met. They've been bitching and laughing about that play ever since.

"Charlie Hustle my ass," Dad says. "If he'd hustled he would have made that play easy."

Pete says, "I seem to remember one of us caught the ball, and his name wasn't Boone."

Two outs. But the Phillies were still in a fix. The bases were still loaded and McGraw was pitching hurt, wincing every time he threw his out pitch. The screwball is a nasty, unnatural pitch that kills elbows. Maybe that's why no major leaguer throws one anymore. Tug McGraw was thirty-six years old, and he'd thrown thousands of them in his fifteen years in the majors. Now his left elbow barked every time he twisted it sideways to spin one away from a right-handed hitter. If each screwball was a bullet, Tug was out of ammo.

Willie Wilson came up. All he'd done for the 1980 Royals was hit .326 with a league-leading 230 hits.

Dad went to the mound again. "We'll get him out with screwballs," he told McGraw.

Tug shook his head. "Boonie, my fingers are numb. I might have one screwball left."

"*Screwballs*," Dad said.

They got a strike with a first-pitch screwball. So Dad put down the sign again: *screwball*. McGraw shook him off. Dad didn't care. He put down four fingers and wiggled them—the sign for a screwball. McGraw shook him off again. As Tug remembered, "I shook him off four times. And now Willie Wilson's looking confused, thinking, *He ain't got that many pitches!* Finally I throw him a slider. He fouls it off. Now the count's oh-and-two, and Boonie and I are at odds again. He wants a screwball, of course." Finally they agreed to waste a fastball up and in, to set up what might be the very last screwball in Tug's sore left arm. Only he didn't get the fastball under Wilson's chin, where he wanted it. It came in letter-high, right over the heart of the plate, "and Willie was so surprised that he *took* it!" The Series might have ended there, but umpire Nick Bremigan called the pitch a ball, a fraction of an inch high. Now the count was 1-2. Just then McGraw noticed a policeman on a horse near the home dugout. The cops were on the field to keep a Phillies victory celebration from getting out of hand, but McGraw took another message from what he saw. "The horse lifted his tail and did his business right there on the field. I looked at that pile of you-know-what and thought, *If I don't get Willie Wilson, that's exactly what I'm gonna be.*"

Dad knew Wilson would be looking screwball. Everyone in the stadium was looking for a screwball. Fifty-five million TV viewers were looking for a screwball.

Dad hung one finger. *Fastball.* And McGraw gave it all he had. Years later he remembered watching the pitch leave his hand and thinking, *Hurry up and* get there! The ball got there a fraction ahead of the screwgie Wilson expected. He swung and missed. McGraw leaped toward the sky. The Philadelphia Phillies were World Champions for the first time! Dad, too worn-out to jump, trudged toward the mound while McGraw and Schmidt hugged and the Philadelphia crowd started a party that lasted a day and a half.

I remember every second of it. That game was played on a school day, but I got to play hooky to watch the Phillies. I was the eleven-year-old kid running around the clubhouse while Dad and his teammates lit cigars and sprayed champagne all over the place. We were still celebrating when Pennsylvania governor Dick Thornburgh declared the next day Philadelphia Phillies Day, complete with a victory parade.

Dad and Pete Rose must not have been too mad at each other, because I wound up going home with Rose. Pete was practically an

uncle to me, and his son, Petey, was like a cousin. That was my favorite sleepover—staying up late with Pete and Petey, watching TV.
Every newscast showed "World Series hero Pete Rose" snagging the
pop-up that went off Dad's mitt, which Pete thought was funny as
hell.

The next day—Wednesday, October 22, 1980—was my first parade. I joined up with Dad again, and we rode a float down Broad
Street with his teammates. The streets were jammed with half a million cheering, singing, happy fans waving pom-poms and Phillies
pennants. I was sleepy and a little smelly, still wearing the champagne-
stained corduroy pants and velour shirt I'd slept in the night before,
but who cared? Not those 500,000 fans on Broad Street, or another
800,000 waiting at John F. Kennedy Stadium in South Philly—not
bad for a town with a population of 1.7 million.

Dad leaned over to me. There was confetti falling on us. "Bret,"
he said, "remember this. Because this is what it's all about. And
remember—there are no parades for second place."

3

GROWING UP BOONE

Gramps always swore I came out of the womb hitting. "Bret was born in a bat bag," he told people. I hadn't had the birds-and-bees talk yet, so I might have been a little confused about where babies came from, but I knew it had something to do with baseball.

Start with our family's favorite story—me knocking Wiffle balls over the house at the age of two. Or was it age one? The funny thing about that story is, I seem to get a little younger every time my parents tell it. But then, my parents always said I was a freak—in a good way. "I watched Mike Schmidt and Pete Rose at work every day," my dad told me. "But the way you swung a bat at such a young age—it was freakish. To do that at *less than a year old* . . ." Pretty soon he'll be waving one of those embryo pictures, a sonogram, telling people I was swinging a bat in the womb. My first video highlight.

I didn't buy all that "one-year-old" business until I started working on this book and asked my mom about it. Now, Sue Boone couldn't tell a lie if she tried. She doesn't tell tall baseball stories or brag about her boys. And she swears those stories about me are gospel. "At the age of six months, you crawled for a few days," she says. "Three or four days. It was certainly less than a week. Then you stood up, and you had a surprised look on your little face, like 'What was I crawling around for? This is better!' From then on, you walked. I'd take you shopping at Sears, and other shoppers would stop and stare at this six-month-old child who went up to my knee, walking the aisles like he owned the place."

Around that time Grandma Patsy, the champion swimmer in the family, decided I should join them in the pool. So she tossed me in. She always swore I wasn't scared. I never cried, just splashed around till she reached down and pulled me out. A few months later, I was swimming laps.

I can't explain why stuff came so easy and early to me. It's not like I was the world's greatest athlete. Later in life I'd run into guys who really were great, once-in-a-generation talents, and believe me, I know the difference.

Maybe it's just that I was so eager to get on to the next thing, to get on with *life*. Patience was never my strong suit.

My folks never said I was great or amazing. They wouldn't want me to get a big head. But there was one word they did use to describe little Bret. Gramps, Grandma Patsy, Mom and Dad, my aunt Terry and the rest, they used the same word. *Fearless*.

At least it sounds better than *freakish*.

☆ ☆ ☆

You couldn't script my life any better if you tried.

My first memories are of mornings at my grandparents' house. Waking Gramps up at dawn. That's when we began our tradition of playing ball in his yard. It must have started in 1970, because Dad was serving in the Army Reserves. It was the middle of the Vietnam War. Mom and I went to stay with Gramps and Grandma Patsy in San Diego. I'd toddle into the master bedroom every morning about six, poke him in the foot or the belly, and go into my usual routine: "Ball, ball!"

Gramps dragged himself out of bed, but he wouldn't play with me right away. First he brewed a pot of coffee, the one thing he couldn't do without. Coffee and the sports page. He lifted me onto his lap while he paged through the baseball stories and box scores in the *San Diego Union*. And then, finally, we'd go out to his yard to have a catch.

I didn't know it then, but we were only a couple of miles from the fields where Gramps played when he was a kid, following Ted Williams from the local sandlots to the slightly better field at Hoover High School. Now, almost forty years later, he was stretching his achy legs, underhanding Wiffle balls to his year-old grandson while the sun came up.

Gramps wasn't sentimental about his playing days, but he kept a few old bats around the house. Not in a trophy case or anything. They were just old, tar-stained bats from the 1950s lying around. I liked to feel the grain in the wood. Those dinged-up Louisville Sluggers were as tall as me, and twenty years older. I couldn't swing them yet. I couldn't even pick them up, but something about the feel of the grain stuck with me, like the dry leather of an old glove or the calluses on Gramps's hand. Years later, when other big leaguers started switching to maple bats, I stuck with Louisville Sluggers made from white ash. If old-fashioned wood was good enough for Gramps and Dad, it was good enough for me.

After Dad got back from the army and made it to the big leagues, he played winter ball in Puerto Rico. That's where I knocked tennis balls around with his friend Frank Robinson, the Hall of Fame outfielder who was one of the seven or eight best hitters ever. To me Frank was just the nice man bunting a ball over the net to me. And to him I was Bob Boone's little loose cannon, rearing back and smashing the ball at him as hard as I could.

Frank never saw me plunging into a pool near the tennis courts, but it seemed like everybody else in Puerto Rico did. I was climbing the ladder to the high dive when the poolside crowd started noticing. They'd never seen a two-year-old climb up there. Some of them ran to my parents. "We've got to save him!"

Dad shook them off. "Just watch," he said. The other adults stood around the pool looking worried, pointing at the toddler on the high dive. Finally I toddled to the end of the diving board and leaped off. Everyone was flipping out—till I splashed to the surface, waving to the crowd.

After that, Mom sat in a beach chair by the high dive. When people got scared for me she told them, "It's okay. He's just precocious."

Life was fun, and the best thing of all—hitting a ball with a bat—was easy. We lived in Medford, New Jersey, across the bridge from Veterans Stadium in Philadelphia. My parents settled there during Dad's rookie year with the Phillies. I played T-ball in the local Little League, but let's get one thing out of the way. My dad didn't teach me to play. Fans picture big-league dads on the Little League field with their sons, showing them how to grip and swing a bat. But ask yourself—when would that happen? My Little League games were on weekend afternoons. Dad was either catching at the Vet, a twenty-minute drive away, or on a road trip. Gramps had more to do with my early days of swinging plastic bats at Wiffle balls, but except for the year Mom and I spent in San Diego, he lived three thousand miles away. I saw Gramps mainly on Thanksgiving and Christmas.

So who taught me?

That's a question every second-generation player has to answer. It's a sore point to some. Barry Bonds wanted his dad to come to his Little League games, but Bobby Bonds—a three-time All-Star who hit 332 home runs—was busy playing for the Giants and seven other teams. The McRaes were like that, too. Hal McRae, a 1970s star, never saw his son Brian play a single ballgame until Brian was a pro. Same for my Seattle teammate David Bell and his father, Buddy, a great third baseman of the 1970s and '80s. David and his brother Mike idolized their dad when they were young, but it's not like Buddy was in the backyard, having a catch with them. He was playing for the Indians, Rangers, and Reds.

I was talking with Dad about this. He said, "Your grandfather was right. You were a born hitter, that's all." And while Dad never showed me how to swing a bat, he taught by example every day of the week. One day when I was five or six, he was in our backyard, building a swing set for Aaron and me, when his back locked up. He yelled like he'd been shot. The Phillies had a game that night, so our neighbor Greg "the Bull" Luzinski, the Phils' homer-hitting left fielder, picked him up and helped him to the car. Greg drove them to the stadium, where the trainers shot Dad up with painkillers. Then he went out and played. For the rest of the season, Dad's back would seize up in the late innings. He'd twist and stretch and stay in the game.

He played with a broken finger on his throwing hand and torn cartilage in his knee. He played the 1980 World Series on a broken foot, and never complained. Aaron and I saw all that. Even if nobody ever said a word about it, we saw what it meant to be a gamer. While my father might not have been around to teach me how to grip a bat, he taught me how to be a pro and how to be a man.

But I'm my own ballplayer, always was.

☆ ☆ ☆

In those days, we had a tri-level house in a woodsy part of Medford, at the end of a cul-de-sac called Sunrise Court. There was a basketball hoop, a pool in the backyard, three cars in the driveway. One of the cars was a black El Dorado, a free lease to Dad from a Phillies-fan Cadillac dealer. Then there was Dad's Datsun 280Z, also black, the sports car he loved to drive fast. He and Luzinski drove to work together, zipping across the Walt Whitman Bridge from New Jersey to

Philly, waving to fans who waved and honked their horns. Dad might have gotten a lot more speeding tickets if most of the cops hadn't been Phillies fans, too.

Mom's station wagon got the most mileage. She'd drive us kids to school and the mall and about a hundred ballgames a month, especially after Aaron joined the home team in 1973. Dad had promised my mom he'd never miss the birth of any Boone of his after he missed mine, but Aaron came along when Dad was on the road. There was no paternity leave in those days. He didn't lay eyes on Aaron until Mom took us to meet the Phillies on the road six weeks later. At that point, in 1973, Dad was 0 for 2 in terms of seeing his sons enter the world.

But he was moving up in the world, making $100,000 by the time I got to grade school. That's worth about half a million today. Before long he'd be up to $400,000, thanks to Marvin Miller and the players' union. So we were comfortable, but not snooty about it—Bob and Sue Boone never put on airs. They never let Aaron and me think we were anything but regular American kids. It might seem a little weird when we'd make a family trip to the grocery store and other shoppers asked Dad for his autograph, but he said that was nothing special. "They see me on TV, that's all." The only autograph seeker who annoyed him was a fan who asked me to sign a baseball. I was still a Little Leaguer, but the guy must have thought I had a big-league future. Dad stepped between us and told him, "Leave my boy alone. Just let him be a kid." Other than that, he said signing autographs was just part of the game, and he felt lucky people cared so much about baseball that he could play it for a living.

That was Dad all over, Mr. Good Citizen. Aaron was like that, too, the Boones' little angel, but I had some mischief in me. Okay, maybe a lot. Nothing nasty or malicious, but if a kid was building a ramp to fly his bike over trash cans in the driveway, Evel Knievel–style, it was probably me. If a mouse turned up in the laundry, or the dog was on the roof or the mailbox caught on fire, I was the prime suspect. Dad had the idea that he was the disciplinarian in the house, the sheriff of Sunrise Court, but it never quite worked out that way. He was busy catching 140 games a year for the Phillies. That left Mom in charge of the Boone boys, and I was faster than she was.

If I was in for a spanking, I'd take off running around the yard. She'd chase me till she got winded and gave up. "Just wait," she'd say. "Wait till your father gets home!" But by then it would be late at night. Dad would have caught nine innings, talked to reporters, showered and dressed and made the drive home, and we'd all be so happy to see him that I got off scot-free.

Our house was like a theme park for Aaron and me and our friends. We had the swimming pool, plus a tree house and a zipline between oak trees, one of the first backyard ziplines in New Jersey. After school, we played pickup games. Every sport in its season, plus a lot of street hockey; it's the national pastime of suburban New Jersey. Kids strap on roller skates, set up a couple of goals, and pretend they're the Broad Street Bullies of 1975. This wasn't the neighborhood moms' favorite game, due to the traffic on Sunrise Court. But we had it under control. When a driver came around the bend we'd yell "Car!!" and hustle up the driveway. After the car went by and the coast was clear, we'd get back to the game. It was the kind of spontaneous, unsupervised fun today's overscheduled kids never seem to have. We'd just get a bunch of kids together and play, with no adults keeping stats, nobody taking pictures, nothing to gain except fun.

Our three-car garage was full of footballs, basketballs, and soccer balls, as well as bats and baseballs Dad brought home from the Vet. With buckets of baseballs in the Boones' garage, no kid on our street ever had to pay for one. We had bikes, a moped, and a couple of snowmobiles. In the winter we'd snowmobile around the neighborhood, dodging trees. Then we'd pile into the basement and put on a show.

That basement was Dad's favorite room. There were a couple of couches and a pool table down there. Framed pictures of his team-mates and friends—Schmidt, Luzinski, Tom Seaver, Carlton Fisk—lined the walls. There was a bar where Dad could serve friends and teammates the latest cabernet recommended by Philadelphia wine connoisseur Steve Carlton. There was a trophy case for Dad's plaques and trophies, like the Gold Glove he won in 1978, his first of seven. Over the years Aaron and I would add trophies of our own to that display case, but when we were little we contributed mainly noise. We'd get tired of watching *Happy Days* or *Laverne & Shirley* and chase each other around the couches, jumping over the dog, Wegian, a nervous Norwegian elkhound. Then we'd climb onto the carpeted platform at one end of the room. Aaron and I and the neighborhood boys used that platform as a stage to entertain the grown-ups. We'd act out the latest Wrestlemania, with me as Hulk Hogan, in front of a wall covered with giant paintings of Bob Boone.

Paintings? Oh yeah, Mom hired a local artist to cover the wall with life-size pictures of Dad catching and hitting. To me, that basement wall seemed as normal as the picture window upstairs. Same for the buckets of baseballs in the garage, the mitts with Dad's name stamped in the leather, the Bob Boone–model bats, and the big, muscly team-mates who were his friends—none of that struck me as anything special. I mean, didn't everybody have Pete Rose and Greg Luzinski drop by after work, and action paintings of their dad on the wall?

The Boones and Luzinskis were tight. Dad and Greg met as team-mates in the low minors in 1969, the year I was born. Dad and Mom were twenty-one years old, living in a little apartment in Durham, North Carolina. The Bull was eighteen, a year out of high school, already six one and about 225, when he pulled my mom aside and said, "Sue, my girlfriend's coming to town. What do I do? Can you help me out?" Mom must have been a good helper. She showed Greg's girlfriend around Durham, and Sue Boone and Jean Luzinski have been friends ever since.

"We went through the minors like baseball wives do," Mom says. "It was guys on the road and girls together, helping each other. Cooking together, doing laundry, babysitting—all the glamorous stuff."

Ten years later we lived up the street from the Luzinskis in Medford, on opposite sides of a little lake. I'd hop on my bike and ride over to the Bull's house. Greg and Jean's daughter Kim was my age. Their son Ryan was Aaron's age.

Ryan and Aaron looked up to me, of course, and why not? I was a Little League stud, four years older, while they were topping grounders in T-ball. What I remember about Aaron and me at that age is trying to be a decent big brother to him. I let him tag along and play ballgames with me and my friends, so he grew up competing with older boys, getting better fast. And not just at baseball. In those days, kids weren't so specialized. We played baseball all summer, football in the fall, and basketball in the winter.

I think specialization is a key factor in today's sports, and it's a double-edged sword. Today's kids tend to pick one sport—sometimes even one position—and play nothing else from an early age. They're exclusively pitchers or quarterbacks or strikers or point guards long before they hit puberty. They get better training than ever before, and by the time they get to high school, some of them are as polished as I was in college. By the time they make the pros, they're the best-trained, hardest-throwing, hardest-hitting generation in sports history. That's one reason the talent level keeps going up. Today's average player is better than the average when I came up in 1992. In fact, today's average player is probably better than the All-Stars of Gramps's day.

But do today's players have as much fun as my grandpa, my dad, my brother, and I had? Do they love the game as much? Do they *enjoy* it? I'm not so sure about that. Sure, talent matters. Technique matters. Strength, speed, and high-tech training all have their place. But fun should matter, too.

Here's a related worry—baseball's injury epidemic. Specifically pitchers. Everybody wonders why so many pitchers keep hurting their arms. Back when Dad was playing, only one player in the majors had "Tommy John surgery" to reconstruct his elbow: the Dodgers' Tommy John. Today the number is five hundred and climbing fast. A record thirty-one pitchers had the operation in 2014. Some never made it back to the majors. Others came back better than ever, with an extra tick or two on their fastballs. My dad, who runs the Washington Nationals' minor-league system, says the Nationals plan to give all their kid pitchers Tommy John surgery, "just to get it over with." He's joking, but you get the point.

I keep thinking that a lot of those pitchers with blown-out arms might have been better off trying lots of sports, the way kids did when childhood was less of a job. Instead, many if not most kids now play on Little League teams, school teams, and travel teams from the time they're in first or second grade. Picture the strain on all those young, growing arms. They just throw baseballs as hard as they can, over and over and over, until they learn to twist those muscles and tendons to make the ball curve, and then they repeat *that* motion thousands more times.

Does that sound like fun? Or stress? Kids should have a chance to be kids—and to figure out what their favorite sports are, without specializing at such a young age.

Of course, for Aaron and me, baseball season was the best—especially when the Phillies had a home stand. I'd come home from grade school with a full head of steam. "Dad, c'mon, let's go!" We'd pile into his car—Dad, Greg Luzinski, Greg's son Ryan, Aaron, and me—for the twenty-minute drive to the ballpark, with us antsy kids climbing all over our dads.

Phillies manager Danny Ozark was like the world's coolest uncle. A round-faced, grizzled old baseball lifer with a quick smile, he was friendly and funny. It was Ozark who once claimed, "Ninety percent of this game is half mental," a line most people think Yogi Berra said. And thanks to him, the Phillies had the family-friendliest clubhouse in the league. (Note to readers who didn't grow up in a ballpark: a baseball *clubhouse* is the locker room. It just sounds friendlier.) Aaron and I had our own locker and mini-uniforms. We'd bomb around the clubhouse on our Big Wheels—plastic tricycles that were a popular toy in those days—rolling over Ace bandages, jerseys, and jockstraps. We took grounders on the field before the game, and shagged flies in the outfield while Dad, Schmitty, and the Bull took batting practice. Once the game started we'd explore the stadium, a couple of grade school kids in pint-size Phillies uniforms playing tapeball in the equipment room. Swinging yellow Wiffle bats, we'd knock a rolled-up ball of duct tape off a wall—that was a single—or a roll of tarp for a double, or off a John Deere tractor for a homer. Later on we'd join Mom to see if the good guys won the game.

In the middle of July 1979, Mom was nine months pregnant with her third child. Her due date happened to be the same week Dad was selected as the National League's starting catcher in the All-Star Game at the Kingdome in Seattle. He couldn't miss that. Who knew if he'd ever start another All-Star Game? Dad swore he'd play the game and fly straight home the next day, probably in time to catch the baby. So she told him to go to Seattle. "And take Bret and Aaron with you." She didn't need me doing dirt-bike tricks in the driveway when she went into labor, which is why I wound up on national TV at age ten.

The All-Stars were the main attraction. Steve Carlton and Dad were the National League's starting battery, going up against Nolan Ryan and an American League lineup featuring George Brett, Carl Yastrzemski, Jim Rice, and Fred Lynn. But some of the biggest cheers came an hour before the game, when the stars took batting practice. In those days before fears of legal liability ruined all the fun—*what if a child got hurt?*—players' kids got to field the balls that stayed in the

4
THE LITTLEST PHILLIE

While I was entertaining the All-Star Game crowd in Seattle, my mother was back in New Jersey, giving birth again. My second baby brother wasn't going to wait for Dad to fly home from the game. So the 1979 All-Star break left Bob Boone 2-for-5 as an All-Star and 0-for-3 in the seeing-your-kids-born department. Not that it bothered my parents. After all, Mom had encouraged him to go to Seattle. "You can't miss the All-Star Game," she'd said. "Don't worry, I'll be fine." So he'd given her a kiss and said he'd be with her in spirit. As it turned out, he'd be with her on TV, too.

Jean Luzinski was there in person. The Bull's wife spent the night in Mom's hospital room, serving as her designated helper for the birth. Jean was one of the first to hear the new baby's name. "We've decided to call him Joshua," Mom told her. Then they tuned in the All-Star telecast. After the National League's 7–6 victory, the postgame show featured some of the winners, including catcher Boone. He gave TV announcer Joe Garagiola a few happy comments, and then looked at the camera lens and waved to his wife.

"Hello, Sue! I was talking with the guys in the dugout," he said.

"About the baby's name." Mom saw what was coming—he was changing signals again, just like with my name. "We like *Matthew*."

So Matthew it was. There's another baseball first for the Boones. I'm pretty sure my brother Matt is the only person ever named on TV by a bunch of baseball All-Stars.

He was still in diapers while my unusual childhood ramped up in the early '80s. Aaron was four years behind me, getting bigger and better all the time, but hustling to keep up with my friends and me. For reasons we both forgot long ago, I called him "Arnie." Maybe it sounded less formal than "Aaron." Anyway, kid brother Arnie and I spent so many school nights and weekends running around Veterans Stadium that we thought of the place as our second home.

I still remember the layout of the clubhouse. Greg Luzinski's locker was in the corner, next to Larry Bowa's. Bowa's was next to Mike Schmidt's. Dad's locker was two over from Schmidt's, and Carlton's was two over from Dad's. And with our own locker and little uniforms, Aaron and I were charter members of the Phillies-kids' club. Along with Ryan Luzinski, Petey Rose, and Marky McGraw we had carte blanche in the clubhouse, without knowing how special that freedom was.

We got to know the World Champion Phillies in a way fans could only dream of—and not just because we saw them walking around naked, sipping postgame beers and flipping towels at each other. When the stars were out on the field, people in the stands yelled out to them, asking for autographs, calling them Mr. Schmidt or Mr. Luzinski, but to us they were Schmitty and Bull. I remember the tall, quiet Carlton, who always looked like he was thinking deep thoughts, and Dallas Green, the gray-haired manager, who was even taller. There was Tug, the clubhouse jokester, always looking like he didn't have a care in the world. He was the one who set an example for me by catching batting-practice fungoes behind his back. And then there was Garry Maddox, an outfielder with an Afro that bulged out from under his helmet to join his sideburns and his curly beard. Maddox was so fast they used to say that the oceans covered three-quarters of the earth's surface, and he covered the rest. And as much as I looked up to those guys, my real backstage buddy was bigger than any of them and greener than any rookie. He was six foot six, 300 pounds, with crossed eyes, purple eyebrows, and a ninety-inch waist.

The Phillie Phanatic was the best mascot in sports. He came along a few years after the San Diego Chicken, a kind of hyper version of Big Bird, and got a lot of attention. In 1978, Phillies GM Bill Giles said, "We need more excitement in the Vet. Let's get a mascot." Next thing you know the Phanatic was driving an ATV around the stadium, shooting hot dogs into the stands. He'd dance on the home dugout, hex the opposing pitcher, spray Silly String on bald fans' heads, even wrestle with the Dodgers' colorful manager, Tommy Lasorda.

The guy inside the green shag-carpet costume was Dave Raymond, and to me he was almost as cool as Lefty, Schmitty, and the other players. I used to hang out in his dressing room under the stands, keeping him company between innings. Dave was a twenty-two-year-old PR intern, not much more than a kid himself, when he invented the Phanatic. His dad, Tubby Raymond, was the football coach at the University of Delaware, which probably helped him get the gig but didn't make him rich. The Phillies paid him twenty-five dollars a game for amusing thousands of fans in that big furry costume, which was so cumbersome that he needed an assistant—another intern—to help put his head on. And as tough as it is to hit in the big leagues, Dave's job might have been tougher at times. During day games in July and August, the Astroturf field at the Vet got so hot that it was like stepping in a frying pan. It was basically a half-inch layer of plastic carpet over cement. You could see waves of heat coming up off the field. He'd be sweating rivers when he came off the field, guzzling

Gatorade in his cramped little dressing room. But Dave was a good-natured Phanatic, willing to put up with a grade school kid's questions.

"What planet is the Phanatic supposed to be from?" I asked.

"Earth," he told me. "He's from the Galapagos Islands."

"What does he eat?"

"Hot dogs and Silly String."

"How hot is it in that suit? A hundred? Two hundred?"

That's the question that pained him. "Little Boonie," he said, "you don't wanna know." Then he'd duck his head to let his assistant put his Phanatic head back on. The assistant was a member of the Hot Pants Brigade, a cute girl in short shorts and white boots—another reason I liked following the Phanatic around.

Some people didn't like the Phanatic. Baseball purists, mostly. Lasorda hated him, especially after the Phillies whipped Tommy's Dodgers in the 1983 National League Championship Series. Tommy was a sore loser who didn't appreciate it when the Phanatic carried a mannequin in a Dodgers jersey—a jersey with LASORDA on the back—and started kicking and stomping the dummy. That brought the real Lasorda running out of the L.A. dugout to attack the Phanatic in one of the dumbest baseball brawls ever. YouTube it—it's hilarious.

The Phanatic was one of my heroes. Not just because he was funny or because he was nice to me when I was a kid, but because he was a gamer. He gave his best every day and never griped.

☆ ☆ ☆

I lived for home stands. If my dad didn't take me to the ballpark with him, my day was ruined.

The manager, Green, was an intimidating figure, but he let me take hitting and fielding practice with the team. That's something that never happens in today's more corporate game. And it mattered.

I think it helped make us ballplayers. Far from being intimidated when we made the majors almost twenty years later, Aaron and I felt like we belonged. And while we didn't get formal instruction from Dad and his teammates, if you're taking hacks in the batting cage and Mike Schmidt says, "Get your hands a little higher," you listen.

But I wasn't really looking for technical advice. I was born to swing a bat. What really made a difference was something more like osmosis. More like soaking up what it means to be a big leaguer. Growing up around some of the best players in the game, you can't help picking up on their habits. Not just how a big leaguer acts and moves and talks, but how he believes in himself. How he acts and talks the same way if he hits two home runs or goes 0-for-4, if he's a gamer.

Pete Rose was one of the all-time gamers. He used to sit in the dugout with his son, Petey, who was about my age. He'd say, "You don't have to think, just look. Look at how Joe Morgan plays second base. Watch Schmitty play third. Watch *me*. That's how to play this game."

Yes, Rose gambled on baseball, and that's one of the game's mortal sins. Major League Baseball Rule 21(d) is posted in every clubhouse:

> Any player, umpire, or club official or employee, who shall bet any sum whatsoever upon any baseball game in connection with which the bettor has no duty to perform shall be declared ineligible for one year. Any player, umpire, or club official or employee, who shall bet any sum whatsoever upon any baseball game in connection with which the bettor has a duty to perform shall be declared permanently ineligible.

The rule doesn't say anything about the Hall of Fame. The Hall changed its policy to keep ineligible players out in 1991, *after* Rose lost his job as the Reds' manager for betting on his team. As a *player*, my dad's teammate Pete had 4,256 base hits. Go back and look at that number for a second. Four thousand two hundred and fifty-six hits is more than 21 years' worth of 200 hits a year. It's not just 67 more hits than Ty Cobb had in his 24-year career, it's almost 1,000 more than Willie Mays had in his 22-year career. There may be spitballers, racists, drug addicts, and all-around bad guys in the Hall of Fame, but there's no room for a player who had almost half again as many hits as Tony Gwynn or Rod Carew or Wade Boggs? More often than not, the Hall of Fame voting is a joke. Pete Rose was a 17-time All-Star who won the Rookie of the Year award, an MVP award, three batting titles, two Gold Gloves, and a World Series MVP. On the field, at least, he epitomized what a ballplayer should be.

Okay, he was a family friend, too. But friendship has nothing to do with my views about the Hall of Fame. In fact, Pete was no big fan of mine, at least at first. Watching batting practice in the early '80s, he'd tell his son to watch Morgan and Schmitty and the others, and then he'd point out one lousy example.

"Look at Boone's kid out there," he'd tell Petey. "Stylin' and show-boating, catching long fly balls behind his back. That's *not* the way to be." Of course, this was coming from baseball's leading showboat, a guy who sprinted to first on walks and spiked the ball on the stadium's Astroturf after third outs. But let's give Pete a break. He was never the top talent in the game, but to me, he was always the ultimate *ballplayer*.

Pete had a name for me, too: "mullion." That was a ballplayer's word for an ugly girl, but he gave it to anybody he wanted to needle. Some nights when I'd go home from a game with him and Petey, and sleep over at their house, Pete would wake me for breakfast, saying, "C'mon, mullion, up and at 'em. But don't look in the mirror—you'll break it." That didn't bother me. I thought I was pretty cute. Pete's view of my "showboating" didn't bug me, either. We just didn't see eye to eye about that, and being old didn't make him right. I didn't see my outfield catches as stylin' or showing off. I saw them as fun.

It all seemed normal at the time, but now I keep thinking how abnormal my childhood was. In a good way.

I liked to sit in the clubhouse with Manny Trillo, helping him paint his gloves. Manny, the second baseman from Venezuela, liked them black. Rawlings didn't make black gloves yet—that came later—so I'd help him use shoe polish to get the job done. He didn't speak much English, and my Spanish was pretty much limited to *bueno, beisbol,* and *caca cabeza* (poop head), but he'd ruffle my hair and call me *niño simpático*.

During games, I sat in the dugout every chance I got. That was a game-time decision, depending on how the team was doing. If the Phillies were winning, Green let the players' kids into the dugout. If they were losing, we were expected to disappear. Nobody had to tell us. Dad would give me a look—*See ya*. I'd head for the Phanatic's dressing room, or other parts of the stadium the fans never saw. Players' kids could join our moms in the wives' and girlfriends' section behind home plate, but sitting still for nine innings was more than our preteen attention spans could handle. We hit against pitching machines in the batting cages under the stands. We played tapeball in the equipment room. Or pickle, a tag-the-runner game you might know as "rundown," in the hallway outside the clubhouse. We followed hot dog and peanuts–and–Cracker Jack sellers up and down the aisles. I liked the ones who fired packs of peanuts to customers with behind-the-back throws. Just showin' off! A couple of them had control like Carlton. They never missed.

When that got boring, my brother and I would watch a few innings.

I liked to sit with the grounds crew. They were hardworking guys who got paid even less than the Phanatic. I used to sit on a rolled-up tarp talking with them, just me and these "old guys," some of them nineteen or twenty. They'd needle me if Dad had a bad at-bat. "Oh, you got the strikeout gene!" Not to be nasty, just to see if I'd get mad.

There's no needle like a baseball needle; it's usually good-natured, but with an edge. If you're touchy, it can get under your skin. The thing to do is needle the needler right back.

I'd say, "Don't worry about Dad striking out. I'll make up for that one someday."

They liked that. And they weren't really ripping Dad anyway. They knew that he hardly ever struck out. And while he might not have been one of the big stars, he was a Phillie and they loved him. When the Phils won and we watched Dad shake hands with the pitcher and walk off the field with his teammates, the grounds crew guys would pat me on the back like I had something to do with it.

Once a year, the Phillies put on a father-and-son game at the Vet. They moved the bases in to Little League dimensions. Carlton and Tug McGraw pitched underhand. The other dads kicked ground balls and made blooping throws so their kids could be safe on every play, and the next day's *Inquirer* would run pictures of all the smiles and fun family moments of the father-and-son game. I wasn't in those pictures because I wasn't smiling. I was twelve years old, and I was pissed. Because I didn't want any free outs. I wanted to *win* the father-son game. *Don't condescend to me, Bull! You better play me deeper, Schmitty!* Sometimes I'd smoke a liner up the middle. The dad who was pitching would back up and throw overhand, trying to get me out. Even then I'd foul the ball off or hit a grounder. Then I'd run past the shorter bases to the full-field sliding pits because *I came to play.*

Rose used to act a little annoyed at my antics. He liked to tag me out. "Yer out, mullion. Now get off the field." But then he'd grin and give me a slap on the back pocket.

☆ ☆ ☆

I was a B student at school. Not too good, not too bad, not too interested. No straight-A's Bob Boone type, that's for sure. The schooling that mattered to me was going on at Veterans Stadium. Before I ever got to elementary school, I knew where I was going in life—nowhere but the big leagues. If you'd asked if I planned on going to college, I would have said, "Why?" I must have been three or four years old the first time Gramps asked me what I wanted to be when I grew up. I told him I was going to be a ballplayer like him. When Dad asked the same question, I said I was going to be a ballplayer like him, only better.

Our dinner table talk revolved around a particular subject. You can guess what it was. As Dad likes to say, "If you put a bunch of Boones around a table, we won't be talking about modern art."

We talked baseball day and night, breakfast, lunch, dinner, and midnight snack. Shop talk was the background noise of my boyhood.

"Warren Spahn!" Gramps would say. "Now *there's* a pitcher. Do you know he struck me out in the World Series?"

Dad would nod and say, "Yes, sir, we have heard that. Nineteen forty-eight, Boston Braves against the Indians. But you were only a rookie."

"Warren Spahn! There's never been a better left-hander."

"Well, there was Koufax . . ."

"Better than Spahn?"

". . . and I've been catching a fellow name of Carlton. He won twenty-three games last year and struck out two hundred eighty-six. That's about a hundred more K's than Spahn in his best year."

Gramps wasn't convinced. I don't think there was ever a man who was prouder of his generation. "Carlton's good," he admitted. "But did he face Joe DiMaggio? Did he face Ted Williams?"

Sometimes Dad pushed back. Sometimes he said no, Lefty Carlton never faced DiMag or Williams, but he faced Tony Gwynn and George Brett. Mostly, though, he let Gramps sound off. It was only after Aaron and I got to the big leagues that our dinner table talks would get really interesting. When we were little, Dad, the ever-respectful son, let Gramps sound off on the wonderfulness of the olden days, *his* playing days. After all, Gramps was our patriarch. We owed him everything. Suppose he'd followed his father into the carpentry business instead of running off to play pro baseball—today we might be Boone & Sons, Woodworkers. And while there's nothing wrong with carpentry, it would have taken a lot longer to make a million dollars.

And thanks to Marvin Miller and the players' union, Dad was earning almost a million a year in the '80s. Aaron and I were earning postgame Slurpees for Little League victories.

With Mom in the bleachers, keeping score, little brother and I dominated local and regional competition. (Matt would do the same a few years later.) Travel teams were still new in the '80s, not nearly as dominant as they are now, but we dominated them, too. It was like the other teams were playing in slow motion. I mean, at the same age other players were trying to catch pop-ups and hit 50-mph fastballs, I was snagging warning-track drives and smacking 75-mph fastballs during major-league batting practice. Compared to that, Little League wasn't just easy. It was too easy. So I tried mixing things up.

Like most future big leaguers, I played shortstop in Little League. But now and then I'd strap on a mask and chest protector. "Look at me, I'm just like Dad!" That lasted until the day my dad made a surprise visit to our neighborhood field. And he was *fuming*. He moved me—physically—out from behind the plate. Then he made me give the catcher's gear to another kid.

"You're not a catcher," he said.

Now I was mad. "Why? Because I'm not as good as you?"

"That's not it." He said there were only a few things he knew for sure about baseball. "One is that you play shortstop until they tell you that you can't."

"But Dad—you're a catcher."

"You catch because you have to. Because it's the only way to get to the next level," he said. "That's how I got to the big leagues. Let's see if you can do better."

I got my glove and played short. By then I had an inkling that I might not be a born shortstop. The second baseman's footwork and throws felt more natural to me. But Dad turned out to be right anyway. I would wind up playing short for years, until a college coach said, "Boone, you're at second today."

When middle school classmates talked about going to college someday, I said they'd be going without me. By the time they were freshmen at Rutgers or Temple, I planned to be a bonus baby, a first-round draft pick driving my own Beemer around the high minors on my way to the big leagues. It was around this time that a Philadelphia reporter wrote a story about Bob Boone and his precocious kid, the one who was stylin' at the All-Star Game. That was the first time anyone in the media mentioned the three-generation angle. If I made the majors someday, I might be the first one to follow his father and grandfather to the game's highest level—the first third-generation big leaguer.

Which meant zilch to me. Who cared about ancient history? I was burning to leave my brand on the game. Me, *Bret Boone,* not *the third Boone* or *the latest in a bunch of Boones.* Of course I loved Gramps and Dad, but at that age I thought my future was so bright I had to wear shades and lampblack under my eyes. I was on my way . . .

Till I stopped growing.

At the age of fifteen, I was five feet tall. Not five one or five feet and half an inch. Five zero. All but one or two of the other ninth-grade boys at Medford's Shawnee High School were taller. So were most of the girls. Shoot, a lot of the seventh-grade girls were taller than me. And what I lacked in height, I also lacked in bulk. I tipped the bathroom scale at 110. That was about the same as one of Greg Luzinski's legs. It wasn't much more than half what my six-two dad and six-foot grandpa weighed. My physique was a daily shock to me, and it surprised the whole family. Mom would mark my height on the wall with a pencil, and the pencil mark never moved. Dad used to tell me I'd probably be taller than he was. After all, I was the new generation, better fed than old guys like him and Gramps. Instead I leveled off at the height of Sneezy, Dopey, and Bashful. I could hit, field, run, and throw—everything but grow.

I made Shawnee High's varsity baseball team as a freshman, but so what? High school bats were too heavy for me. The coach didn't even let me hit. I'd play shortstop, and then sit in the dugout while the DH batted in my place. Our pitcher got to bat, but not me! Finally, late in the season, I got into the lineup as a hitter. Batting ninth.

One night I asked Mom if we could speed things up. "What things?" she said.

"My growth," I said.

She laughed. "You'll be all right. Let nature take its course. Now go to bed." So I went to sleep and dreamed of being six three.

☆ ☆ ☆

That was the year the Phillies decided their catcher was too old. Dad was thirty-three, which is about ninety in catcher years. He was coming off a 1981 season when he was hurt most of the year. He batted .211 with only 4 home runs and 24 RBIs. So Philadelphia traded for twenty-nine-year-old Bo Diaz—a deal that cost the Phillies a young outfielder, Lonnie Smith—and sold Dad to the California Angels.

As it turned out, the washed-up catcher had some baseball left in him. Nine years' worth, to be exact, including five Gold Gloves and another All-Star appearance.

The Angels' arms couldn't match the Phillies of Steve Carlton and Tug McGraw. Their pitching staff was led by Geoff Zahn, Ken Forsch, and Mike Witt. Dad helped lead them to the 1982 AL West title. He also took his family home to Southern California—to Orange County, an hour's drive north of San Diego. He and Mom said we'd love it there. The Angels played in Anaheim, ten minutes from Disneyland!

Mom and Dad loved the Philadelphia area, but they were glad to go home to SoCal. Gramps and Grandma Patsy, still living in San Diego, were thrilled, too. My little brothers were too young to know the difference. All they cared about was the Disneyland part.

That left me, throwing a fit in the driveway.

"I'm not goin'!"

Dad said I'd be crazy about California, where kids played ball year-round. I didn't want to hear it. I was a Jersey boy. Dirt bikes, not surfboards. The Boss, not the Beach Boys.

"You can't make me!"

Of course he could. His job was in California now. So I said goodbye to all my friends, and our home with its tree house and zipline, and the basement with its Wrestlemania stage and paintings of Dad on the walls. I enrolled at El Dorado High School in Placentia, California, and tried out for the baseball team. All five foot zero of me.

I made the team, too, and that turned out to be a mixed blessing.

A couple of years after being the superstar of Medford Little League, I was the runt of the roster. The fields were bigger now, but not me. The bats were heavier, but not me. Some of my teammates were six feet tall, with mustaches, while I still looked like a child. All over. I mean, I didn't have a hint of body hair on me, and I was showering with teammates who looked like men. That's embarrassing for a kid.

I felt washed up at the age of fifteen. It's hard to feel smaller than that.

For the first time in my life, baseball was no fun.

5

THE EDUCATION OF A BALLPLAYER

What's the old saying? "The older you get, the smarter your dad gets." Invented by a dad, probably. But I can't argue with it. The more I grew, the more I saw that my father was right about most things.

California, for one.

At first I hated being the squirt with the Jersey accent at El Dorado High, a few miles from the stadium where Dad played for the Angels. I was totally out of place, not just pint-size but dressed all wrong. The other kids dressed like surfers and skateboarders. They wore Keds and jams and T-shirts, while I stood out like a manicured thumb in my Calvin Klein jeans and button-down shirts. Preppy, they called me. But I adapted. You might say I hit puberty the way Hank Aaron hit fastballs. Pretty soon I was decked out in 501s and a T-shirt, hanging on the beach with girls in bikinis while the other guys surfed. I never learned to surf, mainly because it was more fun staying on the beach—for obvious reasons.

Baseball was literally the key to my family's move from New Jersey to California. At first Dad rented a house from pitcher Frank Tanana, who'd been traded by the Angels to Boston (for Fred Lynn) before signing with the Texas Rangers. Next we crammed into a condo Dad bought from another Angels teammate. California girls aside, there were two great things about that period. Little brothers Aaron and Matt shared a room, while I got my own room, and I finally hit a growth spurt. During my second season playing short for the El Dorado Golden Hawks, I sprang up six inches! Not enough to make me big, exactly, but at five foot six and 140 pounds, I now cast a shadow that could cover second base. Those six inches and extra poundage made the game fun again. A 29-ounce bat that had felt overwhelming the year before began to feel like a toothpick. Now I was hitting bullets off six-foot pitchers.

Facing good pitching was another benefit of moving to my parents' and grandparents' home state. In California just about everybody plays year-round, so the competition's at a higher level. With rare exceptions, California high schoolers threw harder than anyone I'd faced in New Jersey. No more than 1 in 50 ever touched 90 mph—today it's more like 1 in 10 in Sun Belt high schools—but plenty could reach the high 80s, and some of them threw curves, too. I even swung at a high school slider or two. It would be years before I learned to hit a good breaking ball, but once I got a little muscle on me, I could turn a fastball around. What's it take to do that? Start with a lot of fast-twitch muscle fibers. Most people's muscles are about half fast-twitch and half slow-twitch. Endurance athletes have mostly slow-twitch muscles, while athletes in sports that call for short bursts of action—sprinters, football and baseball players—have more fast-twitch. I was in the 80 percent fast-twitch range, which means it's a good thing I wasn't a marathoner. My muscles were made for the quick, explosive reaction it takes to hit major-league pitching.

Once the swing starts, it's a matter of delivering the bat's sweet spot squarely to the middle of the ball. That's when contact feels perfect. All the force of your swing gets transferred into the ball, so the bat doesn't vibrate. Your hands don't sting. You don't feel contact at all, but the ball goes back where it came from, faster.

As I grew, my ground balls to infielders turned into base hits. (As a sophomore, almost all my hits were singles.) Then, as I continued growing—eventually to five foot ten, where I stopped—the singles turned to doubles. Finally, some of the doubles started flying over the fence.

One day my guidance counselor asked about my career plans. It was a standard question. Was I planning to go to college? If so, I might want to give more than a passing thought to my grades. If not, what sort of crummy job did I expect to qualify for after high school fun and games?

I sat there looking at the counselor like he had three eyes. A backup plan? *Me?*

He was only being realistic. The counselor knew that my dad was the Angels' catcher, but he also knew that the vast majority of big-league players' sons never play a single game in the majors. To his credit, he'd gone to the trouble of looking it up. Out of all the thousands of major-league baseball players dating back to the 1900s, fewer than a hundred were the sons of major leaguers. And almost all of them were underachievers. Sure, my dad had followed Gramps to the bigs, and eventually to the All-Star Game. Along with Buddy Bell, the Rangers third baseman whose dad, Gus, made four All-Star teams in the '50s, Dad was the most accomplished second-generation player in baseball history. But that was practically a double whammy. My guidance counselor asked if I knew how many third-generation players had reached the majors.

That was a math question I could handle. "Zero."

"That's right. Zero," he said. "So you'll need a backup plan. If baseball doesn't work, what's Plan B?"

"More baseball. *Pro* baseball. You can write it down in my file. In five years I'll be in the big leagues."

Looking back, I can't believe how naïve and immature I was. (As it turned out, I was wrong, too. I wouldn't be in the big leagues in five years.) I just didn't think the usual limits applied to me, because I was born to play ball. If making the majors meant being the only third-generation player ever, fine, that's what I'd be.

Unless somebody beat me to it.

The funny thing is, there was another candidate for the three-generation trophy, and what seemed like a trivia question to me— Which high school hotshot has a father and grandpa who played in the majors?—was more like a mission to him.

The *other* funny thing is, there were about 24,500 high schools scattered across the United States, and he went to the one closest to mine.

Jim Campanis was the tall, sandy-haired catcher for Valencia High School, our rival, a mile down Yorba Linda Boulevard and Bradford Avenue from El Dorado. Two years older than me, he stood six foot one and tipped the scales at 200, while I was still the smallest guy on my team. Scouts drooled over Jim, not just for his size and home run power but for what they called his bloodlines. His dad, Jim Campanis Sr., had been a backup catcher for the Dodgers, Royals, and Pirates. His grandfather, Al, played a week for the Brooklyn Dodgers in 1943 before becoming the scout who discovered Sandy Koufax and going on to be a team executive. Al Campanis would lose his job as the Dodgers' GM after telling Ted Koppel on a 1987 *Nightline* episode that blacks "lack the necessities" to be managers or club executives. But in 1985, when Jim was a power-hitting senior at Valencia, Al was one of two prominent grandpas watching high school games in Orange County's Empire League.

As the GM who brought Fernando Valenzuela, Orel Hershiser, and Pedro Guerrero to the first-place Dodgers, the team that always overshadowed Dad and the Angels, Al Campanis was the bigger name, but Gramps had been a far better player. His 151 big-league homers and 1,260 hits looked pretty imposing next to Al's zero homers and 2 career hits. Jim Campanis Sr., with his 4 career home runs and 32 hits, looked puny compared to my dad, who would wind up with 105 homers and 1,838 hits. I needled Jim Campanis about those stats. I'd yell across the diamond: "Hey, big guy, my family's better than yours!"

He'd ask, "Who's the little guy with the big mouth?" And our long, twisty relationship was under way.

One Saturday night when his parents were away, Jim hosted a kegger. It was an invitation-only gathering of top jocks and cool upperclassmen. Naturally, I crashed it.

As Jim would remember that night, "I walked into my kitchen and saw this preppy-looking kid and thought, *What's he doing here?*"

I guess my Jersey roots were showing. Instead of cargo pants and a T-shirt, I wore slacks and a button-down Pierre Cardin. Hey, that's respect. I dressed up for your party, Jimmy! And if some of the other kids laughed at my outfit, that was as cool to me as the beer we weren't quite old enough to be drinking (as the cops who broke up the party pointed out). My attitude, then and now, was, *If they don't like me, it's their problem.*

☆ ☆ ☆

I was still going to the ballpark with Dad every chance I got. We didn't talk baseball during those freeway drives to Anaheim. He wasn't the type to share his thoughts about the starter he'd be catching that night, or how he was hitting, or how his beat-up knees and feet hurt so much he sometimes had trouble sleeping. No, he saw those drives mainly as a chance to discuss my approach to schoolwork, which was still, um, how should I put this? Less than diligent? Somewhat indifferent?

Sucky? Here was Stanford grad Bob Boone, one of baseball's high-IQ guys, driving to work with his eldest son, who was barely pulling B's in high school.

"How's your algebra going?" he asked.

"Great," I lied.

El Dorado baseball coach Steve Gullotti's wife was a math teacher. She tutored me after practice every day. I was fine at computation—divide your hits by ABs to get your batting average; multiply a pitcher's earned runs by nine, then divide by innings pitched to find his ERA—but algebra was Greek to me. What did πr^2 have to do with anything in real life? Even now I think it's crazy that anyone but math specialists has to learn algebra. We've got a generation of kids who can't make change for a dollar or find their way around their hometowns without a phone app, but they're still taking algebra.

"Mrs. Gullotti knows her stuff," I said. I didn't tell Dad that we'd worked out a study plan. She liked baseball almost as much as math, so we skipped the math and talked baseball.

"Good. You'll need algebra for your SATs. You know that's what colleges look at first, don't you?"

"Yes, Dad. I know, Dad." I didn't add that my SATs didn't matter because I wasn't going to college. There were two reasons for that: a) the best players signed pro contracts right out of high school and b) I was one of the best players. You don't need algebra to see where "a + b" was going.

All the Boones agreed on one thing—it was great to get to the ballpark. As a teenager I wasn't as bright-eyed and bushy-tailed as the little kid growing up in the Phillies' clubhouse, but I still loved the sights, sounds, and even smells of the game. Walking into Anaheim Stadium, the Big A, hours before the game, Dad and I took in the bright green grass and red clay dirt of the infield, and the sweaty leather-and-aftershave scent of the clubhouse. Pretty soon we split up. Dad went off to exercise. He started his workday with yoga and kung fu, which I thought was comical. Kung fu might help you in a bench-clearing brawl, but I'd rather take BP. Once, when he asked me to join him for a workout, I said, "I don't have to. I can *hit*."

After kung fu he'd huddle with that night's starting pitcher, to hash out how they'd go after the other team's lineup. I headed for the visitors' clubhouse. In those days I was the new kid working for Brian "Bubba" Harkins, the Angels' legendary visitors' clubhouse manager. His job was to keep the visiting team as comfortable as possible in a locker room half the size of the home team's. Bubba coddled the visitors, since most of his pay consisted of tips. At that time the major-league minimum salary was $109,000. The minimum tip for a clubbie was $35 per series. Even rookies had to give Bubba that much. The big-dime stars might tip him $100 per game, so he did his best for all of them. Bubba knew which superstar liked a postgame Budweiser, which utility infielder liked a Dr Pepper with extra ice. Carlton Fisk, for instance, liked to have a chilled Coors Gold waiting for him after a game. Cal Ripken Jr.'s only requirement was a brand-new pair of sanitary socks for every game, while the Indians and Yankees outfielder Mel Hall needed a new box of Fruity Pebbles every day. Hall just loved his Fruity Pebbles! Bubba could also line up dinner reservations for you and your wife, or a car and driver after the game (maybe for you and your girlfriend), or Disneyland tickets if your family was flying in tomorrow, or all of the above.

My job was less glamorous—laundry, mainly. Plus errands that came up when the clubhouse manager was busy. One ruckus came after Yankees manager Billy Martin corralled me and said, "Kid, bring me a bottle of vodka." Which I did. The executive suites were stocked with liquor. All I had to do was say, "It's for Billy," and a server handed me a bottle. (Maybe I should have told Jim Campanis and his buddies about this gig.) Later, after I mentioned my errand to Dad, he charged into Martin's office and told him, "You'd better *never* use *my* son to fetch *your* liquor *again*!" And Billy never did. I went back to throwing jockstraps into the industrial-strength washers under the stands at the Big A. Yes, I carried Cal Ripken Jr.'s jock. Roger Clemens's and Don Mattingly's and Rickey Henderson's, too, but it's not like I got a kick out of it. I just wanted to be at the ballpark with my dad, even it meant washing socks and jocks and jerseys. I planned to be back here in a few years, and not as a no-name kid scoring an occasional ten-dollar tip from a guy who hit a homer that night. I planned to be the guy who hit the homer.

Bubba never forgot how I pointed at a particular locker and told him, "That's the one I want when I'm a big leaguer." It wasn't a corner locker like the big stars get, often along with an adjoining locker for their fan mail and all the free stuff people give them. It was just a good locker, in a row with the everyday players. Bubba said, "Forget it. You've got no shot." He asked if I had any idea how long the odds were that a kid whose dad and grandpa had been big leaguers would make it a family trifecta.

"Just you wait," I said.

Meanwhile I played other positions fans never hear about. Once the game started, it was my job to go down the right-field line and warm up the Angels' right fielder between innings. Now, the 1986 Angels had a pretty star-studded roster. First baseman Wally Joyner was so popular that the papers called the stadium "Wally World." Pitcher Don Sutton was on his way to the Hall of Fame. But right fielder Reggie Jackson was their biggest star by far, and he never let you forget it. I'd stand in foul territory, tossing a ball with him so he could keep his throwing arm loose. It was as commonplace as a practice swing, but Reggie, being Reggie, expected perfection. If I threw a ball he had to reach for, he gave me a dirty look. If I threw one over his head, he looked pained and threw up his arms, like *How can I, the great Reggie, put up with this?*

Reggie was such a star that he got a piece of the Angels' gate receipts. On top of his $3.6 million salary, he got 50 cents for every ticket the club sold beyond a certain level. The fans knew all about his attendance clause. They liked to rag him—and support him for his homers—by throwing quarters and half-dollar coins onto the field. "Here you go, Reg. Here's my fifty cents!" He'd nod and bow and put the coins in his pocket. Sometimes I helped him avoid bad hops by putting some of them in my pocket.

Reggie impressed me but didn't intimidate me. When he gave me the evil eye for a bad warm-up toss, I thought, *Okay, you're great and all, and I respect your Reggieness, but I'm doing the best I can. I grew up taking infield with Mike Schmidt, so don't give me attitude.*

After nights at the Big A, I spent afternoons on the high school field at El Dorado. Orange County was a hotbed of high school ball. Still is. Perfect weather and affluence are good for growing ballplayers. I was still getting used to the perfectly manicured field at El Dorado when our team went up against Los Alamitos High with its superstars J. T. Snow (son of the Los Angeles Rams' wide receiver Jack Snow), who would play fourteen big-league seasons, and Robb Nen, who went on to save 314 games for the Marlins and Giants. Another local rival, Lakewood, had Damion Easley, who would play seventeen big-league seasons and make an All-Star Game for the Tigers.

Coach Gullotti told me I could learn from watching guys like Snow and Easley, but I wasn't listening. I mean, I'd grown up watching Schmidt, Pete Rose, and Rod Carew. Not to mention my dad, who sometimes annoyed me by staying in the background all the time. Back when I was a five-foot freshman, Dad thought it would be better for me to play every day on the junior varsity instead of playing short for the varsity and sitting in the dugout while a bigger boy batted in my place. But did he tell the coach what he thought? No, there'd be no catcher's interference from Dad. He didn't want to be one of those overbearing baseball dads who ruin everything for everybody. He wanted me to make my own way. Fifteen years after Grandma Patsy pitched me into the swimming pool, it was sink-or-swim all over again.

As a junior, I batted a school-record .423. Even better, I turned sixteen. The rich kids, the cool few whose dads were CEOs or real estate developers, drove shiny sports cars. I wanted one of my own. Being a high school baseball stud wasn't bad, but a baseball stud in a Porsche had a better chance with the girls who did the best job filling their bikinis.

I learned to drive in Dad's turbocharged Datsun 280Z, and he knew how I was dying for a sharp set of wheels. As the son of a local baseball hero, I thought I deserved one. He didn't.

"You need to learn the value of a dollar," he said. I was thinking, *That's not algebra. The value of a dollar is a hundred cents, so I'm going to need about five hundred thousand cents.* But Dad was determined to make this a learning moment. I was his number one son, the one who was supposed to set an example for my brothers, and he was worried I'd get spoiled.

Maybe he felt guilty about being away from us so much of the time. Nobody complained, but he wasn't much of an everyday part of our lives, and he knew it. So he made the most of the chances he had. He said, "Bret, it's time you got your own car. But I'm not buying you one."

"You're not?"

"You need to earn it."

I knew my dad well enough to know that there was no point in arguing. He'd thought it through, pro and con, and worked out what was right and what was wrong. That meant exactly two things: he was right, and I had to go along.

That meant working during the summer. Baseball practice, *then* work. He said he'd match whatever I earned. "And then we'll go get you a car." So I spent the summer of 1985 washing and detailing cars.

I earned almost $2,500. Dad matched it, and off we went to pick out my car. Being a major-league player, Dad knew plenty of car dealers. One of them sent us to an auction where he promised we'd get a great deal. All day I pictured pulling into our driveway in a sports car even slicker than his. Instead he picked out a used Nissan truck with rust around the rims. I said, "Dad, I want to drive the girls to the beach, not a demolition derby."

He said, "Do you know what it costs to insure a sports car for a teenage driver?"

"How much?"

"More than you can afford."

He offered me the keys to the Nissan, take them or leave them. Of course I took them. And it turned out that old truck went zero to 60 faster than he could say, "Mind the speed limit!"

Dad couldn't make many of my games, but Gramps made the trip from San Diego every chance he got. He'd come off a thousand-mile scouting trip for the Red Sox and drive straight to the field at El Dorado. He was sixty-three years old, climbing the bleachers on those creaky knees of his, looking unimpressed. I'd go 3-for-4 with two homers and he'd talk about the out. "A fat fastball, and you pop it up." It drove me nuts. Gramps had been my best baseball friend since I was in diapers, pulling him out of bed for a catch first thing in the morning, and he wouldn't give me a pat on the back.

One day he gave me such a hard time I quit listening. *See you later, old man.* I stomped off to my position at short, but I'd left my glove behind. I was jogging back to get it when I heard Gramps talking to another scout.

"Yeah, the shortstop," he was saying. "That's my grandson, and he can *play*. You watch—he's going to be a star in the big leagues."

That was the day I figured something out about my grandfather. Ray Boone was a man of his generation. He was never going to praise you to your face. It just wasn't done. He was the same way with the person he loved most in the world. I remembered how he used to hold his coffee cup up in the air, waiting for Grandma Patsy to serve him. He wouldn't thank her when she refilled it, wouldn't say a word. But as soon as she was out of earshot, he'd lean over to me and say, "Bret, did you see who just went by? That's the most wonderful woman in the world."

But he couldn't come right out and tell her. Or tell me he thought I had a future in baseball. That would have been too mushy for a man like him. And you know what? It made me love him even more.

One time he surprised me during a high school game we played against Lakewood High. The umpire had a chip on his shoulder—he didn't like the cocky second baseman with the big-shot baseball name. A Lakewood player slid into me at second on a double-play ball. Our legs got tangled up. A second later we're scrambling to our feet, and it's possible that it looks like we're fighting—if you're half-blind. The ump came running over the mound and thumbed me out of the game.

You should have seen Gramps. The moment the game ended, he followed the ump to his car, chewing him out the whole way, defending me, and telling him that he'd tossed a kid he'd be asking for an autograph someday.

It was worth getting ejected to hear that.

Gramps was almost as respected for his scouting as for his big-league career. In thirty years of driving around the Southwest for the Red Sox, he signed future stars like Marty Barrett, Sam Horn, Phil Plantier, and a cocky, chunky junior college kid named Schilling.

That was in 1986, my junior year at El Dorado. Gramps drove to Phoenix to meet Curt Schilling and his father, Cliff. He wasn't all that crazy about Schilling, a nineteen-year-old nobody from Yavapai College, but he liked the kid's size (six five, 200 pounds) and heavy fastball. He figured he could sign him for a modest bonus because nobody knew the ins and outs of scouting better than Gramps. Most of them started with the prospect's father.

Cliff Schilling was an army veteran and Ray Boone was an old navy man. That helped. By 1986 Cliff was manning the night desk at a Ramada Inn, chain-smoking even after doctors told him he had lung cancer. He urged his son to sign with the Sox for the $15,000 Gramps was offering, but Curt wanted more.

Gramps knew that $15,000 was more than Curt's dad made in a year at the Ramada. He said, "Son, if you're as good as we both think you are, fifteen thousand is going to be meal money in a few years. But if you're going to jerk me around, I'm going home."

Curt said, "Where do I sign?"

Two years later, Cliff Schilling died of lung cancer. Eight months after that, Curt made his major-league debut. He took his first big-league paycheck to the bank, cashed it, and took the money to his hotel room. Six thousand dollars in twenty-dollar bills. He threw all those twenties on the bed and said, 'Dad, you were right!' "

For the next twenty years, whenever Schilling started a game, he left a ticket at the will-call window in his father's name. To this day, when Curt sees me or my brother Aaron, he tells us that story about signing with Gramps. He faced our dad a few times in 1990, Dad's last year in the majors, and today he works at ESPN, sometimes with Aaron. In baseball, family stories keep coming around.

☆ ☆ ☆

"The Boone kid," which might as well have been my full name in high school, had a big senior year at El Dorado. After batting .500 with 10 homers in 30 games, I joined a California All-Star team that won the 1986 Connie Mack World Series. Jeff Kent played third base on that club. Kent and I would play 31 big-league seasons and make 8

All-Star games. He didn't have his mustache yet, and I hadn't started bleaching my hair surfer-dude blond, but we figured we'd meet in the majors sooner or later. Correction: sooner. The 1987 major-league draft was coming up, and everybody said my hot-prospect self was sure to go in the first few rounds. That could mean a signing bonus up to $100,000. *Suck on that, doubters,* I thought. *Maybe you'd like to buy a used Nissan truck.*

Today, baseball's June draft of amateur players is must-see TV for hard-core baseball fans. In 1987 it was still just a conference call. Team took turns phoning their selections in to Major League Baseball (MLB) headquarters on Park Avenue in New York City. Each club's GM or a selected scout then phoned the player's home with the good news. On June 2, 1987, the last-place Mariners surprised nobody by selecting Ken Griffey Jr., son of a still-active Braves outfielder, number one overall. Griffey was one of the best prospects ever. After the phone rang at the Griffey house in Cincinnati, he gave reporters his ear-to-ear smile. "I'm happy being me!" he said. He signed for a record bonus of $160,000.

At the Boone house in Orange County, the phone did not ring. The first round seemed to take forever. Jack McDowell went fifth overall to the White Sox. Other first-rounders included Delino DeShields, Chris Carpenter, future Hall of Famer Craig Biggio—chosen twenty-second overall—Pete Harnisch, Travis Fryman, and a bunch of guys you never heard of. In round two, the phone rang for Albert Belle and Derek Bell, but not me. I was disappointed but not crushed. The draft lasted three days. I could still go on the second day, score a five-figure bonus, and prove myself in the minors.

I didn't sleep much that night. But I was determined not to let anybody see me sweat. Instead of sitting around staring at the phone, I went to the beach on the second day, and only called home seven or eight times.

"Did anybody call?"

Mom said, "Not yet, dear."

Ray Lankford went 72nd overall, Scott Coolbaugh 77th, Steve Sparks 123rd. In the sixth to tenth rounds, Dave Hollins, Kevin Belcher, Reggie Sanders, and Derek Lee got the call. The Orioles selected Mike Mussina in the 11th round, 273rd overall. Steve Finley went 425th, David Segui 455th, Jeromy Burnitz 617th.

In the 26th round, with the 680th selection of the draft, the Mets tabbed catcher Dan Wilson. Still no call to Casa Boone.

Finally, on the third and last day, with the 711th overall pick, the Minnesota Twins chose me. When the phone rang and a Twins scout gave me the news, he sounded like I should thank him. I said, "How could you let me drop to the twenty-eighth round? You passed on me twenty-seven times."

At that moment, I would have bet him that at least six hundred of the guys picked ahead of me would never make the majors. And I would have been right. The Twins' first-round pick that year, Willie Banks, who signed for the same $160,000 Griffey got, would be one of the exceptions. He'd go 11-12 in his best big-league season and win 33 games in nine years.

I was crushed, but the more I thought about it, the clearer my future looked. *I'll show them,* I thought.

The Twins scout came to our house. He sat at the dining room table with Dad and me and made his offer. The bonus would only be $40,000, but he said I could make a lot more later, if I was as good as he thought.

Here was my chance to be a professional ballplayer. He put the contract on the table. All I had to do was sign it.

6

THE OLD COLLEGE TRY

The Minnesota scout sat in our living room, waiting for my decision. Dad and I listened politely to every word the man said. I was a little fidgety, thinking *Let's get this over with*. I had a baseball scholarship offer from the University of Southern California, so the choice on the table wasn't much of a choice. A $40,000 bonus, or a full ride to USC that was worth about $200,000?

The Twins wouldn't add a dollar to their offer, so Dad and I shook the scout's hand and told him, in the nicest possible way, to get lost. And that's when it really dawned on me: I was going to college.

More school. That was the last thing I'd expected after hitting .500 as a high school senior. Dad was the college man in the family; he actually liked hitting the books. I didn't. But now, instead of going straight from high school to pro ball like Gramps, I'd be going forty-five miles up Interstate 5 to one of the most academically demanding colleges in the country.

It was 1987. Michael Jackson's "Bad" was on the radio, matching my mood while I loaded my gear—bats, gloves, schoolbooks, shaving kit, and a backpack stuffed with clothes and family pictures—into Mom's car for the drive to USC. Dad joined us. He'd be catching for the Angels that night, but he wanted to help me move into my dorm room.

On the way north we drove past his workplace, the Big A. A couple hours later I was settling into my new home. Fluor Tower, one of USC's athletic dorms, is a red brick box eleven stories high, about as homey as a hospital. Mom and Dad hugged me and drove home. My suitemates hadn't arrived, so I sat on my bed, looking out the window toward the baseball field, feeling all alone in the world. I could almost hear my dad's voice. The night before, he'd given me one of his father-son talks. It was brief, maybe a minute long. After roughly nine million arguments with umpires and mound conferences with pitchers, he knew how to make his point in a few words.

Dad told me not to be bummed about going to college. After turning down the Twins' offer I wouldn't be eligible for another major-league draft for three years. But I could still get drafted in 1990 and sign for a fortune. Meanwhile, college ball would refine my game, maybe even refine *me*. "You're still a kid," he said. "College will make you a man."

I only heard a couple of the words he said. *Three years!*

At first, USC was an eye-opener. I was a suburban kid and the campus is in Watts, one of the poorest, toughest neighborhoods in Los Angeles. Other kids told me to be careful walking the streets near the campus. They were "full of Crips and Bloods." But this is America, isn't it? A guy's got a right to a Big Mac and fries. So I took my life in my hands and walked to McDonald's. No problem . . . until the day I had to shoot my way out of a gang war.

I'm kidding. Yes, there were gangbangers around. I'm no criminologist, but if you see a guy wearing a red bandanna leaning on a lamppost, with a bulge in the *back* of his waistband, he's probably not a crossing guard. But they were taking care of their business, and I was taking care of mine. Which meant cutting classes to spend time in the batting cage.

Other students asked, "What's your major?"

"Communications," I said, thinking, *I'm learning to communicate with the opposite sex and hit more balls to the opposite field.* Truthfully, as with a lot of Division I athletes, my sport was my major.

At first I gave the books a shot despite the fact that *King Kong* was the only book I ever read all the way through. (Thirty years later, this book makes two.) But why waste a USC education? "I'm changing my ways," I told my parents. "You're looking at a real student-athlete." Please ignore the sound of Aaron laughing in the background, because I meant it. In my first English class, Comp 101, the professor had everyone write an essay about something we loved. I forget my topic (if you're betting, take the odds on baseball), but I wrote feverishly. And when the prof read an essay to the class, it was mine. He actually praised my writing! At that point there were fireworks going off in my brain. And my ego. I spent a semester slaving over essays for that professor . . . and he gave me a C. That's when I thought, *Shoot, I can pull C's cramming Cliffs Notes the night before the final.* After that I cut more classes than I attended. Athletes had to maintain a 2.0 grade point average, a C average, to stay eligible. My GPA as a freshman was exactly 2.0. As a sophomore . . . 2.0. As a junior . . . you guessed it.

This is *not* an academic approach I recommend. Looking back, I wish I'd been more of a self-starter in school. I've always been good with numbers, but even today, when my kids come to me with homework on anything from algebra to Shakespeare, I tell them, "Call your grandpa."

It's not like I was lazy or dumb. I've got enough of my father's genes to be intrigued by stuff that matters—how money and politics and other forces make the world go around. It's just that I never found much of that in the classroom. Besides, what preoccupied me was the simplest sort of math, like, it takes two hits in five tries to bat .400. And in spite of being passed over 710 times in the '87 draft, my career plans hadn't changed. I was as single-minded as Tommy Trojan, the

ancient mascot whose statue stands in the middle of USC's campus.
Warrior Tommy had two goals in life:

1) Beat the Greeks in the Trojan War of the twelfth century BC,
   and
2) Beat UCLA

I had two of my own:

1) Make it to the big leagues, and
2) Make it to the big leagues

So I report to my first USC practice and run into the team's stud
catcher, a six-one, 200-pounder who looked a little familiar. Jim
Campanis!

"Hey, Boonie, welcome to Watts," he said. "I'm still going to beat
you to the big leagues."

I just gave him a nod. "Good luck with that."

Jimmy Campanis was two years ahead of me, two years closer to
the goal that meant more to him than it meant to me. I mean, as much
as I loved Gramps and Dad, my plan was to tear the cover off college
pitching, zoom to the majors, and make fans forget everyone who
wasn't named Bret Robert Boone.

Unrealistic? Sure. Naïve? Absolutely.

Would I have had any chance *without* that sort of crazy confidence?
Maybe not.

☆ ☆ ☆

I played second and batted fifth for coach Mike Gillespie's USC Trojans. Not a bad life. We rode a luxury bus to play UCLA and flew to
the other schools in the Pac-10. We were welcome at every frat party
on campus. And we had a hell of a club. There was catcher Campanis

thumping home runs, with shortstop Bret Barberie getting on base ahead of him. Barberie, who went on to play six years in the majors, was all business. He'd talk the maintenance men into turning on the stadium lights so he could take grounders at night. He and I gave Gillespie the only team in baseball history with two one-*t* Brets up the middle. Better yet, we had future big leaguer Damon Buford in the outfield and future All-Star infielder Jeff Cirillo (later a teammate of mine in Seattle) *pitching*. Our biggest name was Rodney Peete, who joined us every spring to play third base after quarterbacking USC's football team to the Rose Bowl. Rodney led the football Trojans past a UCLA team starring Troy Aikman (twice!) and bopped homers for us as a hobby.

We had plenty of baseball bloodlines between the foul lines— not just Campanis and me but Buford, whose father, Don, was a big leaguer. Barberie's dad had played in the minors. Utility man Jay Hemond's father, Roland, was the longtime general manager of the White Sox and Orioles. Jay wasn't the type to fill up a box score, but a couple of years later he left his own impression on the game as baseball instructor for the movie *Field of Dreams*.

I batted .326 as a freshman, with 8 home runs and 53 RBIs, second on the team behind Campanis. There was nothing wrong with my glove, either; Coach Gillespie called me "a magician on defense." So what's not to like? Well, I might not have been the Pac-10's Mr. Congeniality. People said I had a short fuse, which wasn't so bad until they added, "like Mike Tyson." In the first national story about me, the *Los Angeles Times* told the world, "Boone's freshman season was noteworthy not only for his bat, but for the loud and visual outbursts that followed his own perceived failures." Before long, *Sports Illustrated* mentioned my "helmet-throwing."

Outbursts? Helmet-throwing?

Okay, maybe I bounced a few helmets on my way to the dugout after striking out. My language wasn't always G-rated. But I'd only get mad at myself, nobody else. Looking back, I'm amazed by my immaturity in those days. I had no idea how hard the game could be. How hard it's *supposed* to be as you climb the ladder from high school to college and finally, hopefully, to the pros. I was still kicking myself for every ball that wasn't smoked for extra bases. Bloop single? *Sonofa-bitch!* I'd practically bust a vein cursing it.

It would be a few years before I learned one of life's great lessons: Every flare that falls in is a gift from the baseball gods.

At least my attitude helped keep me in shape. I ran many a lap for Coach Gillespie. "You're not a bad kid, Boone, but you're your own worst enemy!" he'd yell while I cussed myself out. "Give me a lap around the diamond!"

Everyone expected me to be like my dad, the calm, coolheaded catcher for the Angels. To his credit, he wasn't one of them. Dad told people that he was the boring one in the family. "Bret's passionate," he said. "He wants to get a hit every time. He's *eighteen*."

Was he always on my side? No. One day, Gillespie batted me fourth. I came up late in the game with two runners on base, nobody out. Gillespie, coaching third base, flashed the bunt signal. (In college and the low minors, the head coach or manager usually doubles as third-base coach.) I'm thinking, *What, me bunt?* I gave it a couple of halfhearted tries, then ripped a double off the fence. A Campanis grounder got me to third, where Gillespie was waiting with a homework assignment. He said, "I want you to go home and ask your dad what a hitter should do in that situation."

I did as I was told. At our next practice I reported to Gillespie, "Dad said you were right. The cleanup hitter should bunt." He looked happy until I went on. "And that's why my dad bats ninth. I think you're both wrong."

That line was worth a couple of laps.

☆ ☆ ☆

After sprouting from five foot to five foot ten in high school, I was sure I'd keep growing. I expected to pass six-foot Gramps and six-two Dad. Wrong. Thirty years later I'm still five ten. "Little" brother Aaron grew to six foot two, and baby brother Matt matched him at six two, leaving me as the runt in the Boone bunch. That's another double-edged part of my story, since size matters in baseball. If everything else is equal, a six-two, 220-pound hitter's fly ball clears the fence while a five-ten guy's fly ball falls a little short.

Lucky for guys like me, everything else is never equal.

In baseball, more than other sports, heart matters. Heart, guts, brains, instinct, luck—all those other things that make life interesting. That's why baseball is the best game in the world. And as it turned out, being the shortest Boone boy was a blessing. It gave me extra motivation—a chip on my low-altitude shoulder. More important, my compact size helped me stay in the middle infield, where I belonged. Taller guys tend to wind up at other positions.

The power alleys at USC's Dedeaux Field were 375 feet from the plate. The prevailing wind whistled in over the tennis courts beyond the left-field fence. Right-handed hitters like me lost some homers to that breeze, though it didn't seem to bother some guys. Four years before I got there, a rangy first baseman named Mark McGwire swatted 31 homers for the Trojans.

I wasn't a prospect on McGwire's level, but every year you'd find me on a handful of preseason All-America teams. Then I'd hit a smattering of homers and drive in about 60 runs. Good but not great. My average dropped to .273 in my sophomore year. My reputation still got me onto a preseason Team USA that toured Cuba, where we waited for Fidel Castro's motorcade to deliver *El Presidente* to the ballpark. He whooped it up while Team Cuba beat the snot out of us. The Cubans, led by third baseman Omar Linares, were *men*. We were still boys. When we flew home and told our friends and college teammates how good the Cubans were, nobody believed us. America would find out soon enough.

Back at USC, I learned that playing home games near Hollywood has its benefits. One day, Doug DeCinces, an Angels teammate of Dad's, called me and asked, "Bret, you want to be in a movie?" "Hell yes!" I said. (Now, as a rule, I can't stand baseball movies. Most of the dramas are fake and most of the comedies are dumb. I love parts of *Bull Durham,* including Kevin Costner's efforts to look the part on the field. He worked just as hard on his pitching motion in *For Love of the Game,* but that was ruined for me by his heat, which was way short of lukewarm. His windup and delivery looked fine, but then his fastball took half an hour to reach the plate. Why didn't they speed up the film?)

For this movie—*Mr. Baseball,* starring Tom Selleck—DeCinces wanted me to play shortstop. Frank Thomas would play first base. Frank was the American League's Rookie of the Year, but everybody knew who the movie star was. Selleck strutted around like the big man on campus. He had a decent swing for an actor but no idea that he couldn't hit a real home run even if you moved the plate to second base. Everything about the movie was amateur hour. The director, an Australian named Fred Schepisi, thought he could have a bunch of extras dance around the field, chewing tobacco, and they'd look like ballplayers.

Fine by me—I was getting two hundred dollars a day to field grounders. "Just make it authentic," the director said.

The batter hit a grounder to short. No problem. I fielded it, and then fired the ball to Thomas at first. *Cut!*

"That's not how to do it," Schepisi said. So we tried it again. Grounder to short, throw to first.

"*Cut!* No, that's not how."

I looked at Thomas and DeCinces. They shrugged. I walked

toward Schepisi. "Tell me something. How would you know how it should look?"

"I'm the director!"

"You know shit about baseball," I said. Selleck stood there looking shocked. I apologized to DeCinces, saying, "Doug, they can keep their two hundred bucks. Thanks for the chance." Then I walked off the field feeling like I'd stood up for the game. I guess that last one was my only walk-off grounder.

☆ ☆ ☆

If Hollywood baseball wasn't working for me, the real-world version wasn't much better that year at USC. While Jimmy Campanis made first-team All-America, I lost out to shortstops who outplayed me: Mickey Morandini of Indiana, Dave Silvestri of Missouri, Fresno State's Eddie Zosky, and Iowa's Tim Costo. They were All-Americans while I was a perennial underachiever.

Why? Was I was pressing? Gillespie thought so. As we went into the 1990 season, my junior year, he told me to enjoy myself. He'd seen junior year ruin other players. It's the season when collegians who turned down pro deals coming out of high school become eligible for the draft again. "Don't think of it as your draft year," he said. "Just be yourself. Let the scouts see what you can do."

Instead I twisted myself in knots. I stubbed my brain. (Is that a psychological term?) Every line drive at an outfielder ticked me off. Every long fly the wind knocked down made me think of how Campanis, Morandini, and a hundred other guys were getting ahead of me. Going into the 1990 NCAA tournament I had a decent average of .313 for the season, but only six home runs. No wonder I was nowhere near the first-team All-America squad, or the second or third team, or the honorable mentions. Then we went to Baton Rouge, Louisiana, for the NCAA regional, and something clicked. I figured I'd already messed up my chances in the upcoming draft. A great junior season might have made me a first-round pick, but after a disappointing year I realized I'd probably fallen to the second or third round. With nothing to lose, I blanked out everything but the simplest thought. *See the ball, hit the ball.*

Talk about a fun tournament. With a slew of pro scouts behind the backstop, I had half a dozen home runs and 13 RBIs in five games. After a regular season with only six homers, I showed them six more in a week. While we lost the regional final by a run, I won the MVP award. Gillespie told me I'd just changed my future. "A first-round pick's performance," he called it.

There were still doubts about my attitude, though. "Bret's headstrong, no question," Gillespie told reporters. "That's one reason he's so good." As June's MLB draft approached, the *Los Angeles Times* called me a likely first- or second-round pick. That annoyed me. *First or second?* How many middle infielders hit six homers in five games?

Dad told me not to get too hung up on which round I went in.

"Easy for you to say," I told him. "You went in the twentieth round."

"Sixth," he said.

The Braves chose Larry "Chipper" Jones first overall in the 1990 draft. Chipper got a $400,000 signing bonus. Tony Clark, who's now executive director of the players' union, went second overall to Detroit. To sign Clark, a six-eight basketball star who might have had a future in the NBA, the Tigers gave him even more than Chipper got. Half a million dollars.

Then the waiting started.

Mike Mussina, Jeromy Burnitz, Rondell White, and Dan Wilson went in the first round. Not me. Okay, the second round's better than nothing. I waited for a phone call as the . . . clock . . . ticked . . .

The Angels, Dad's team, took Garret Anderson in the fourth round.

The White Sox chose Ray Durham in the fifth round.

Finally, with their fifth draft choice of the 1990 draft, 134th over-all, the Seattle Mariners selected USC shortstop Bret Boone.

I thought I'd been crushed three years before. This felt worse. Three years to go from the twenty-eighth round to the fifth! When Mariners scout Ken Compton called, asking if he could bring a contract for me to sign, I wanted to give him directions. I wanted to say, "Go south past Disneyland, then take the off-ramp to hell. Don't come around my house with your fifth-round money."

Dad was the voice of reason. As usual. he reminded me again that he'd gone in the sixth round, back in 500 BC, and hadn't he done okay? He was now catching for the Kansas City Royals, finishing out a nineteen-year major-league career. The year before, he'd won his fourth straight Gold Glove Award, at the age of forty-one. Crouching on knees that sent stingers of pain up his legs every inning, he was the oldest player in the big leagues. At the end of the 1990 season he would retire with a résumé worthy of the Hall of Fame: seven Gold Gloves, four All-Star appearances, a World Series title, 1,838 career hits, and more games caught than any other catcher in history. Before he retired, he wanted to pass the torch to me.

He came back to Orange County on a road trip with the Royals and we had another heart-to-heart. This one was more like a brain-to-gut. My gut told me to reject Seattle's $90,000 offer, but Dad talked me down. "Life's not fair," he said. "The draft's over with, and they're not going to redo it for you."

Gramps was plugged into the nationwide network of pro scouts, so we knew what big-league clubs thought of me. One scout told his bosses I had "average speed, average arm strength, and average big-league power." Another said, "His hitting is suspect. He's just getting a lot of attention because of his name." Even the Mariners had their doubts. General Manager Woody Woodward, a former major-league infielder, wasn't crazy about my glove or the temper that led one scout to call me "a helmet-throwing terror." (Cheap-shot stat: In nine big league seasons, Woodward hit a home run. That's right, one home run.) The Mariners wouldn't have drafted me at all if not for scouting director Roger Jongewaard. He liked my attitude. "Bret Boone is the most self-confident player I ever scouted," Jongewaard said.

I told Dad I couldn't accept fifth-round money. "How *dare* they? I'm not signing."

He said it wasn't so simple. "You can pout and hold out. Maybe they'll give you a few thousand more, but you'll lose time." If I held out and missed that summer's short-season schedule—three months of games for Peninsula, Seattle's so-called advanced A-ball team—I'd have to start the next season there. But suppose I signed right away. "Kick butt in your short season and they'll start you at Double-A next year. You can save a whole year that way."

I said, "Maybe you're right, Dad. I still want to say, 'Screw 'em.'"

"Don't screw 'em," he said. "*Show* 'em."

So I signed.

Next thing you know I'm getting out of a taxi at War Memorial Stadium in Hampton, Virginia, home of the Peninsula Pilots. War Memorial Stadium, across the James River from a place called the Great Dismal Swamp, looked like it had been there since the Stone Age. I found my way to the home team's clubhouse with its dripping shower and rusty lockers. This made college ball look fancy.

Welcome to the minors.

7

YOU FIGHT YOUR WAY UP

The Peninsula Pilots had a tough assignment that night. The Frederick Keys had Arthur Lee Rhodes on the mound. My new teammates warned me about Rhodes. A hulking lefty, nineteen years old, he was one of those hard-throwing kids who are just wild enough to intimidate hitters. Rhodes threw between 95 and 100 mph, and the dim lights at War Memorial Stadium made his heater look a few ticks faster.

Somebody said, "Kid, you picked the wrong night for your debut."

But I didn't care if Arthur Lee Rhodes threw hard. I was confident I could hit just about anybody's fastball. I might have lacked experience, but not balls.

Another thing I lacked was a bat. As in every other minor league, it was wood bats only in the Carolina League. That put me at a disadvantage, because I'd never swung one in a game. From Little League right up through high school and college ball, I'd used aluminum. As you probably know, the ball springs off a metal bat with a *ping* you can hear half a mile away. It's got a much bigger sweet spot, and the ball goes farther. But metal bats are illegal in the pros. They make hitting too easy. If you gave one of today's major leaguers a metal bat from my era, the game wouldn't be fair anymore.

So I marched to the bat rack with no idea of what I was doing. What sort of lumber did I want? A toothpick? A tree trunk? There wasn't much time to decide, because Rhodes was striking out the two guys ahead of me.

You may be wondering why I'd go into pro ball without at least trying a wood bat. The answer: Dad's advice. He knew I was being scouted from my first days at USC. He figured I'd look better to the scouts ripping liners than blooping bloopers. "Don't give them a reason not to like you," he said. It made sense at the time. Nobody could say I had a weakness—"Kid can't hit with wood"—if I never tried it in the first place.

I'm not sure our plan worked. It sure didn't seem to help my draft position. And now here I was at the bat rack in pro ball, reaching for . . . this one. No, that one. Finally I took the lightest bat in the rack. Not much heavier than balsa wood, it felt like the Easton aluminum bat I used in college. With Rhodes on the mound, I wanted to be quick.

A voice on the loudspeakers—"Now batting, Bret Boone!"

Sometimes hitting is simple. *See the ball, hit the ball. Ignore the butterflies in your stomach.* Rhodes wound up and . . .

I ripped a bullet to the gap that one-hopped the wall, and I was 1-for-1 as a pro. The fans clapped politely, but to me it sounded like a standing O. I cruised into second base with a smile so big it must have gone into short left field.

After the game the other Pilots and I rolled into our leaky locker room, looking for a postgame meal. I was starving. "Where's the spread?"

And then I saw Tiny lug in a tin box full of hot dogs. Tiny, who weighed about 400 pounds, was the Peninsula Pilots' clubhouse man, handyman, and you-name-it man. Most teams in the low minors have somebody like that. Tiny did laundry and sometimes filled in on the grounds crew or in the ticket booth, whatever it took to get the Pilots through the day. He even sold me his junker of a car for eight hundred dollars. One of Tiny's duties was to dispose of all the soggy hot dogs that didn't get sold that night. So he dumped them on a table in the middle of the locker room. He said, "There's your spread, kid." And my teammates dug in. The lucky ones got a bun to go with their hot dog. I was standing there thinking that A-ball was going to be a hell of challenge. Nutritionally, at least.

☆ ☆ ☆

Fans like to think of minor-league baseball as a downsized version of the majors, but it's not even close. As a twenty-two-year-old Peninsula Pilot I made $700 a month. Okay, $700 went further in those days, but not far enough. A Big Mac cost $2.25 in 1990. You remember that kind of thing when the paycheck you get every other Friday says *Pay to the order of Obscure Minor Leaguer, $350,* and has no taxes deducted because you're well below the poverty level. My $175 a week came to a little less than $30 a game.

I bunked in a crummy condo with three teammates, eating fast food and driving the others around because I was the only one with a car. One day I drove a bunch of guys to a water park. Just being a prince of a teammate, you know? We probably left a trail of baseballs and tobacco spit on the road to the park, because the heap Tiny had sold me had a hole in the floor. The car broke down on the way back. We decided it was a lost cause, so we called a cab and left Tiny's heap by the side of the road. Hampton, Virginia's a sleepy enough town that it might still be there. If you ever drive through there and see a rusty junker on the side of the road, it's mine.

We drew pretty good crowds on weekends and fireworks nights, but most nights we entertained thousands of empty seats. Sometimes there were two hundred fans in the ballpark and a million mosquitoes. I'll admit I was spoiled by first-class college ball—flying to road games with the USC baseball team, eating room-service dinners in Hiltons. The Peninsula Pilots rode buses. We stayed at Travelodges and Motel 6s in Frederick, Maryland, and Salem, Virginia, and Durham, North Carolina. Some of the Carolina League ballparks had no visitors' locker room, just a dugout, so we'd dress in our motel rooms and clomp through the lobby in our spikes and unis for the bus ride to the park. At home we'd hope for hot water in the showers at War Memorial Stadium, where you could trip over the athlete's-foot fungus.

And you know what? I loved every day of it.

This was pro ball! *Finally* I was a professional ballplayer like Dad and Gramps, even if I was making $3.30 per inning.

Kevin Costner wasn't around for our road trips to Durham—they'd shot his movie *Bull Durham* three years before—but we used to quote the movie on our team bus. "*You gotta learn your clichés.*" *Bull Durham* was funny and even realistic to a point. We had our bush-league fun like the guys in the movie. There were goofy pranks. Superstitions. Bench-clearing brawls. There were minor-league groupies in every town, girls who were crazy for ballplayers. Some of them wanted autographs, some wanted something a little more personal to remember you by. We were young, dumb, and full of, um, enthusiasm, but somehow we always made it to the ballpark the next day.

Of course I was too focused to waste much time with something as distracting as a groupie. By game time every day I wanted to get called up to the majors by the seventh-inning stretch, if not sooner.

☆ ☆ ☆

That year with the Pilots was also the year I learned to hit a cowhide ball with a wooden bat. Dad goes back to the days when the ball's skin was horsehide, but in 1974 the game switched to cowhide—tanned leather. I grew up hitting cowhide-covered balls with metal bats, never giving much thought to either one.

Bats have changed a lot over the years, and not just in what they're made of. Size matters, too. In my era, the early 1990s to mid-2000s, a typical big-league bat was 34 inches long and weighed 32 ounces. That's exactly two pounds. It's about what a liter bottle of soda weighs. In the olden days, sluggers like Babe Ruth and Lou Gehrig swung bats made of hickory, a wood that's denser than ash. You'll hear old-timers swear that the Babe used a 36-inch bat that weighed 40 or even 50 ounces, but that's a crock. I've swung one of Babe Ruth's game-used bats, and there's no way it weighed even 40 ounces. Thirty-six, maybe. "My idea on weight is that you should use a bat as heavy as you can handle," Ruth said. I'm saying that was 36 inches and 34 to 36 ounces for him. Gehrig's bats were supposedly the same length—a yard to the inch—and 40 or 41 ounces. Don't buy that, either. Sure, bats were heavier then, mainly because their weight was more evenly distributed, with more weight in the handle. I'm still betting somebody in the Yankee clubhouse had his thumb on the scale when they weighed Ruth's and Gehrig's bats, if they even had a scale.

There are a lot of myths about the legendary players, partly because reporters wanted to make them seem larger than life. That might be one reason you hear that Babe's bat was a tree trunk and Lou swung a phone pole. I've also heard Joe DiMaggio's bat was 38 inches and 40 ounces. I'll believe that when I see one. Ty Cobb might be a different story. He claimed to use hickory bats that were 34½ inches long and anywhere from 36 to 40 ounces. That might be true because Cobb, whether you think he was a racist or not, was also a scientist at the plate, choking up and slapping the ball to all fields.

My Gramps could have told you who changed the game for good. It was his idol Ted Williams, the ultimate hitting scientist. When

Williams came to the majors in 1939 he brought a bat bag full of white-ash Louisville Sluggers that weighed 33 ounces apiece. He could swing them faster than old-fashioned hitters with their hickory tree trunks.

That's the trade-off: you want the heaviest bat you can swing *fast*. A lighter bat means swing speed, while heavier lumber adds density—and power. Williams, the Splendid Splinter, was the first to really optimize the trade-off. His bats were 35 inches and 33 ounces. In the jargon of the game that's a *bat drop* of minus two. For almost a hundred years the difference between a bat's length and weight went the other way, but after Williams started hitting rockets with his "tooth-picks," everybody switched to ash bats with more inches than ounces. With a lighter bat, Ted could watch a pitch a split second longer and trigger his swing a split second later. Ever since his day, bat drops have been in the minuses. No hitter from high school to the major leagues would even dream of using one with a bat drop of zero. That's just one of the ways the game has evolved.

As it turns out, Williams's minus two was pretty close to perfect. (Gramps, you were right—old Ted was a genius.) By the time I reached the majors I'd settle on a 34-inch, 32-ounce Louisville Slugger, for a minus-two drop that's pretty close to universal in 2016. I've seen scientific studies showing that the ideal bat for a modern power hitter is within an inch and an ounce of the bats I used to swing.

Of course it's not quite that simple. The bat that squares up a 98-mph fastball in April might start feeling heavy in August, when you're achy and sleep-deprived. At that point, if you're smart, you go to minus 2½. In August, 34 inches and 31½ ounces gets the bat to the same spot in the hitting zone.

Like Williams and most of my contemporaries, I liked a wide grain in the wood. You hear a lot about grain in wooden bats, but what does that mean?

Everybody knows that trees have age rings. Ash trees, hickory trees, maple trees—they produce a new ring every year. Each ring represents a year's worth of growth for the tree, and a wide grain means the tree grew fast that year. That's the wood I want in my bat, because a healthy tree makes strong, dense lumber. A wide grain might add a couple of ticks to one of those trendy stats you keep hearing about: exit velocity. These days, teams release players or trade them if their exit velocity—the speed of the ball off the bat—isn't up to snuff. You can think of exit velocity as the flip side of fastball speed. A hundred miles an hour is terrific, 90 is decent, and below that you should probably think about another line of work.

You gotta love the science of the game. It comes down to the simplest thing in the world—hit a ball with a stick—but there are so many variables, so many details. When I broke in, big-league hitters still weighed bats on a bathroom scale. In the late '90s electronic scales came in. Edgar Martinez and I brought one of the first into the Mariners clubhouse. We discovered that hardly any of our 32-ounce bats weighed 32 ounces. They weren't far off, almost always between about 31.8 ounces and 32.2, but that could be enough to turn a double into an out. So we'd toss any bat that didn't meet our specs. Not in the trash. The rejects were still good bats, good enough for anything but big-league combat, so we'd give them to rookies or to the clubbies who look after the players and earn most of their money in tips.

We got our bats for free, of course. If you signed a deal with Louisville Slugger, like about 60 percent of major leaguers at the time, you got a few grand a year from Hillerich & Bradsby, plus all the bats you needed shipped to you wherever you were, usually by UPS. A typical big leaguer goes through 150 to 250 bats a year, depending on how persnickety he is and what kind of wood he prefers.

From Ted Williams's time to the 1990s, just about everybody swung an ash bat. Then hitters began switching from ash bats to maple. It's a denser wood, a little harder. People who care about stuff like this—woodheads, you could call them—usually give Barry Bonds credit for bringing maple to the majors. It's true that Bonds's 73 homers in 2001 made other players think, *I want a bat like Barry's,* but the Blue Jays' Joe Carter got there first. Carter won the 1993 World Series with a maple-bat homer off the Phillies' Mitch Williams.

At first, maple bats had a scary tendency to shatter, sending sharp pieces flying all over the lot. The Cubs' Tyler Colvin was leading off third base in 2010 when a teammate ripped a broken-bat double. A chunk of the bat stabbed Colvin in the chest, puncturing his lung and sending him to the hospital. It could easily have killed him. After that, Major League Baseball conducted a study of maple bats and put in quality-control regulations to make them safer. Then, when Oakland's Brett Lawrie broke his bat grounding out in 2015, a piece of his maple bat hit a fan in the face. She lived, but it was another horrible moment.

Some people say we should ban maple bats. I don't see that happening. Too many hitters have switched to maple, and the companies that make and sell their bats would raise hell. They'd probably sue MLB. Today, more than half of all major-league hitters use maple bats. It's about two-thirds maple, one-third ash, going more toward maple every year. I'd say 80 percent of players under twenty-five years old use maple bats. Are they dangerous? Yes. But the real question is, are they significantly more dangerous than ash bats? I doubt it. Still, recent incidents with maple bats have led teams to consider building new screens to protect fans in the front rows. Would that make more sense than banning maple bats? Maybe. That's not my jurisdiction. What I know best about bats can be boiled down to this: hitting's hard, and so's a good piece of wood.

☆ ☆ ☆

It took me about a week in the Carolina League to find a wooden bat that suited my all-or-nothing swing. That bat had the drop-two specs

I would use with rare exceptions for the rest of my career: 34 inches, 32 ounces. I was ready to set the league on fire.

So one night I'm at War Memorial Stadium and who's standing in the dugout, strapping on his shin guards? Don't guess, because it's too much like a bad movie—hungry hotshot starts his pro journey, reaches for his bat, and sees . . .

Jim Campanis.

"Hello, Boonie," he said.

"Not you again."

He said, "I'm still going to beat you to the Show." His favorite topic.

I was just getting used to life in the minors. The Show was a thousand miles away. I said something like, "Good for you, Jimmy."

"Want to bet on it?"

That got my attention.

"I'll bet you a car," he said. Jimmy never lacked for motivation.

I said, "Well, I'm not driving some Pinto."

"A BMW. I'll bet you a BMW that I beat you to the big leagues."

I had to think about that for one-tenth of a second. "You're on."

I had a lousy vehicular history. My last car was still rusting by the road in Hampton, Virginia. The one before that was long gone, too. I'd gone out and spent most of my pro signing bonus on a jet-black Ford Bronco I tricked out with a quadraphonic Blaupunkt sound system you could hear from space. My A-ball teammates would feel the ground shake and say, "Boonie's in the parking lot." Then came April 1991. Tax time. To my surprise, Uncle Sam wanted a third of the bonus I'd already spent.

I called Dad. "Help!" He helped, but I had to sell my pimped-out Bronco. That was one of my first lessons in professional baseball: no matter how much you make, it's not as much as it sounds like.

☆ ☆ ☆

I hit eight home runs that first summer with Pilots, and they came with a slash line of .267/.383/.427. For those who don't follow baseball stats, a slash line is your batting average, on-base percentage, and slugging percentage. My slash translated to fair/pretty damn good/decent. What mattered to me was that it got me promoted to Double-A ball the next spring, just like my dad predicted.

Like Dad said, I could have pouted and held out when the Mariners drafted me in the fifth round, but it would have cost me a year. Instead I went straight to short-season A-ball and kicked ass. Or at least nudged ass. So the next April, the month when I turned twenty-two, the Mariners called me up to their Double-A farm club, the Jacksonville Suns, two steps from the majors.

At the Double-A level you're halfway up the minor-league chain. You play in bigger towns. You're in Orlando and Memphis instead of Winston-Salem and Lynchburg, and believe me, a Holiday Inn in Orlando is nicer than the Lynchburg Motel 6. Double-A ballparks are bigger, too. Most nights, you can actually hear the fans. The players' postgame spread is more like sandwiches and Caesar salad instead of hot dogs. The buses don't break down as much. The girls are prettier. It makes you picture how amazing the majors are going to be if you ever make it that far. Not that I had any doubts on that score.

One night we played the Birmingham Barons, the Royals' Double-A farm club. Bo Jackson was spending a couple of weeks with the Barons, rehabbing an injury. We knew each other because he'd been a Royals teammate of Dad's. And while Bo may have been one of the best pure athletes who ever played the game, his baseball instincts weren't perfect. He was always a football guy in a baseball cap. Early in the game he smashed a single and gave me a wink as he rounded first base. "I'm coming for you, Boonie," he said. We instantly picked him off. But instead of diving back toward first, he took off for second at top speed. The first baseman threw me the ball, and I was thinking

this was fun. We had Bo in a rundown. Except that he kept barreling toward me. I showed him the ball, like you're supposed to do,
and instead of turning back toward first, he sped up. I thought, *Does
Bo know he's not allowed to run over the second baseman?* Here he came at
Mach 12. Then he stopped a foot away from me. On a dime. Stopped
and touched his toe to second base. I put the tag on him. I was too
late, but the play was just so weird that the umpire called him out
anyway. Bo wasn't upset; it's a minor-league out. He tapped me on
the butt and said, "You know I was safe."

Yeah, Bo, but I still don't know how you did it.

That season, I represented the Jacksonville Suns at the 1991
Southern League All-Star Game. By then I was starting to get known
for my glove as well as my bat. I'd heard that Mariners GM Woody
Woodward didn't think much of my defense. Or my bat, for that matter. Or my infectious charm. But the thing about baseball defense is,
it's a craft. A lot of hitting, maybe most of it, is God-given talent, but
defense is something you can learn by repetition, especially infield
defense. That's why I spent hour after hour in the Florida sun, taking
ground balls before most of the guys showed up. Infield defense is a
little like dancing; it's footwork and timing. Field 100 ground balls
and you might get a little quicker to the baseball and better balanced
on the balls of your feet. Field 10,000 and you might get better than
Woody Woodward ever expected. That may sound like a whole lot
of grounders, but do the math: 100 grounders before every game for
100 games, that's 10,000. Enough to make a difference.

I wound up smacking 19 homers for Jacksonville that year. Jim
Campanis, who'd been promoted to Double-A along with me (of
course), had 15. The minors' biweekly bible, *Baseball America,* named
me the game's 99th-best prospect. Not so bad, I guess, for the 134th
pick of the 1990 draft. But I was dying to make up ground on Chipper
Jones, Jeff Bagwell, and the others ahead of me on *Baseball America*'s

minor-league list. So I stepped up my game. Thousands of grounders. More hours in the batting cage. In 1992 I got another promotion—to the Calgary Cannons of the Triple-A Pacific Coast League.

Now we're getting somewhere, I thought. This was Triple-A ball, the minors' highest level, one phone call from the majors. It felt like I'd taken forever to get here, but I was still only twenty-three. That was three years younger than the average Triple-A player. And I was learning intriguing details all the time.

For one thing, it's easier to hit in Triple-A baseball than in Double-A. That probably sounds crazy. Double-A pitchers may be more talented than Triple-A pitchers but the Triple-A guys are more polished. They're older and wiser. A big part of hitting—one of the biggest—is thinking along with the pitcher's pattern. Outsmarting him. You can do that in Triple-A (and in the majors) because he *has* a pattern. He has a pretty good idea where the ball's going before he throws it. He might even get a breaking ball over the plate *on purpose.* That doesn't happen so much in Double-A ball, where pitchers are more like Nuke LaLoosh, the wild phenom in *Bull Durham.*

For another thing, I found out I could make it at the minors' top level without learning to hit a breaking ball. At least a good one. Curveball, slider, splitter, screwball, that ain't my style. And even at the Triple-A level, where the other team's ace might—I say *might*— throw a breaking ball for a strike, it's not happening twice in a row. So I developed a simple plan: sit on fastballs.

To sit on a pitch means you won't swing at anything else. Throw me a curve and a couple of sliders that catch the plate in Calgary, Mr. LaLoosh, and I'm your strikeout victim. But if you throw me one fastball anywhere near the middle of the plate, I'll be waiting for it.

Using that approach, I batted .290 with 48 homers in 402 minor-league games.

Meanwhile, I enjoyed baseball life at this new, higher level. At first it was strange playing home games in Calgary, in western Canada, holding my cap over my heart for two national anthems before home games. But do you know what really weirded me out? Canadian restaurants serve Coke with no ice.

"Can I have some ice in my drink?"

"We don't do it like that," they tell you.

"But I like ice."

"It's cold already," they say. Canadians hate ice. Or maybe they're saving it for hockey rinks.

In 1992 I batted .314 with 13 homers and 73 RBIs for the Calgary Cannons. When *Baseball America* published its new list of the 100 best prospects, I'd moved up. Two whole spots, to 97th place. Oh, I was pissed. It took me two good years to pass the 98th-best guy! At this rate I'd be older than Gramps by the time I got to Seattle.

A year later I was hitting .332 in Calgary. The parent club was running last in the AL West. Fans in Seattle were booing, and Mariners second baseman Harold Reynolds, a two-time All-Star, was slowing down a little. There was talk that the Mariners might call up the Boone kid. And hey—wouldn't that make him the first third-generation player ever?

I heard the talk but tried not to listen. My job was to keep my head down and keep hacking.

Our manager at Calgary, Keith Bodie, was a minor-league lifer from Brooklyn. Good guy, but gruff. If you needled him when we were losing he could get as prickly as his big black disco-era mustache. But this one night we were winning, so everybody was getting along. I smoked a single to right. I was rounding first base when Raul Mondesi, the right fielder, threw behind me, to the first baseman. Mondesi loved to show off his arm. I was safe—it wasn't even close—but the next thing you know, Bodie sent another player out to replace me.

"What are you doing here?" I asked him.

"Pinch-running," the guy said.

"Not for me you're not."

I held my ground while Bodie came steaming out of the dugout. "You lazy-ass motherfucker!" he said. "Get off the field."

"I beg your pardon?" I said. Or words to that effect.

"You want to play for me, you run hard."

"Fuck you, Keith. I always run hard!" It was true. I may not have been the most virtuous guy, but I always hustled, partly because every leg hit got me a little closer to the majors. Now my manager was showing me up in front of the fans. In front of my teammates. Even worse, he was going to send a report to the parent club after the game. If Bodie said I was dogging it, the Mariners might never call me up.

"Sit your ass down in the dugout!" he yelled. "You're out of the game!"

At that point my blood pressure was off the scale. My fists were clenched. If I'd gotten near the dugout I'd probably have started smashing it up. That's when Bodie stepped closer and pointed right at my nose. And he had a big grin on his face.

"Get out of here," he said. "You've got no business on my team. You know why? Because there's a car outside, waiting to take you to the airport. You're going to the big leagues."

8

THE ROOKIE

I'd been punk'd! As soon as Bodie told me I was going to the majors, he hugged me. A couple of photographers popped out of the dugout, snapping pictures. My Calgary teammates gave me a round of applause. They must have been wishing it was them going up, but they were happy for me.

I called my mom first, then Dad, then Gramps, saying "I'm goin' up!" Too excited to sleep, I stayed up all night playing solitaire.

The next morning, I flew to meet the big club in Baltimore, where the Mariners were playing the Orioles that night. For the first time in my life I flew first-class, because that's how they do things in the majors.

There was a businessman across the aisle from me. "Where you headed, son?" he asked, looking me over. I guess he wasn't used to seeing twenty-three-year-old kids wearing jeans and sneakers in the first-class cabin.

"To the big leagues," I said.

"Come on."

"It's true. Come out to the park and you can watch me."

The businessman was an Orioles fan. He said he couldn't make it to the game, but he'd watch on TV. "Tell me something," he said. "How do you think you'll do your first time up?"

"I don't know, but don't miss it. You're gonna see a ball hit hard somewhere."

This was going to be nothing like my debut with the Peninsula Pilots. If I needed a reminder, all I had to do was check out all the cameras in my face at Camden Yards. The Mariners had tipped off the press to a feel-good story. Bret Boone was on his way, following his father and grandpa to the major leagues.

The reporters crowded around. They wanted to know how proud I was.

"What's it like to be the first third-generation player ever?"

"Have you called your dad yet? Does your grandpa know?"

"How do you *feel*?"

To be honest with you, I felt bleary from my solitaire-y, sleepless night. Bleary and a little pissed-off.

Yes, I was proud to be a Boone. Of course it was special to be part of something that never happened before, part of baseball history. But the Mariners weren't calling me up because of my name. They were calling me up because I earned it. I had worked my ass off to prove myself in the minors. The Mariners wanted a second baseman who could field his position and hit some balls hard. That was me. But try telling that to the writers following me off the field in Calgary and the TV crews meeting me at Camden Yards. To them I was a one-day human interest story. I was starting to wish my name was Bret Smith.

I'm not proud to say that. Like I told you before, I was immature. Thinking back on that day, it's a little embarrassing that I didn't spend more time telling everybody how special it felt to carry on the big-league tradition Gramps started and Dad passed on to me. But that would have been a lie. All I can say is that I had blinders on. I just didn't want anybody saying I got a pass because of my name.

I had a lot to learn.

Starting with how to hit big-league pitching.

It's a cliché, but it's true—hitting a baseball is the toughest job in sports. It never seemed that way in Little League, high school, or college because I was a natural hitter. When reporters asked Gramps if he thought I could match him and Dad now that I was in the majors, he told them *match* wasn't the word.

"Bret has more talent that we did," he said.

I was ready to prove it.

It was Wednesday, August 19, 1992. A hot night in Baltimore. Seattle manager Bill Plummer had Ken Griffey Jr. batting third and Lance Parrish hitting cleanup. Junior was seven months younger than I was, but he'd been in the majors since he was nineteen. He had already hit more than 100 homers for the Mariners. We'd known each other since we were kids. Back when his father was playing outfield for the Reds, Junior and I goofed around a few times when they played my dad and the Phillies. Now he came up to me with a big smile on his face. He stuck out his hand and said, "Welcome to the big leagues." A few minutes later we went out for batting practice. That was a real eye-opener, the first of my Welcome to the Show moments—watching Junior Griffey take BP. The ball made a different sound when he hit it. A smack like the ball must be *hurt*. And his BP homers didn't just clear the fence; some of them were still going up when they started bouncing around the upper deck. That moment—batting practice at Camden Yards in August of '92—taught me a lesson I never forgot. It taught me that there was at least one guy with so much talent that he made whatever I had look ordinary. A once-in-a-generation guy so good I don't mind calling him a sort of a genius. To play in a lineup with a guy like Griffey, I was going to have to work harder than ever.

Plummer wrote *Boone* in the seventh slot. In the top of the second inning, Jay Buhner doubled and I came up to face Orioles starter Arthur Lee Rhodes. Yes, the same flamethrowing kid I'd faced in my first pro at-bat two years before. Throwing as hard as ever. I gave Rhodes a look, like, *You again?*

Rhodes threw a fastball. I ripped it to center for an RBI single.

Let me tell you, that was one hell of a feeling—hearing my teammates clap while I rounded first base with a 1.000 batting average, seeing an ump take the baseball out of the game. My first big-league hit. Randy Milligan, the Orioles' first baseman, gave me a smile. "Two thousand nine hundred and ninety-nine to go," he said.

That's another moment I never forgot. Here's Milligan, a veteran, saying I could end up with 3,000 hits. I guess he'd heard I was a hotshot.

I couldn't agree. I was thinking, *Shit, why would I settle for three thousand?*

A week later I was 3-for-22.

For a month, every ball I hit hard was an atom ball. Right at 'em. Except that I'm lying. I might have told Dad and Gramps I was hitting nothing but atom balls, but mostly I was striking out, popping up, hitting weak little grounders to infielders. You know all those terms announcers use so they don't repeat "grounder" all the time? They say you hit a roller, a nubber, a chopper, a tapper, a hopper, a bleeder, a comebacker. Throw in a couple of strikeouts and you've got a doubleheader for me around that time.

One day in Detroit I'm sitting in the dugout with Mike Blowers. Going crazy. "The big leagues is hard," I said.

Mike was a veteran who'd been up and down his whole career. He was never more than a bad month from getting shipped to the minors. "You bet your ass," he said.

I was discovering a major difference between the major leagues and the minors. In a nutshell, it's this: Minor leaguers pitch to their strength. Major leaguers pitch to your weakness.

That's why I could make it all the way up through the Mariners' farm system without learning how to hit a decent breaking ball. In the minors, a pitcher's strength is almost always his fastball. That's what got him to pro ball in the first place. It's the pitch he can throw where he wants it, or at least pretty close. He figures that if he can get two strikes on you, he'll strike you out with it. Meanwhile he's just learning to throw a breaking ball. With a few freaky exceptions (I'll talk about them later), nobody succeeds throwing only one pitch. So even if a pitcher throws 100 mph, he's learning a slider, a curve, or some other pitch to mix in with the hammer he wants to bring down for strike three.

But because he's still learning, your enemy's all over the place with that breaking pitch. I can't tell you how many bush-league at-bats start like this: slider for ball one; slider for ball two. After that I'd be sitting fastball, waiting to pounce on the heat I knew was coming next. On the rare occasions when a minor leaguer got three breaking pitches over or blew a fastball by me, I'd strike out and tip my cap to him. But that didn't happen too often, as you can tell from my .332 average for the Triple-A Calgary Cannons.

It's different in the majors. As I was discovering, big-league pitchers aren't just better, they're better in a very particular way. They won't *let* you sit on fastballs.

The night I put on a big-league uniform, my at-bats started going like this: slider for ball one; slider for ball two. Now I'm sitting fastball. Instead I got slider for strike one; curveball for strike two. Now I didn't know what to expect. He could get me with another breaking pitch. Or he could get me with a fastball—the first one I'd seen this at-bat—while I was looking for something else.

Instead of sitting on a fastball, I was taking a seat on the bench.

Six weeks into my major-league career, I checked my average on the scoreboard at the Kingdome in Seattle. In numbers ten feet high, it read .197. Ow.

That's when Edgar Martinez took me aside. He said, "Kid, you're going to have to make an adjustment."

"Huh?"

"You've got to hit the breaking ball to get to the fastball."

Let me tell you about Edgar Martinez. He was our third baseman and DH, which in Edgar's case stood for distinguished hitter. He came from Puerto Rico, had dark curly hair, and always looked like he needed a shave. He had a quick smile and an even quicker bat. He was only twenty-nine, but guys looked up to him so much they called him "Papi" years before David "Big Papi" Ortiz came along. By 1992, when he pulled me aside for a veteran-to-rookie talk, Papi had batted .300 or better two years in row. He was on his way to his best season yet—a .343 average with 18 homers, a league-leading 46 doubles, and only 61 strikeouts all year. And yet this baseball veteran took time to help a stubborn, clueless rookie survive in the majors. It was Edgar who taught me about the Adjustment.

"You've got to hit the breaking ball," he said, "to get to the fastball."

What did he mean by that? Simple: I had to prove I could cope with major-league sliders, curves, and splitters, or why would a major-league pitcher ever throw me anything else? That's why I couldn't keep sitting on fastballs. If I did, I might never see one again. Big-league pitchers are the best in the world; they'll prey on your weakness until you adapt.

The minors are full of guys who couldn't adapt. I wasn't going to be one of them. So I changed my style of hitting, even changed my stance. Instead of sitting fastball, I looked for breaking balls. I hung back in the batter's box, learning to recognize a breaking pitch on its way to the plate. That's hard to explain without getting too technical, but it comes down to how a pitch appears as it leaves the pitcher's hand. A breaking ball looks a little higher coming off his fingers.

Maybe that's because it stays up at the level of his fingers a split second longer, while the fastball starts bearing down on you right away.

For me, at least, that split second made all the difference. Once I started watching for that telltale sign—the ball finger-high for an extra hundredth of a second—I started hitting again.

It felt weird at first, letting fastballs go by. They'd been my meat for so long. Sitting on breaking balls takes more patience than I thought I had. It means waiting, holding back. It feels like sitting in a rocking chair, and from that position you can't trigger your swing fast enough to catch up with a fastball. But you can time the shit out of a curve.

After my sit-down with Edgar, I started sitting on breaking balls. Leaning back in my rocking chair, I'd rock forward to handle sliders and curves. Pretty soon I got my average up to .200, then .210 and .220, with a couple of upper-deck homers.

In the major leagues, word gets around. Pitchers and catchers notice a hitter's tendencies. So do advance scouts, the guys big-league clubs send ahead of the team to watch the next couple of opponents on their schedule. "The Boone kid's starting to hit off-speed pitches," they reported. And before you know it, enemy pitchers changed their approach to beat my new approach. This is the game within the game, the chess match that never ends. As soon as I adjusted to the pattern that was getting me out, they ditched it. "If he's going to hit breaking stuff and let fastballs go by, we'll throw him fastballs."

So I went back to sitting on fastballs.

One night at the Kingdome, we were facing a starter who'd thrown me nothing but junk a week before. First pitch, fastball. I crushed it over the center-field fence. The fans cheered me around the bases and into the dugout. They were yelling so loud I couldn't hear Edgar, but I didn't have to read his lips to know what he was saying.

"You gotta hit the breaking ball . . ."

I filled in the rest. "To get to the fastball!"

☆ ☆ ☆

One crisis down, one to go. You might think that making the Adjustment would be the biggest fight a rookie faces, and you might be right.
Of course it's always temporary. You make the Adjustment, but it
never stays made. If you're lucky enough to stick in the majors, you'll
be making adjustments to pitchers' adjustments to your adjustments
for the rest of your career. That can be fun once you get the hang of
it. But there's another game within the game, an off-the-field contest
the fans never see. You have to fight for your place on your own team.

Every major leaguer spends most of his time in a high-pressure
workplace with twenty-four other men at the top of their game,
which happens to be the national pastime. Like most teams, the 1992
Mariners were led by a handful of veterans who set the tone for everybody else. Edgar liked me, but Edgar was the quiet type. Some of the
others wanted to put me in my place. Believe it or not, they thought I
was a little bit full of myself.

"Step aside, rook."

"Here's a dime. Shine my shoes."

"I'll be checking out at ten. You can carry my bags to the bus."

"We've got a dress code for rookies," one of them told me. "So we
chipped in to buy this, just for you."

A dress. They made me wear a frilly dress on a road trip to New
York.

Fine, I thought. It's all in fun. Dad and Gramps had gone through
the same crap when they were rookies. You wear a dress, you sing a
song on the bus, you fetch coffee for the veterans and carry their lug-
gage. They treat you like a turd. Like a rookie. Fine. Except that it's
supposed to stop. You lug four heavy bags and a cup of coffee through
the Seattle airport, wearing a dress and a blond wig, getting laughed
at all the way. You've been hazed.

For me, it didn't stop. I was the rookie wearing a dress on a team-
record three road trips. Did it make me mad? No, I embraced it. Why

did they single me out? Because of my name? No, because of my attitude. They thought I was way too smug for a rookie. Mr. Bret Fucking Full-of-Himself Boone. That's how a lot of people saw me, and I probably deserved it, because that's the persona I projected. If you didn't know me, you might think I was the cockiest sonofabitch this side of Muhammad Ali. I projected confidence—mostly because I was and am confident. But also because I'll never show you the doubt inside. The worries. Until now, I never admitted that I had swarms of butterflies in my stomach before the first game of every spring training and the first at-bat of every season. I was scared I'd strike out or fall on my ass, scared to embarrass myself. And nobody knew it but me.

When the Mariners veterans kept giving me hell for my attitude, I thought, *Screw 'em. I'm just trying to stay in the big leagues like everybody else.* But I knew they'd keep it up unless I did something about it.

On the third and last time they made me wear a dress, I changed my approach. I went commando. There I was, giving everybody a moon's-eye view on the team bus. Pretty soon I'm waltzing off the bus at the team hotel, waiting for an updraft to make the Seattle Mariners synonymous with balls-out baseball.

What happened? Nothing official. Maybe word came down from the front office, and Plummer, the manager, told the veterans to back off. Maybe they got tired of giving me a hard time, or even liked how I fought back. The point is, I was done wearing dresses.

Baseball's all about making adjustments.

The hazing I got as a rookie reinforced that lesson and taught me another one. Not all traditions are worth following. I happen to think rookie hazing is stupid. Years later, when I became a veteran, there were a few cocksure rookies who joined the teams I was on. My attitude was, let's not give them a hard time. That kid might be the real deal *because* of his attitude. We don't have to humble him; the pitchers will do that. If they don't, good for him—he'll help us win.

Jay "Bone" Buhner was one of the established players giving me hell. Buhner was a big Texan with a buzz cut. He hit 44 homers one year and got so popular in Seattle that the team had Buhner Nights when fans got their heads shaved. Griffey was our superstar but Buhner was the Mariners' leader, and he got a kick out of putting me in my place. I'd come out of the shower after a game and find my street clothes cut to shreds. No legs on my pants, no buttons left on my shirt, no laces in my shoes. Somebody said, "Bone made some alterations!" while the other guys yukked it up.

One day Buhner confronted me. He said, "Kid, I'm the one who fucked up your clothes." He leaned in close enough to head-butt me. "You know what's next?"

I thought about poking him in the eye. Instead I said, "No. What's next?"

"We're going to lunch, and then I'm buying you a new suit."

Buhner treated me to lunch in the best steak house in the next town. Then he bought me a custom suit that was better than anything I could have picked off the rack. I guess I'd passed the rookie test. Or maybe not. Maybe he was just one of those old-school ballplayers who like to see a rookie sweat before treating him like a teammate. Either way, he went straight from my shit list to my bucket list. To this day, I'm thankful that Jay took me under his wing.

Bone, if you're reading this, I'd like to buy you a steak and a suit.

About the same time, he bought a house and moved out of his apartment in Seattle. "Catch," he said, tossing me his keys. So I moved into Buhner's apartment, and when it was time to pay the rent, he paid it. "Forget it," he said. "Maybe one of these days you'll help another snot-nose rookie who doesn't deserve it."

I was starting to feel at home in the big leagues.

On a road trip to Anaheim, I shook hands with Bubba Harkins, the clubbie I used to help do players' laundry. He pointed me to a locker labeled BRET BOONE—the same locker I'd told him I wanted when I was a kid.

And on a road trip to Oakland, I came out of the cage after BP and who's standing there? Reggie Jackson. I guess he forgave me for making him reach for a few balls while I warmed him up at the Big A. Reggie had a tear in his eye. He gave me a bear hug and said, "Boone kid! I knew you'd make it."

Had I made it? I guess so, for the moment. But I still had to prove I could hit big-league pitching for more than a month. A late-season slump left me with a rookie-year batting average of .194.

Even that was worth a Beemer. Jim Campanis, still catching for the Double-A Jacksonville Suns, sent a package to *Bret Boone c/o Mariners, Kingdome, Seattle WA 98134*. It was a small package, maybe three inches long, the size of a set of car keys.

I tore it open. Sure enough, Campanis had paid off our bet. He'd sent me a BMW. A Hot Wheels BMW you could hold in your hand.

9

RED ALERT

Tempe, Arizona, 1993: I spent my first spring training as a big leaguer hitting fastballs in gaps and breaking balls off walls. Harold Reynolds had gone free agent after ten years in Seattle, so second base was mine.

Then came our last spring game. Lou Piniella, Seattle's new manager, sent utility man Rich Amaral out to play second.

I turned to Mike Blowers. "Lou's just resting me, right? I mean, I'm making the team."

Blowers had been up and down between Triple-A and the majors enough to read the signs. "Don't count on it," he said.

"Mike, be honest with me. What's going on?"

He nodded toward second base. "Who's out there? Not you. That's not an accident. And they won't keep you around to pinch-hit. You're either going to start or go down."

"Bullshit. You don't know."

"Maybe they want to take you down a peg," he said. "Maybe they think you need more at-bats at Calgary. More seasoning—that's what they always tell the press."

A couple of hours later John McLaren, Piniella's bench coach, came by my locker with a message you don't want to hear at the end of spring training, the kind of message that makes your balls retract:

"Skip wants to see you."

My testes must have been halfway to my chin by the time I got to the manager's office. Piniella was shuffling papers on his desk. As a sweet-swinging, hot-tempered outfielder he'd helped the Yankees win back-to-back World Series in 1977 and '78. Now pushing fifty, he still had the square jaw and sly smile that made women swoon over "Sweet Lou."

The nickname was facetious. Everybody who knew Sweet Lou knew he was never more than an inch from a shouting match. He'd managed the 1990 Reds to a World Series title, sweeping an Oakland A's club featuring Rickey Henderson, Mark McGwire, and Jose Canseco. Two years later, Piniella's Reds went 90-72, second-best in the NL West, but owner Marge Schott fired him anyway, partly because he got in a clubhouse punch-out with Rob Dibble, his closer. Lou had a great baseball mind, but he wasn't the type to play well with others. He once yanked second base out of the ground and chucked it at an umpire. His face got so red during arguments that you'd swear he was about to have a stroke. I always saw him as a cartoon character, sort of a cross between Yoda and the Tasmanian Devil.

Piniella looked calm enough when I knocked on his door. He looked up from his paperwork and said, "Son, I want you to work on hitting the ball the other way."

I said, "Where?"

"Calgary." He could see I was mad, but somehow we both kept our cool. "I want you to go down and hit," he said. "Hit to all fields. Show us what you can do, we'll call you back up."

So I went back to the land of Cokes with no ice and seats with no fans. Pretty soon I was hitting .327 down there. The Mariners called me back to Seattle, where Piniella put me in the lineup against Cleveland's Eric Plunk.

Plunk set me up with a couple of sliders. Strike one, strike two. He and his catcher, Junior Ortiz, figured I'd be looking for another one, but I was a step ahead of them. I thought they'd try to cross me up with a fastball. Now, they might suspect I was thinking that way, and double-cross me with a third straight slider, the obvious choice. But I doubted they'd give a second-year kid that much credit. So I was sitting fastball.

Plunk wound up and here it came. Fastball.

It's so fun to outthink a pitcher and catcher who think they're outthinking you. I watched that heater as it came off Plunk's fingers. I triggered my swing. Unfortunately, this particular fastball went nowhere near Plunk's target. Ortiz had to stand up to catch it. The ball was nose-high as I swung under it.

Piniella met me as I trudged to the dugout. He gave me his most exasperated look, threw his hands in the air, and said, "Son, what are you swinging at?"

I was in no mood for quizzes. "You know what, Lou? Maybe you forgot that it's hard to hit at this level. You think I was *trying* to strike out?"

"You want to go back to Calgary?"

I offered him my bat. "Fuck you. You go hit it."

"Fuck me?"

I was kicking things around my locker when McLaren dropped by again. "Skip wants to—"

"Yeah, I know."

Piniella sat at his desk, working on a lineup card without me on it. "Son," he said, "I'm sending you out for ten days. This is the last time. When I bring you back up, you'll either be my second baseman for the next fifteen years or I'll trade you. For a jockstrap if I have to."

That night I called my dad to bitch and moan. He gave me his usual advice. Life's not fair, don't bitch, just do your job, etc.

I said, "Yeah, yeah. But it's not right. They treat you like shit. Like a boy."

"That's just it," he said. "They expect you to mope and bitch like a boy. So you prove them wrong. Go down and kick ass."

I heeded Dad's advice, but not right away.

Under the contract between owners and the players' union, demoted players have three days to report to their minor-league teams. Management doesn't like it if you take the full three days, but they can't force you to go faster. So I took my sweet time. Roughly 71½ hours after Piniella sent me down, I rolled into Foothills Stadium, home of the Calgary Cannons. And bore down. And kicked ass. Over the next week and a half I had a hitting streak, a couple of homers, and a Pacific Coast League Player of the Week award. Keith Bodie was still managing the Cannons; he didn't have any tricks up his sleeve this trip, and most of his nightly reports to the parent club started with my name.

Finally my ten days were up. Everybody on the team knew about my ten-day trial in Triple-A. On the eleventh day, the other guys gave me a few sideways looks. Most of them were career minor leaguers. By the twelfth day they were laughing at me. "Oh look, it's Bret! Hello, Boonie, we didn't expect to see you here. What happened to ten days? Did Lou forget you?"

I could have called my agent. I could have called my dad. But I'm the direct type. If I've got a beef with you, let's have it out face-to-face. Or as close to face-to-face as possible.

I called Piniella's office at the Kingdome. I said, "Lou, why am I still in Calgary?"

"Hi, Bret," he said. "I hear you're raking down there. Hitting four-something, aren't you?"

"Screw that! You said ten days."

"Well, it took you a while to get down there." Turns out he was miffed that I took the full three days to report. "When I send a guy down," he said, "I don't want him taking his own sweet time to report. I don't care what the union says. File a grievance. It might take me three days to bring you back up. . . ."

At the same time, he was amused to have a player call his office to yell at him. The next day, Piniella brought me back to Seattle. He stuck me in the starting lineup, batting second or sixth most nights, and we got along fine after that. Seattle reporters saw us arguing and wrote about a "feud" between Boone and Piniella, when we were really kindred spirits, a couple of hot-tempered baseball lifers. In fact Lou paid me a hell of a compliment that year, without saying a word.

We were playing Minnesota on the second-to-last night of the '93 season. The Twins were out of the AL West race and so were we. When we took a big lead in the eighth inning, Piniella pulled his stars from the game. It was a curtain-call moment, a chance for Mariners fans to cheer their heroes, Junior Griffey and Jay Buhner.

And me. While the others finished the game, Lou gave Griffey, Buhner, and Boone an early shower, the best shower I ever had.

I guess I'd made it. I was set to be Piniella's second baseman "for the next fifteen years," Lou told me.

Seattle fans who loved Griffey and Buhner were warming up to me. Seattle General Manager Woody Woodward, not so much. Woodward still had doubts about my fielding and my attitude. The guy had been a light-hitting middle infielder. If I hit, he said I couldn't field. If I turned a double play, he said I couldn't hit the ball the other way. And he needed a catcher.

Jim Bowden, Cincinnati's thirty-two-year-old GM, had a top-notch young catcher named Dan Wilson. Bowden needed a second baseman to replace streaky Juan Samuel, who'd gone to Detroit as a free agent. On November 2, 1993, the Mariners traded me, plus pitcher Erik Hanson, to the Reds for Wilson and pitcher Bobby Ayala.

Dad and Gramps told me all about Wilson, the Reds' first-round pick in the 1990 draft—the year I went in the fifth round. Wilson was my age, twenty-four, with a rep as a future Gold Glove catcher. He would go on to spend a decade with the Mariners, hitting 15 homers a year with a solid average of .270 or so, but his real value was as one of the best defensive catchers ever. Wilson was a modern-day Bob Boone.

Gramps told me to keep my head up. "It's no shame to get traded. Happened to me four times," he said. "It means somebody wants you."

I was in California, spending the holidays with a bunch of Boones at Mom and Dad's house in Orange County, when my new manager phoned me. "Hiya Bret," Davey Johnson said. "I want to welcome you to the Reds." Johnson had led the 1986 Mets to a World Series title, and kept them in the race year after year, only to get fired when the owners decided he wasn't tough enough. "Toughness" is one of those dumb ideas that owners sell gullible fans and reporters—the idea that a manager who stomps his feet is a tough guy, a real disciplinarian. In fact, players laugh behind that guy's back. Fines, tantrums, curfews, clubhouse speeches, and the rest of the crap you see in sports movies don't motivate players. Professionalism does. Players want a manager who treats them like fellow professionals—like grown men—and that's pretty much the end of it.

By phoning me, Johnson was acting like the pro he was. Some managers act like they're above you. They like you to feel uncomfortable, so they'll wait for a new player to come up and introduce himself at spring training. But most of them follow the usual protocol, which calls for a phone call to the new guy within a day or two of a trade.

"I want you to know how glad I am to have you," Johnson said. "You're going to help our offense, and you and Larkin can be a hell of a double-play combination. I think we're going to win our division."

Now I was feeling better about the trade. I thanked him. We were saying goodbye, see you at spring training, when he said he had a question for me. "Can you help me get in touch with your dad?"

"That's easy," I said. "He's standing right here."

Dad had retired after nineteen big-league seasons that put him up there with the best catchers in history. A four-time All-Star with a World Series ring to go with his rep as one of the coolest heads in the game, he won seven Gold Gloves and spent 2,225 games behind the plate. At the time, that was more games caught than by any other catcher *ever*. He'd spent 1992 and '93 managing the Tacoma Tigers, Oakland's top farm club, proving himself as a manager.

I handed him the phone. "Davey wants to talk to you."

They spoke for a few minutes before Dad hung up. "He offered me a job," he said. "Bench coach." He'd be the manager's right-hand man—sort of a lateral step from managing in Triple-A, but a return to the majors.

"And?"

"I took it."

I couldn't believe what I was hearing. "Without asking me?"

At that moment, it didn't occur to me that Johnson's offer could be a step toward the managerial job Dad wanted, or that Johnson had a right to hire whoever he wanted, or that this was another all-time first for the Boone family: the first welcome-to-the-team phone call to add a player's dad to the team. What occurred to me was, *Shit! I'm twenty-four years old, moving to a new team in a new town, and I'll have my dad looking over my shoulder? Welcome to Booneball.*

There wasn't much time to mope about it. Three months later, Dad and I flew from Orange County's John Wayne Airport to Orlando, Florida. We rented a car and drove an hour to the Reds' spring-training complex in Plant City, where I met my new double-play partner.

☆ ☆ ☆

Remember when I said that hitting's mainly a talent but fielding's a craft? Today, when I work with young infielders as a special instructor for the Oakland A's, I drill that into their ears until they're sick of hearing it. Defense is work, repetition, muscle memory. That's how you develop the footwork and timing that make tough plays look easy. It has next to nothing to do with your hands.

When an infielder makes a slick play, you often hear TV announcers say he has "great hands." Why do they say that? Because they don't know what they're talking about. What the announcers think is great hands is actually bad feet. Watch enough games and you start to see how many fielding gems are caused by lousy, lazy footwork. An infielder hangs back on a hard-hit ball. His first step is sideways instead of toward the ball. He's out of position. At the last instant he stabs at the ball. If he comes up with it, throws to first, gets the runner by a step, the TV guys get all excited. "Great hands!"

Then there's the fielder who moves toward the ball with the crack of the bat, hands low, weight on the balls of his feet. His footwork turns the other guy's bad hop into a routine play. The announcers don't notice that play, but baseball people do.

Players I respected had told me about Barry Larkin. They said he was one of those shortstops who make life easier for second basemen. That spring, with about twenty fans in the Reds' little six-thousand-seat ballpark in Plant City, I found out they were right. Playing the infield with Larkin was like taking BP with Ken Griffey Jr.

The Reds finished fifth the year before, when Johnson replaced Tony Perez in midseason, but our '94 team was better. We had Jose Rijo and John Smiley at the top of the rotation. We would have Larkin, Tony Fernandez, Hal Morris, and me in the infield and a potent outfield—Kevin Mitchell in left, Reggie Sanders in right, and (after an early-season trade) football-baseball star Deion Sanders in center. We had a loose clubhouse featuring vets like catcher Joe Oliver, a big, friendly dude who put up with my jokes about his huge head. (I once asked all our teammates, "What would you rather have, a million dollars or Joe Oliver's head full of nickels?")

With "Neon Deion" stealing bases and headlines, the Reds took an early lead in the NL Central Division and stayed on top all season. I batted .316 in April and stayed hot, but that's not what stands out when I look back on 1994. What stands out is what fun I had learning telepathy.

That's how it feels to be in sync with your double-play partner. I'd played with another great shortstop, Omar Vizquel, during my two years in Seattle. On a grounder to me, Omar would move toward second base, rounding toward the bag like a baserunner going the other way, while I fielded the ball. I'd lead him so that my throw reached him just before he got to the base, then he'd drag his toe across the bag and fire a strike to first.

That's the optimal double-play ball. Sometimes you have to improvise, and Vizquel was a wizard at that. Throw the ball behind him and he was liable to spin around, barehand it, and still get the runner at first. Omar was a wizard, but I can't say he was my favorite double-play partner. I was still a newbie in Seattle, kind of a major-league apprentice still learning my craft. We worked well together, but our shortstop–second baseman relationship was more of a solid marriage than a bromance.

Then I met Lark. Cue the violins.

Barry Larkin turned thirty the year I got to Cincinnati. He was a five-time winner of the Silver Slugger Award as the National League's best-hitting shortstop, an All-Star who had already hit .342 in a season and swiped 40 bases in another. Larkin was the only base-stealer I'd put in Rickey Henderson's class. Pretty soon he'd be voted Most Valuable Player of the National League. None of which meant nearly as much to me as the way he played short. Like a jazzman. Reacting, improvising, never losing his composure, every move as cool as could be. It all started with the sort of footwork that fans, announcers, and even baseball men tend to miss. He seldom backhanded a ball, because he was in position before it got to him. He might have to backhand a rocket to the hole, but that was a ball other shortstops would dive for. He would go on to win three Gold Gloves, the fielding awards voted on by managers and coaches. But he deserved twice as many, if not more. Larkin wasn't seen as Vizquel's equal as a fielder, but nobody saw him up close like I did, and I think he was as good as Ozzie Smith.

Purists and Reds pitchers knew how special Larkin was. I guess I was one of the purists because I felt something weird when we worked together—kind of like meeting a twin you never knew you had. I'd be diving for a ball up the middle, chasing one behind the first baseman, or charging a bunt, and I knew where he was. I could sense it. Lark knew where I was, too. There were times when we made no-look throws to empty spaces, tosses that should have rolled into the outfield or foul territory, and the other guy was there. If one of us broke his toe, the other would probably holler in pain.

Not too many second basemen and shortstops have that kind of mind-meld, but the ones who do turn a lot of double plays.

Every double-play combination's different. Some guys like to shovel the ball underhand, while others set themselves for an overhand throw with more zip. Some like a chest-high relay toss, some like the ball a little higher. Some push off the bag and jump to make the throw to first, others stay lower and cross second base while they throw. And all our preferences go out the window when we have to improvise, reacting to the speed of a grounder, the speed of the batter, and the runner sliding—or barreling—into second base to break up a double play.

There's a code to cover that situation. You won't find it in the rulebook. The code is an unwritten set of rules that ballplayers understand because . . . well, just because. There's no rule against stealing a base when your team's ahead 10–0, but you don't do it. It's against the code. It's wrong and stupid to show up the other team, especially in baseball, where tonight's losers can blow out the winners tomorrow night, and if you're the guy who stole with a ten-run lead, tomorrow's starting pitcher might stick a fastball in your ear. Which would also be against the code. Usually.

The code says you don't throw at somebody's head—except in retaliation for serious code violations by the other team, like throwing at somebody's head. You don't walk a guy late in the game if he's working on a hitting streak of 15 or 20 or more games (unless the game is on the line). You don't bunt for a hit against a pitcher who's working on a no-hitter (unless you hate his guts). Because you'd be a jerk if you did. A busher, an amateur. The code comes down from veterans to rookies, generation after generation. It hasn't changed much since Dad's day, or Gramps's day, and it has nothing to do with fans, managers, agents, reporters, or anybody outside the foul lines. It prevents more fights than it causes.

Like I said, one subsection of the code covers the double-play pivot. The shortstop or second baseman taking the relay throw is often a sitting duck. Sometimes he's in midair, sometimes he's pushing off second base with one leg. A clean, hard slide can disrupt the double play but a dirty one can hurt or even cripple the fielder. If my spikes catch in the dirt and a runner crashes into me, rolling up my ankle, he could snap my leg in half. I want to avoid that, and as a fielder I've got one weapon to fight back with. I've got the ball.

A minor-league coach of mine, Marty Martinez, had a saying: "Somebody screws with your family, you screw with his." By family, Marty meant your health, your career, everything family relies on. A runner barreling into second with his spikes high, or going ten feet out of the baseline to knock you down, or blocking your throw by waiting too long to slide, he's antifamily. You have every right to throw the ball between his eyes.

I practically killed a guy on a play like that. This was in Double-A ball. A runner came charging into second as I was making the relay throw, and I don't know if he was mad or just absentminded, but he *did not slide*. Now, you don't need the code to know that nobody breaks up a double play standing up. So I did what I was supposed to do. I fired the ball at his face. It's his job to get out of the way. The next thing I heard was a crunchy clanging sound. The ball banged right off the bill of his helmet. It bounced all the way to the first-base stands on the fly. He stood there blinking like the ball just woke him up. Lucky guy—he needed a new helmet instead of a new nose.

Best of all, the ump called him out for runner's interference, so we got the double play.

☆ ☆ ☆

By the middle of 1994 Lark and I had settled in as one of the best double-play combos in the league. Some people would go further than that. They'd say "the best in Reds history, one of the best ever." I'm way too polite to disagree. We made tough plays look routine. Our footwork was like clockwork. When it broke down due to a bad hop or a swinging bunt or a ball that got tipped by the pitcher or another infielder, we improvised. Double-play balls or other force plays at second meant one thing to me: get the ball to Larkin ASAP. Nothing means more to a middle infielder than an extra split second. On a grounder between me and Hal Morris, the first baseman, I'd go into short right field for the ball, then spin toward center field with my back to the plate to make the throw to second. If I knocked down a shot up the middle and my momentum took me past the ball, I might try to kick it to Barry. Whatever it took to get him the ball. He did the same for me. The difference between us and an ordinary shortstop and second baseman might be an extra out every game or two, but the difference adds up. Sometimes I'd actually smile in the middle of a double play, knowing we were turning one that most teams wouldn't.

I was happy to be in Cincinnati, fired up about the Reds' future.

The main weirdness we had to deal with was when the owner stuck a dead dog's fur in our pockets. Marge Schott, the colorful, chain-smoking, maybe slightly crazy owner, adored Schottzie, her St. Bernard. Schottzie was Marge's good-luck charm. He used to romp around Riverfront Stadium, peeing on the Astroturf. Till he died. She kept a bunch of his fur, and told us it was lucky. I'd be coming down the tunnel from the clubhouse to the field when I felt a hand in my back pocket. It was Marge, sticking some Schottzie fur in there. "Boonie," she said, "you're going to have a big night."

Larkin was an All-Star in 1994, as usual. Maybe I should have been, too, but the National League second basemen that year were Craig Biggio, the Dodgers' Mariano Duncan, and the Pirates' Carlos Garcia. (Carlos Garcia? I was hitting .310 at the break with 49 RBIs to his .267 and 20.) I wound up the season batting .320, fourth in the National League. Davey Johnson's Reds led the NL Central wire to wire, but we picked the wrong year to win the division, because our toughest opponent wasn't the second-place Houston Astros. It was a bunch of old men we couldn't beat. The owners.

☆ ☆ ☆

Remember my worries about having Dad on the Reds' bench? Forget 'em. I should have known we'd be fine because he's the ultimate pro. At the park he was purely professional. We were player and coach. He never looked at me or spoke to me any differently than he dealt with anybody else. Then we'd go to dinner and be father and son again. He'd fill me in on what the rest of the family was up to back home in Orange County. Matt was a freshman at Villa Park High School, where he'd soon be a pro prospect, and Mom was busy driving to his high school ballgames, keeping score as always.

Aaron had gone on to star for Mike Gillespie at USC. (What a copycat!) He sat by the phone during the major-league draft that June, but didn't have to wait as long as I did in 1990. The Reds selected Aaron in the third round, 72nd overall, making Cincinnati the game's first three-Boone franchise. Nomar Garciaparra, Paul Konerko, and Jason Varitek went in the first round that year. A. J. Pierzynski, who was still catching for the Braves last time I looked, went one pick ahead of Aaron. A few weeks later my little bro Arnie started his climb to the majors by reporting to rookie ball in Billings, Montana.

Dad and I sat in the home dugout at Riverfront Stadium, looking forward to the playoffs. In August we were half a game ahead of an Astros club featuring Jeff Bagwell and Craig Biggio, and then the season stopped. The players went on strike. We walked out and stayed off the field. Why? Simple: The collective bargaining agreement between owners and the players' union was about to expire. The owners wanted a better deal in the next agreement—a historically, radically, screw-you-dumb-jocksically one-sided deal. They had colluded—cheated—to hold players' salaries down in the late 1980s but swore they were losing money. They said there'd be no new agreement unless the players accepted a salary cap. That was the one thing we'd never agree to. Baseball had never had one, and never will as long as sports' best union exists.

Our leverage was limited. The players could wait till the off-season to negotiate, or we could stage a walkout, threatening the owners' fattest cash cow, the pennant races and postseason, with their megamillions in ticket sales, concessions, and TV revenue. We figured that Bud Selig, the Milwaukee Brewers owner who was the game's acting commissioner, and his fellow owners wouldn't want to screw the fans by refusing to negotiate in good faith. That might threaten or even eliminate the playoffs and World Series.

So we went on strike. On August 12, the players refused to play. We invited the owners to sit down with us and hash out an agreement in time to save the postseason.

I was 100 percent behind the union. In fact I was the Reds' assistant player representative, working with player rep Hal Morris. That was unusual for a guy my age. Unusual and risky, since I was still establishing myself in the big leagues. I was a third-year player, new to the team, and management didn't like uppity players. Most union reps were older, better-known guys who couldn't disappear without making news. Younger players who got active in the union tended to get traded or sent to the minors for mysterious reasons.

Why did I take the risk? Pride, for one thing. I'm conservative by temperament, a Republican my whole life. I'm pro-business. When Democrats say we should take from the rich and give to the poor, I say, Why? This is America—we're all about competition. Let's compete and applaud the winners because they earn it.

Sports is different. Pro athletes aren't interchangeable workers. We're entertainers. Nobody expects Tom Cruise, Taylor Swift, or Jay-Z to settle for a pay scale, and ballplayers are no different. We're the top 1 percent of the 1 percent of college players who sign pro contracts. We're the ones you pay to see. In fact, I'll bet you never once said, "I can't wait to see my favorite owner's team in action."

Over dinner one night, Dad told me about his work with Marvin Miller in the 1970s. Miller, the players' union chief, went to federal court to beat the reserve clause tying players to their teams forever. His legal victories over the owners led to free agency, arbitration, and all the other manifestations of players' right to a fair slice of Major League Baseball's $10-billion-a-year pie. As we finished eating, Dad urged me to get involved in the union. "Educate yourself," he said. "It's your turn."

That's what I did. I joined Morris, our team's player representative, on conference calls with union chief Donald Fehr and player reps from the other twenty-seven clubs. Fehr was one of the sharpest men I'd ever met. His mastery of the legal issues, the game's economics, and our long- and short-term strategy blew me away. I was also impressed by union leaders like Steve Rogers, the Expos pitcher.

Veterans like Rogers, Tom Glavine, Paul Molitor, and Doug DeCinces proved they were true leaders as the strike went on for weeks and months. It helped that we were in the right, while management was greedy and selfish enough to blow up the game if it helped break our union. Yankees owner George Steinbrenner and Orioles owner Peter Angelos were exceptions. "The game's healthy. Let's make a deal and get our teams back on the field," Steinbrenner said. Acting commissioner Selig and most of the others disagreed, with White Sox owner Jerry Reinsdorf leading the union-haters. They were willing to risk the playoffs, the World Series, and even the 1995 season to put us in our place.

How could Selig, the Brewers' owner, be "acting commissioner"? Good question. Ever since Kenesaw Mountain Landis, a federal judge, became the first commissioner in 1920, the commissioner of baseball was supposed to be an impartial figure who could act "in the interests of baseball." Not the interests of owners or players, but of the game. Still, the owners had the power to hire and fire commissioners, and in 1992 they fired Fay Vincent for being impartial. Vincent called the owners' collusion in the '80s "a $280 million theft by Selig and Reinsdorf from the players. I mean, they rigged the signing of free agents. They got caught and had to pay $280 million to the players." He was the last independent commissioner. Once they dumped him, the owners gave the job to one of their own.

Now they were threatening to hire more than seven hundred "replacement players" and go on without us. Did they really think fans couldn't tell the difference between the best players in the world and a bunch of minor-league scabs? We didn't. We knew we could win if we stayed unified. That's why I got so angry at players who griped about the union. In almost every case, they knew nothing about the issues.

"Boonie, we've got to get this over with. It's costing me money."

These were teammates, even friends. Guys I used to respect. They weren't interested in how players in Gramps's generation got swindled their whole careers. They didn't care about the sacrifices Dad's generation made while Marvin Miller and players like Curt Flood, Andy Messersmith, and Catfish Hunter won the court battles that were making us millionaires—battles that we were now fighting for ourselves and the players who'd come up after us. They didn't know or care that the owners had broken the law by colluding to hold our salaries down. All these guys cared about was their next paycheck.

"This strike is bullshit," they'd say.

I went off on a couple of them. "Go educate yourself, then I might listen to you. Till then, you've got no right to an opinion."

Fehr arranged for a bunch of us player reps to go to Washington, D.C., to lobby Congress. That trip was an eye-opener. I was paired with the Orioles' Eddie Murray. The two of us put on suits and ties and spent a couple days on Capitol Hill, explaining the union's position to senators and US representatives. We wanted them to back legislation to end MLB's antitrust exemption, a law dating back to 1922 that kept owners from getting sued for unfair labor practices.

A few congressmen listened to us, but most of our meetings went like this:

Eddie and Bret enter Senator So-and-So's office. We all shake hands. Then a staff member brings in a box full of stuff for us to sign. "For my kids," the senator says. "They're big baseball fans." He must have a lot of kids, because it takes us ten minutes to sign all the balls, gloves, and posters in the box. After that, Eddie talks about our cause. He reminds Senator So-and-So that the owners cheated us and want to break our union. I add a few words, but I can see that the senator's not listening. He's looking right through us. More handshakes, and the staffer leads us out. We were wasting our time.

And there wasn't much time left. At one point we held a players-and-owners summit in Phoenix. Fehr and several of our leaders stated the players' case. We would never accept a salary cap, but just about anything else was on the table. We wanted to play. Then Selig, Reinsdorf, and one of their attorneys, Rob Manfred, rejected everything we had to say. Manfred was a hotshot young lawyer, determined to bust our union. I don't say that as a slam. He was doing his job. Today, of course, former union-buster Manfred is commissioner of baseball.

That meeting really showed me what the owners thought of us. They sat on a stage, looking down their noses at us. I could practically hear what they were thinking. *Dumb jocks.* They saw the players as interchangeable pieces in their game. They were the kings and we were the pawns. When we talked back, they repeated their party line as if we were too stupid to understand it the first time. Fehr kept saying no to a salary cap. He said we'd whip them in court again if we had to, but we'd rather get back on the field. Selig and Reinsdorf and Manfred weren't listening. They said we had two options. We could agree to a salary cap or get another job.

This went on for hours. Finally one of the American League player reps, one of the game's biggest names, stood up. He was an intimidating man, a home run hitter who towered over the owners and their lawyers. He stubbed out his cigar and went to the front of the hall, where he loomed over Selig.

"Bud," he said, "go fuck yourself." And walked out of the room.

The meeting broke up with no progress. The owners told reporters they might cancel the postseason. We didn't think they'd go that far. They'd never call off the World Series.

Or would they?

10
AN INTERVENTION

World War I couldn't stop the World Series. Neither could World War II. In fact, in 1942 President Franklin Roosevelt, who once served as student manager for Harvard's baseball team, told Commissioner Landis, "It would be best for the country to keep baseball going" through the war. The Show went on.

Fifty-two years later, acting commissioner Bud Selig called off the World Series. Why? Because the players wouldn't go for a salary cap. Of course Selig blamed us, and at least half the fans bought his blame-the-players line.

So much for the idea of the commissioner acting in baseball's best interest. Selig acted purely in the interest of himself and his fellow owners. He and other hard-liners like Reinsdorf canceled the 1994 Series and made plans to replace seven hundred major-league players with strikebreakers in 1995. "Replacement players," they called them. We used different words.

As the '95 season approached, I got phone calls from friends I'd known in the minors. They asked if they should cross the players' picket lines. I answered the question with one of my own. "Have you got a shot in hell of making the majors? The real majors?"

If they said yes, I told them they'd be crazy to cross the players' union. "You'll be a scab forever. An outcast. When the strike's over, we'll freeze you out and you'll *never* have a chance."

But if they said no, they'd never make it on merit, I told them that they had a decision to make. "You can cross the line. I'd never do it, but I won't tell you not to." They were ballplayers, and every ballplayer dreams of making the big leagues. I wasn't going to tell them to miss their one chance, even if it was the wrong way to get there.

In April 1995, the day before a new season could start with all-scab teams, the strike ended. Federal judge Sonia Sotomayor, now a Supreme Court justice, ruled that the players were right and the owners were wrong. We won. Not that it helped our image much. After the season began three weeks late, I looked up at the sky over Cincinnati's Riverfront Stadium. A plane was pulling a banner reading OWNERS & PLAYERS: TO HELL WITH ALL OF YOU!

☆ ☆ ☆

My first at-bat after the strike came with the usual case of the nerves. The rest of the year, I'd step out of the shower, pose naked in front of a mirror, and say, "There he is, the best second baseman alive!" But the first trip to the plate always scared me. Maybe that's because it meant so much. *Here I am in the big leagues. It matters.* I wanted to honor that feeling by hitting a ball hard.

Jim Bullinger was pitching for the Cubs on Opening Day 1995. I smacked his second pitch to right field. Going, going . . . *caught* on the warning track by Sammy Sosa. I was 0-for-1, but the anxiety was gone.

We lost our first six games that year, but Davey Johnson didn't panic. His hangdog expression hardly changed as we went on to win

12 of 13 to take over first place in May. Johnson and my dad were a pair of stone faces on the Reds' bench, watching Deion Sanders steal bases while Jose Rijo, our ace pitcher, rubbed snake oil on his elbow and Larkin and I turned double plays. I was twenty-six, just entering my prime, having the time of my life. I loved the bright lights, the big crowds, the locker room spread. In the majors it's prime rib, lobster, grilled chicken, and sushi.

That's why they call it the big leagues. Everything, from the airlines to the bats and balls to the lavish locker rooms to the groupies, is first-class. In Dad's day the groupies were called baseball Annies. Some of today's players use coarser terms like "road beef." I was no altar boy, but the fact is I was too focused on hitting and fielding in those days to play the sexual field like some guys. I needed my sleep! And I remembered something Gramps used to say: "Women are your downfall." He didn't mean all women, just the ones that can slow a guy down when he's trying to make it to the majors. "If you want to be a great ballplayer, that stuff can wait," he said. Which leads me to another family story . . .

Back in A-ball I'd spotted a pretty brunette in the seats behind the home dugout—the girlfriend seats. I asked around. "That's Suzi," somebody said. "Jimmy's girl."

Jimmy Gutierrez was a nineteen-year-old pitcher. As his twenty-one-year-old elder, I could have made a move, but that would have been taboo. The code says you never move in on a teammate's girlfriend. But that doesn't mean you can't find out her name.

"Suzi what?"

"Suzi Riggins."

I was smitten, but I waited. A year later, I heard they'd broken up. Jimmy confirmed it. I didn't want to ask him for her number—who needed Jimmy and twenty teammates knowing I was after his ex? I couldn't Google her, because Google wouldn't exist for seven more years. So I took drastic action that will shock my kids and millions of other millennials. I looked her up in the phone book. There she was in the white pages: *S Riggins*.

"Hi, it's Bret," I said.

"Bret who?"

Our talk went downhill from there. "Bret Boone," I said. The name meant nothing to her. "Come to the ballpark tomorrow. Come see me play."

"Why would I want to do that?" She'd broken up with one ballplayer and could live without another.

"Okay," I said, "but you should know I'm consistent. I'll call you tomorrow, and the day after that and the day after that."

Finally she came to sit in the girlfriend seats at Wolfson Park in Jacksonville. We went to dinner after the game and bingo—we became tighter than Barry Larkin and I would ever be. Within a month, Suzi moved into my parents' house in California and got a job at the local Nordstrom's department store. Dad and I were on the road, so after work it was just Suzi and Mom in the house with my brothers, Aaron and Matt.

That off-season I came home and slept in my old room. Usually. Suzi had her own room down the hall. The sexual revolution never reached Mom and Dad's house, so there was no chance they'd ever let us sleep together. I may have slipped down the hall to Suzi's room a time or ten, but we kept it quiet. When we got married a year later, Mom gave Suzi the same shower gifts she got from Grandma Patsy: a stadium blanket, a seat cushion, a scorebook, and a box of sharpened pencils.

☆ ☆ ☆

I hit .267 with 15 homers in 1995, plus another bomb off Hideo Nomo while we swept the Dodgers in the playoffs. Then we got swept by the

Braves in the NLCS, which was no disgrace since they had Greg Maddux, John Smoltz, and Tom Glavine on the mound. Atlanta went on to win the 1995 World Series. We fell back to third place in 1996 and again in '97, partly because I sucked.

Was it the lifestyle? I'll admit I always liked hearing applause. I never minded smiling for a TV camera. I liked the camaraderie of a big-league clubhouse, and I enjoyed a drink from time to time. In those days there was free-flowing beer in the clubhouse. That was part of treating players like grown men. Today, even light beer is banned from most major-league clubhouses, for two reasons. The first is liability. If a player has one too many and crashes his car on the drive home, the club might get sued. The second reason is more annoying. The clubs want to control players' lives to a degree they never did before, right down to how many hours in a day a man has to himself. In Gramps's era, players might show up at the park an hour before game time. There was more prep by Dad's day and still more by the time I came up. Today teams expect players to show up for stretching, meetings, video study, BP, and media duties five or six hours before game time. Overall, it's worth it. The average MLB salary went up to a record $3.2 million in 2015. But those millions come with a price.

Today I'd be worth $20 million a year. Not that I'm complaining. (Except when I see .240-hitting, 20-homer guys who hurt their teams on defense making $20 mil a year, and even then I usually keep my gripes among family and friends.) I did a lot better than average in my prime—$9 million in my best year—and had a blast doing it.

I loved road games in America's best baseball towns. Fans in Chicago, St. Louis, and Philadelphia know their stuff. They'll get on you about your fielding percentage. San Francisco has been a great place to play since the Giants moved out of Candlestick Park in 2000. But no place compares to New York.

As an infielder, I was far enough from the bleachers to avoid the abuse outfielders got from the bleacher creatures at Yankee Stadium. Most of my interactions were with businessmen in the two-hundred-dollar seats near the visitors' dugout, suit-and-tie guys who'd shout, "Boone, you suck!" while I walked to the on-deck circle. As in the minors, there always seemed to be one loudmouth who'd really done his homework. He'd yell, "You can't hit on Tuesdays! Your dad was on more winning teams!"

"Wait and watch," I'd say. "Let's talk in about four minutes."

If I struck out, they let me have it twice as loud. If I hit a home run, I'd trot around the bases and give my critics a look on my way to the dugout. Most times, to their credit, they'd bow and say, "You da man!"

I liked hecklers who had something witty to say. Any chump can yell, "Boone, you're a bum!" That stuff is easy to ignore. If you want a player to hear you, say something he hasn't heard a million times. One night at Yankee Stadium, a well-dressed fan got on me about my height. "Oh, there's Bret Boone, the big power hitter," he said. "I didn't realize how short you are!"

Such a personal comment deserved a personal answer. Laying it on thick, I said, "Buddy, you should see how tall I am when I stand on my wallet."

The only fans I couldn't stand were professional autograph hounds. Grown men, mostly. You learn to spot them after a few weeks in the majors. They're the rumpled guys hanging out in the hotel lobby, handing you a cap or jersey or mint-condition baseball card to sign. A couple of minutes later, they'll try again with a different cap or card. Some pay little kids to do it for them. It's not about the game for these guys. They're not fans. They only want your autograph to sell it. By signing the items they hand you, you're turning that stuff into collector's items worth ten times what they paid. You're keeping these leeches in business. If you say no, they're liable to call you stuck-up, overrated, and worse. I've seen autograph hounds poke players in the eye with a rolled-up program or a pen. I've gone out with my family and had them horn in on our dinner, asking me to sign two or three things between bites, cussing me out if I say, "Sorry, this isn't the time."

Remember that the next time you hear someone say, "That jerk wouldn't sign his name or take a selfie!" As every player knows, you can sign a thousand autographs and the thousand-and-first person will hate you.

I know it's bad form to complain about a few jerks when you're making $9 million a year. But I could be as rich as Mark Zuckerberg or Mark Cuban and still get mad if somebody's rude. Because I'm human. I can also tell you that when ballplayers say we don't care if fans call us names—when we say we don't read the papers, don't hear fans booing, don't care what people think of us—we're lying.

We care. There's not enough money in the world to make it okay to strike out with the tying run on third. Or to get called a selfish prick when you're trying to eat dinner.

That's the downside of a great job. The upside is the daily thrill of playing the greatest game at its highest level. The challenge of facing big-league pitching. You might be raking, batting .500 for a week. Then you face Maddux and Smoltz. You blink and you're 0-for-8. Then a couple of bloopers fall in. You go 3-for-4 against Glavine and all's right with the world. You suck gas one night and walk on air the next, remembering how one single a week can turn a .250 hitter into a .300 one.

Mulling over numbers like that made me a student of hitting. I wanted to understand the game I loved.

No, I'm lying again. I just wanted to hit .300.

It's a fascinating job either way. For one thing, being a student of hitting makes you a student of pitching. You learn that pitchers with a typical 90- to 92-mph fastball invariably throw a slider between 81 and 84 miles an hour. That's how the human arm works. The instant you recognize a slider—some guys see a pink dot on the ball, an optical illusion caused by the ball's spinning red seams; others, like me, look for a different trajectory as the ball leaves the pitcher's hand— your swing adjusts to that slower range. That's why a pitcher with a different repertoire can make you look sick. When Johan Santana was at his best, he paired a 94-mph heater with a 75-mph changeup. That's a devastating combination, a 20-mph difference instead of the usual 10. Sometimes I outthought Santana—I knew the changeup was coming—and still swung too soon. I could have adapted by slowing down my off-speed-pitch swing, but that would have messed me up for every other off-speed pitch in the league. So I choked up against Santana and tried to slap a single somewhere. Mostly I tipped my cap to him and went back to the bench.

Santana's fastball-changeup combination proved a point that fans, announcers, and even players miss. In pitching, subtraction can beat addition. A 20-mph gap between the fastball and the off-speed pitch can make a pitcher practically unhittable.

Pedro Martinez was a genius at that. In the days when Pedro threw 97 mph, he'd get me down in the count with his fastball. Then, when I was primed for another heater or a slow curve, he threw me a batting-practice fastball so slow and *weird* I couldn't react. A pitch I could hit four hundred feet if I swung. Instead I'd freeze. Strike three.

Some pitchers rely on one pitch. Kevin Brown and Billy Swift used the sinker, a fastball that goes only 89 or 90, with downward movement. A good sinker feels like you're hitting the iron ball in a shotput event. That's what hitters mean when they say a guy throws a heavy ball. A sinkerballer doesn't care if he strikes you out; he wants you to hit the ball on the ground. Today, the Astros' Dallas Keuchel has one of the best sinkers. Ditto Tim Hudson, who was still sinking the ball in 2015 at the age of forty. Hudson used to wear me out. One day he made me look clueless the usual way: sinker, sinker, sinker. Then, for variety's sake, I guess, he hung a curve. My eyes lit up. I knocked it into the second deck and laughed my way around the bases while he glared at me. I said, "Timmy, one more sinker and you had me."

The sinker's just one missile in the pitcher's arsenal. A splitter, or split-fingered fastball, isn't really a fastball. It's slower than a sinker, around 85 mph, but it breaks straight down. Pioneered by reliever Bruce Sutter in the 1970s, the splitter is a swing-and-miss pitch, a strikeout pitch. Roger Clemens and Curt Schilling threw evil splitters. Masahiro Tanaka and Jeff Samardzija throw some of today's nastiest.

The Yankees' Mariano Rivera blew hitters away with his cutter. It veered in on the hands of a left-handed batter, or away from a righthander, just enough to keep them from getting good wood on the ball. Greg Maddux threw a great cutter, too, but Mariano's was heavier. To hit it, I'd forget all about lifting the ball. I'd keep my front shoulder tucked a little longer and try to hit a single up the middle.

That should be your plan against great pitching: do a little something rather than nothing. Find a way to get on base. Facing Clemens, Schilling, Pedro, Maddux, and other all-time greats, I looked for a knock and a walk. A single and a base on balls. Get a knock and a walk and you're helping your team. You're also 1-for-3 on the day. It's the ohfers (0-for-3, 0-for-4) that kill you.

My ohfers started piling up in 1996. I turned twenty-seven that year and batted .233 with 12 homers and a career-high 100 strikeouts. Pitchers had developed a strategy against me. It boiled down to three words. *Smoke him inside.* It's the oldest approach in the book— fastballs on the inside corner.

Getting smoked inside can be tough on a right-handed batter with a closed stance. ("Closed" means that a line connecting my feet points toward the second baseman or pitcher. With an open stance, the line's more toward third base.) If I adjusted by standing farther from the plate or stepping in the bucket—striding toward third base—they'd drop one over the outside corner where I couldn't reach it. The way to adjust is to speed up your hands. Catch the ball as it reaches the front of the plate. That way you can extend your arms and sting the ball.

But my hands got slower. I tried moving back in the batter's box, tried a lighter bat, tried an extra pregame coffee for a jolt of caffeine. Nothing worked. I was losing my swing, turning into the one thing I never dreamed I could be.

An easy out.

The summer of '97 should have been a highlight thanks to another family moment. In June the Reds promoted a skinny punk of a backup infielder, Aaron Boone, from Triple-A to the majors. My little brother Arnie arrived without the fanfare that came with my promotion. And wasn't so little anymore. At six foot two, the same height as Dad, he was four inches taller than his big bro. I was thrilled to see him. Aaron was quieter than I was, more of a listener than a talker, with a "Gee whiz, I'm in the big leagues" look in his eyes. Dad was managing the Kansas City Royals by then, leaving two Boones in Cincinnati, and me with my ohfers and my worries, which I kept to myself. Aaron saw me struggling at the plate, but I moved with the same old swagger. On road trips to Los Angeles and San Diego we'd rent a car and drive to Orange County. The rest of the Reds slept in a four-star hotel while we bunked at home with Mom.

The tough part was going back to work. After my lousy '96 season I'd looked forward to turning my career around. Instead I got worse. In September 1997 my average fell to .218, the worst of any everyday second baseman in the majors. That shit makes you see a different guy in the mirror. Was the game tougher than I was? Would I be out of the majors before I turned thirty?

I never let Aaron see how miserable I was. He was just getting his feet wet in the majors. I'd sneak out of the dugout between at-bats and walk through the dark, cavernous spaces under the stands, crying. There was nobody around to hear me say, "I'm screwed. I lost my swing."

Bret Boone, shitty second baseman for the Cincinnati Reds, would finish the season with a batting average of .223. There were *pitchers* who hit better.

I hid my frustration, but kept hearing Dad's voice. I knew what he'd say. *Grit your teeth. Fight back. If you make an out, take a hit away from the other guys.*

I'd been taking extra grounders, adding muscle memory one ball at a time. Going into September I'd made only 2 errors in more than 500 chances. I worked hard on every play, reading hitters' reactions to Reds pitchers' deliveries, "cheating" to my left or right by leaning that way, going for balls that gave me a *greater* chance of making an error because I'd barely reach the ball and be falling sideways trying to throw it. All to take a hit from the other guys.

I was trying to prove myself—not to Dad, not to Aaron, not to the manager or the fans or the TV announcers. I wanted to prove *to me* that I'd never give up.

And you know what? I finished the 1997 season with that shitty .223 batting average and a fielding percentage of .997. That was historic—2 errors in 607 chances, an all-time record for second basemen.

Which isn't to say I was perfect. Near perfect between the lines, maybe, but not as heroic as Ted Williams. You'll remember that Williams played a doubleheader the last day of the 1941 season and went 6-for-8 to finish with a batting average over .400. In '97, with a fielding percentage of .996705, I sat out the last game of the season. Here's my reasoning: our team was out of the race, so why risk kicking one and losing an all-time record? It wasn't the ballsiest move of my life, but I'm not apologizing.

Houston's Craig Biggio made 25 errors that year to my 2. Yet he won his fourth straight Gold Glove as the National League's best-fielding second baseman. The next spring, when we played the Astros, Biggio told me, "Bret, you should have won. You had a better year in the field." A year later the league's managers and coaches voted for me instead. That trophy might be my favorite. The first of my four Gold Gloves proved how hard I'd worked to help the team one way or another.

But I still couldn't buy a hit.

Finally I phoned Dad. "My swing's gone," I said. "What's wrong with me?"

He'd been watching me on TV. He said, "You stink, but we can fix it."

☆ ☆ ☆

Kansas City fired Dad that summer. His Royals had finished second in the AL Central in 1995, his first season as a major-league manager. They'd fallen to fifth and last the following year and were running last again when they dumped him in July of '97. Dad would never make excuses, so I'll explain for him. Those Royals teams of his would have finished last if you gave them four outs an inning. They proved it by playing worse under his replacement, Tony Muser. Getting fired had to hurt, but you won't be shocked to hear that Dad took it like a man. When people asked what happened in Kansas City, he gave them that level gaze of his and said there were three sure things in a manager's life: death, taxes, and getting your ass fired.

It was a tough stretch for the Boones. Matt scuffled his first year in pro ball, batting .204 for the Tigers' rookie-league club in Florida. Aaron, coming off his rookie season with the Reds, rode the bench in Cincinnati. He also had a medical condition no one outside the family knew about, a heart problem that first came up when he was at USC. Doctors said he could play, but at some point Aaron would probably need open-heart surgery.

My problems were trivial next to that. In four seasons with the Reds I'd averaged 12 home runs and 60 RBIs. Those numbers were about what they expected when they traded for me, but they sounded puny to me—way too similar to my plink-hitting dad's numbers. I'd just become a dad myself—Suzi gave birth to our first child, Savannah, that year—but aside from some sleep deprivation during home stands, parenthood had no connection to my slump. Suzi did the work on the home front with an assist from Mom, who'd fly to Florida (or Mars) if she could rustle up our dinner or change a diaper.

Mom's commute got three thousand miles shorter that off-season. We moved back to Orange County so she could help Suzi while Dad helped me save my career.

Growing up, I never asked for his advice, and, later on, he and I were nothing alike at the plate. I swung for the fences. He tried to put the ball in play. I trained myself to be a Gold Glove fielder, but above all I was a hitter. Dad was the opposite, an elite fielder and game-caller who chipped in enough base hits to contribute now and then. Yet as time passed, I began to appreciate his eye. Like a lot of players who fight for their place in the big leagues, he'd always paid close attention to every aspect of the game. He had to, because other guys had more natural ability. In that way, he was like a lot of managers who rise from the ranks of no-name players. What do Sparky Anderson, Bruce Bochy, Bobby Cox, Whitey Herzog, Tony La Russa, Tommy Lasorda, and Mike Matheny have in common? They were marginal big leaguers who became tremendous managers. Because they learned to outsmart guys they couldn't outplay.

In my ballsy, self-assured, totally naïve youth, I didn't need my banjo-hitting father's help. But, as I said before, the older you get, the smarter your dad gets. By 1997 I was learning to listen. Dad would leave a phone message: "You're pulling off the ball." Or "Your stride's too long." He became my hitting guru. I'd fly him to Atlanta or Pittsburgh to watch me in the batting cage. We got closer than ever before, but it wasn't enough to bail out my season. I'd get two hits the next night, then go 0-for-15. So he staged an intervention.

The Reds' season ended in Montreal on September 28, 1997. Aaron went 4-for-5 with a double and three RBIs, his best game of the year, while I finished with an embarrassing 7 homers in more than 500 trips to the plate to go with my average of .223.

Ordinarily I took three months off at the end of a season, trading my baseball gear for golf clubs and decompressing until New Year's Day, when I'd head for the batting cage to prep for spring training two months later. But this was no ordinary off-season. On Wednesday, October 1, in the middle of the '97 playoffs, I met Dad at a friend's batting cage in Anaheim. Dad never hit much, but he could teach you to hit. Over the next five months we worked seven days a week to make me a different sort of hitter. Starting with my stance.

"It hasn't been working. They keep beating you inside," he said. My closed stance made me vulnerable to inside fastballs. So we moved my front foot away from the plate. Now I could extend my arms and get the fat of the bat on that pitch. I could cover the outside corner by keeping my hands back a split second longer. If the ball was inside I could trigger the big swing; if not, I could shoot it to right field or up the middle.

Sound simple? It wasn't. After five years in the big leagues, it felt bizarre to open my stance to the point where I was practically facing the pitcher. Established major leaguers almost never try something so drastic. At the same time, I saw one benefit right away. Opening my stance brought my right eye into play. Right-handed hitters like me rely on the left eye, which is closer to the pitcher. Lucky for me, my left eye is better than my right. But once I got my own face out of the way, I saw the ball better than ever. It was the difference between watching a crummy old TV and a crisp HD image.

We weren't finished. "Your grip's all wrong," Dad said.

So I changed the way I'd held a baseball bat since I was a year old knocking Wiffle balls over the house with Gramps. I switched from a conventional grip, with my right wrist cocked to the right-hand side of the bat, to what players call a wrapped grip. I moved my right hand counterclockwise, toward the top of the bat. It felt doubly bizarre, like trying to grip the bat with my feet. "It works for Griffey," Dad said. The wrapped grip would keep me from swinging at the inside fastballs I was used to looking for, but that was the idea: to be less of a fastball hitter and more of an anyball hitter. Along with my new stance it would help me spray the ball to all fields. Instead of trying to yank everything over the left-field fence, I'd be able to hit the ball out to right-center and right field.

If it worked.

Two hundred swings a day, seven days a week, six thousand swings a month later, the bat felt almost comfortable. Dangerous, even. By the time I reported to spring training, I was ready.

☆ ☆ ☆

Did you ever have a day when everything went right? Breakfast tastes perfect. The weather clears up the moment you step outside. Traffic parts for you all the way to work, where the boss calls you into his office to give you a raise. You drive home to a loving family, your favorite dinner, and a night of passion with your soul mate, who happens to look like a supermodel.

That's how the '98 season felt. With my new stance and new grip, I started hitting on the first day of spring training and never stopped. That summer I made my first All-Star team. That was another distinction for the Boones. I was the eleventh All-Star in baseball history whose father had been one, too. (How many can you name? Sandy Alomar Jr. and Roberto Alomar, Moises Alou, Buddy Bell, Barry Bonds, Ken Griffey Jr., Mike Hegan, Todd Hundley, Vance Law . . . and Bob Boone.) But how many also had an All-Star grandfather? Just me.

After a two-homer night in August, I smoked down the stretch to finish with a team-leading 24 homers and 95 RBIs. My .266/.324/.458 slash line didn't match Gramps's in 1955, when he led the American League in RBIs (.284/.346/.476), but my 1998 was the second-best offensive year in Boone history. As Gramps himself liked to point out, he made 19 errors in 1955, more than twice as many as my nine in 1998, so maybe my year was the family's best. I'd never say it put me up there with Bonds, Biggio, Tony Gwynn, Chipper Jones, and Larry Walker, but I was in their league, one of the best players in the National League.

So I felt a little proud of myself. At age twenty-nine I'd done the hardest thing in the world, changed the way I swung a bat. I'd grown as a player and as a man, and grown to love the game more than ever. I was looking forward to more All-Star seasons in Cincinnati, playing with Larkin and Aaron.

That winter, Reds executives gathered in Cincinnati. It was the week before Christmas. General Manager Jim Bowden wanted to talk trade with his brain trust, manager Jack McKeon and the club's top scouts and advisors. The Reds needed pitching.

"First things first," Bowden said. "John Schuerholz made us an offer." Schuerholz, the Atlanta GM, was offering a potential ace. Denny Neagle had gone 20-5 to lead a Braves staff featuring Maddux, Smoltz, and Glavine in 1997. He'd won 16 games in '98. But he wouldn't come cheap. "The Braves want a bat."

Bowden went around the table, asking the others what they thought. Finally he got to an advisor he counted on. My dad.

"They want Bret Boone," Bowden said. "Bob, what do you think?"

"Yes," Dad answered. "I'd make the deal."

11

TRADE BAIT

Traded again. Bowden phoned me with the news. He said he never wanted to send me away, but Neagle was a frontline starter. Even Dad agreed.

I said, "Jim, I get it. It's the business of baseball." In fact I was almost flattered to be traded for a 20-game winner. So Bowden and I were okay, but he still had some fences to mend. He had to explain the deal to the press and fans in Cincinnati—a "budding star" like me for a starting pitcher they needed. Even worse, he had to deal with Mom. As Bowden said years later, "Bret understood, and Bob understood, but Sue Boone wouldn't talk to me for a while after I made that trade."

I was starting to feel well traveled. That's a term for a guy who gets traded a lot. At least it's preferable to "journeyman." A journeyman is an aging, marginal guy who hangs on for years by hooking on with different teams, which is better in turn than the lowest of the well-traveled low, a cancer in the clubhouse. That's a jerk who does a Mr. Hyde on your team's chemistry. I've known some of those in my time. Me, I was more of a sunbeam in the clubhouse.

Not that Atlanta needed help in that area. The Braves went from win to win with the sort of cool professionalism that reminded me of my dad. They were the class of the National League, winners of six of the last seven NL East titles. When I arrived they were in the middle of a run of eleven straight first-place finishes, and fourteen of fifteen from 1991 through 2005. The Braves had a star-studded clubhouse: Chipper Jones, Andruw Jones, and that famous rotation of number one starters. With stars and studs like that, they didn't need me coming on too strong, so I dialed down what one reporter called my vaunted charisma. I was a cog and wanted to be a good one. The papers said the Braves had dealt Neagle for "Bret Boone, the second baseman they coveted." As General Manager Schuerholz saw it, "We needed a second baseman and wanted an excellent one. Bret gives us more offense and stellar defense at second base."

Much as I missed Barry Larkin, I got a good thing going with my new double-play partner. Walt Weiss was a former Rookie of the Year. Silky smooth at shortstop, Walt was one of those light-hitting thinkers who'll outsmart you if they can. He's now the Colorado Rockies' manager. We never had the mind-meld I enjoyed with Larkin, but his footwork and positioning on defense were comparable to Barry's, and we didn't have to make a lot of circus catches to keep our team in the game. When you're playing behind Maddux, Smoltz, Glavine, and Kevin Millwood, an 18-game winner that year, your job gets simpler. You have to make the routine plays—*all* of them—or Maddux will give you a look that makes you want to retire on the spot. You should also hit enough to help the team, which I did, with a boost from a side benefit of playing for the Braves: I never had to face Maddux, Smoltz, Glavine, and Millwood.

It was also a pleasure to see Chipper Jones at work. The guy showed up at the park at two in the afternoon for a night game— not to take grounders or hit in the cage but because the stadium was his world. He'd play cards for hours in the clubhouse. He was smart about the demands of the long season, too. In the second half of the season, he didn't even bother taking batting practice. Didn't need it. His swing was dialed in, so why should he wear his body down? A few of our teammates grumbled about that—"special treatment," they called it. *"We have to take BP, why doesn't he?"* I told them there was one good reason. "Because he's The Man. That guy's carrying us all on his back. Let him do what he wants." (You still hear fans and even players say a manager should treat all players the same, but that's a crock. The manager's job is to get the most out of each employee. If that means challenging one guy and babying another, so be it. Back in Cincinnati, Davey Johnson used to yell at me and coddle Reggie Sanders. I didn't understand it at the time, but I do now. Johnson knew that some men respond to a kick in the butt, while others need a pat on the back. The best managers aren't consistent, they're flexible.)

Batting second in front of Chipper, I socked 20 home runs and drove in 63 to offset a lackluster average of .252. My numbers paled beside his .319, 45 homers, and 110 RBIs, but then Chipper was the league's near-unanimous MVP. I scored 102 runs, second on the club to his 116, while we won 103 games and beat the Astros and Mets in the playoffs to face the Yankees in the 1999 World Series.

We had the better team. We'd won five more games that season than New York. The Yankees' aces, Roger Clemens and Andy Pettitte, were coming off 14-win seasons, while our staff, with its three first-ballot Hall of Famers, might have been the best in baseball history. Their top power hitters, Bernie Williams and Tino Martinez, combined to hit 53 homers while Chipper swatted 45 all by himself. Brian Jordan, Ryan Klesko, and I added another 64. They had an edge at short with Derek Jeter slashing .349/.438/.552 to Weiss's .226/.315/.323, but everybody from the Vegas bookmakers to *USA Today* and the *New York Post* made us a clear favorite.

In Game 1 at Turner Field, Maddux dueled the Yankees' crafty Orlando Hernandez, aka El Duque, into the eighth inning. We led 1–0 on Chipper's solo home run, our only base hit. After Maddux walked Darryl Strawberry in the eighth our first baseman, Brian Hunter, booted a bunt. Now the bases were loaded with nobody out. Jeter tied the game with a single to left. That brought our manager, Bobby Cox, out of the dugout. I joined him on the mound along with Chipper, Weiss, and our catcher, Eddie Perez.

Bobby had our closer, John Rocker, warmed up. He would have left Maddux in the game anyway except for the fact that Rocker was a lefty and so was the Yankees' next batter, Paul O'Neill. So Cox waved to the bullpen. Two months later Rocker, a country boy from Macon, Georgia, would become the most hated guy in America for telling *Sports Illustrated* he couldn't stand riding New York subways with "some kid with purple hair next to some queer with AIDS next to some dude who just got out of jail." I had some sympathy for Rocker—not for his intolerance, but because he thought it was off-the-record bar talk when he said it. My immediate concern was the 3-1 fastball he threw O'Neill, who pulled it into the hole between me and Jordan. I dived, but couldn't get it. Two runs scored, and after Rocker walked in a run we went to the ninth inning trailing by three. My single off Mariano Rivera, the Braves' second hit of the night, wasn't enough. We lost 4–1. Advantage New York.

Before Game 2, Braves owner Ted Turner strolled into our clubhouse with his wife, Jane Fonda. Everyone thought Jane looked mighty fine for sixty-one. She smiled while we reached for our towels and uni pants. Ted gave us the sort of rah-rah speech that makes players roll their eyes. "Guys, I'm proud of all you've done this season, winning a hundred and three games." He's the owner, he's got the right. "We're only down one game. Let's go out there and stick it to 'em!" By then my eyes were bulging, not rolling, because I'd seen the Braves' lineup posted in the dugout. With Keith Lockhart at second base.

Lockhart was a journeyman. A good guy with a reliable glove, he was a tough out but didn't have much power. That was the reason

LEFT: *My grandfather Ray Boone was a gamer who became an All-Star and once led the American League in RBIs.*

BELOW: *In 1951 Gramps hit the dirt to complete a double play for the Cleveland Indians.*

ABOVE: *That's my dad—the happy baby with Indians rookie Gramps and Grandma Patsy in 1948.*

RIGHT: *Cute couple! My parents, Bob and Sue Boone, got married in La Mesa, California, in 1967. They were both nineteen.*

RIGHT: *Dad came up through the minors as an infielder, and then turned himself into one of the best catchers in history.*

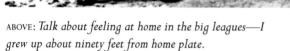

ABOVE: *Talk about feeling at home in the big leagues—I grew up about ninety feet from home plate.*

RIGHT: *Dad made the 1976 All-Star Game in Philadelphia, where I got an ovation for pregame catches like this.*

LEFT: *Spring training 1974 was family time for Mom and Dad and their kids, Aaron (riding high) and me.*

Christmas in California—no snow for the Boone boys, but there might be a fielder's glove under the tree.

ABOVE: *In '93 Dad (left) coached in the minors, Gramps (right) scouted for the Red Sox, and I hit .332 for the Triple-A Calgary Cannons.*

RIGHT: *Rookie infielder Aaron joined me in Cincinnati in '97, the first of our two years as a brother act with the Reds.*

RIGHT: *You've heard of the* Sports Illustrated *cover jinx? I got hotter after* SI *made me its midseason cover boy.*

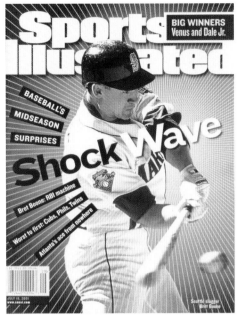

LEFT: *Ka-Boone! Here's one of my 37 longballs in 2001, complete with the bat flip that I should have patented.*

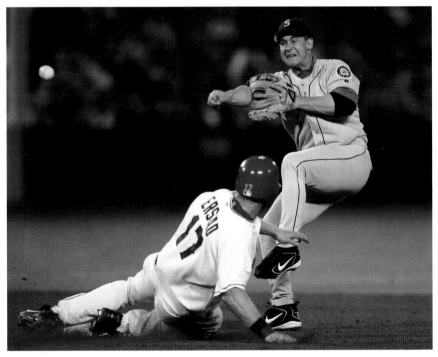

The Angels' Darin Erstad tried to break up a double play in one of my four Gold Glove seasons, but he knew he had no chance.

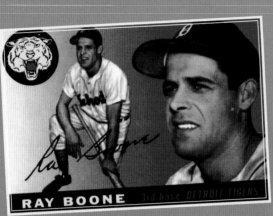

RAY BOONE · 3rd base · DETROIT TIGERS

BOB BOONE

DRAFT '94 PICK

BRET BOONE

MLB DEBUT 00/00/00

Matt Boone

3B

2006 Bowman ROOKIE CARD

Some guys who go into the family trade hand out business cards. We've got baseball cards. That's Gramps in the 1950s, Dad in the '70s, Aaron and me in the '90s, and our brother Matt, who played in the minors before hurting his back, in the early 2000s.

ABOVE: *Aaron (left) and I made the 2003 All-Star Game, where we joined a pair of former All-Stars, Gramps and Dad—another first for the Boones.*

BELOW: *I was in the TV booth when Aaron shocked Boston with a walk-off homer that sent the Yankees to the 2003 World Series.*

RIGHT: *I made my managerial debut in the low minors last year. A wise man once said that all great journeys begin with a single step—in my case, in Beloit, Wisconsin.*

BELOW: *My daughter Savannah, a good athlete in her own right, might be a future sportscaster.*

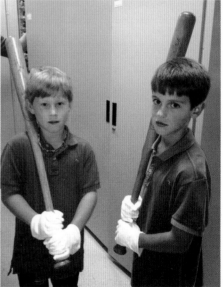

ABOVE: *My twin sons Judah (left) and Isaiah (right) got to hoist Babe Ruth's bats at the Hall of Fame.*

LEFT: *My son Jake's getting serious about baseball. Will he be the first fourth-generation major leaguer? Maybe. just want him to be happy.*

the Braves traded for me in the first place. But Lockhart batted left-handed, and Cox wanted to fill our lineup with lefties against David Cone, the Yanks' starter in Game 2. I thought it was a dumb move. It smacked of desperation. I'd been our second baseman in 152 of 162 games. Now I'm benched for batting right-handed?

To piss me off worse, Cox handled it wrong. Eight-year veterans who play every day shouldn't need to check the lineup when they get to the park. If the manager plans to give them a day off, he's supposed to mention it the night before. That's protocol. It gives the veteran a chance to digest the bad news. But did Bobby do that? No, I found out when I saw the lineup card. Batting sixth, playing second base, *Lockhart*. Benched, grinding his teeth, Boone.

Bobby Cox deserves the Hall of Fame plaque he earned in 2014. But he blew it that night. We were down 7–0 in the ninth when he finally turned to me and said, "Pinch-hit."

You can imagine how eager I was to pinch-hit. I replied with a clever retort. "Fuck that, Bobby!"

Bobby wasn't in the best mood himself. "You don't want to fuck-ing pinch-hit?"

"I can't hit an eight-run homer, Mr. Lineup."

"You're refusing to pinch-hit?"

"Bobby," I said, "you're the manager. I'm the player. I'm pissed as hell, but I respect your position. If you say pinch-hit, I'll pinch-hit."

I ripped a double down the left-field line to drive in Keith Lockhart. We lost 7–2 and flew to New York down two games to none in a Series we were supposed to win.

Damn, but I liked that town. The energy, the swagger, the sex appeal, the fun. New York reminded me of me. I always thought I might wind up with the Yankees someday. The next-best thing was playing for the visiting team at Yankee Stadium in a World Series.

I didn't have to check the lineup card before Game 3. No way

Bobby'd bench me now, not with lefty Andy Pettitte starting against us. In the first inning Gerald Williams singled and I doubled. Chipper's groundout drove Williams home. I doubled again in the third and doubled in a run in the fourth to put us up 4–1. That gave me four doubles in a row, a postseason record. We led 5–3 until Joe Girardi—another light-hitting, cerebral catcher who would become a fine manager—singled ahead of Chuck Knoblauch's homer. In the ninth, with the score 5–5, Yankees manager Joe Torre wanted to put our nuts in a wringer. He went to the best closer ever, Mariano Rivera, to shut us down in a tie game.

I led off the inning. Standing in the on-deck circle I heard Bob Sheppard, the Yankees' legendary stadium announcer, say my name. "Your attention please, ladies and gentlemen," Sheppard announced. "The second baseman, number twenty-four, Bret Boone." Thousands of Yankees fans booed. I told myself they were yelling "Booo-oone." I had to laugh.

There was no point in swinging for the fences against Rivera's sideways cutter. His ball was as heavy as Maddux's. You take what you can get against a pitcher that good. My job was to get on base no matter how, so I shortened my swing and poked a single to right field. That was a heady moment. Rounding first, getting a smack on the butt from first-base coach Glenn Hubbard, I was 6-for-10 in the World Series, 2-for-2 off Mariano. And now Cox, having a less than stellar Series, made another move. He sent Otis Nixon out to pinch-run for me.

Let's stop the tape and discuss this for a second.

I wanted to stay in the game. That's a given. But it also made sense for me to stay in. Suppose we go to extra innings. You'd want my bat in the lineup in the 11th or 12th. You'd want my Gold Glove in the field. Yes, Nixon could fly, but he was forty years old, a 79 percent base-stealer. No sure thing. Yanks catcher Girardi had a strong arm.

Rivera was pretty good at holding runners on, particularly for a right-hander. Only four runners all season tried to steal when he was on the mound.

There's no sure right and wrong in a spot like that one. That's the chess game, the mess of percentages and possibilities that affect every move of every game. In my never-humble opinion, it's one of the things that make baseball the best game of all. If Nixon steals second, maybe we come back to win the Series, and next thing you know we're parading down Peachtree Street in Atlanta with the trophy and I'm smiling and telling Cox, "I guess you were right, you son of a bitch."

Here's what actually happened: Nixon pinch-ran for me. He took off, and Girardi threw him out. The Braves' rally (*triggered by Boone*, the papers would have said) didn't happen. We lost in the 10th and the Yankees led the Series three games to none. We never gave up—we had Smoltz lined up to start Game 4 and figured we could run the table. But the odds were twenty times worse than if we'd won Game 3. The smart money could no longer detect our pulse. In my view that was partly because our manager hurt our chances in the '99 World Series. His calls were defensible, but they didn't pan out. I think we got a little Cox-blocked.

Game 4 was do-or-die. And we'd have to get past Roger Clemens.

I had some history with Clemens. Along with Pedro Martinez he was the most notorious headhunter in the game, a mean SOB who wouldn't hesitate to drill you for hitting a home run off him. Or a double. Or a single. Or arguing a strike call. Or taking too much time adjusting your jock. In Clemens's view, I'd been guilty of swinging too hard.

Back in my first week in the majors, the Mariners went to Boston. First we faced Frank Viola, the tall, mustachioed lefty with a deadly changeup. Viola threw a circle change, a pitch he held between his thumb and index finger and rolled off the other three fingers. It looks like a fastball, but never gets to you. And you just don't see a pitch that nasty in the minors.

Apparently Clemens was working out in the gym under the stands, watching the game on TV, when I came up against Viola. Cramped, ancient Fenway Park happened to be one of the last ballparks where opposing teams shared a weight room, and who do you think was sitting next to Roger? It was Harold Reynolds, the guy I'd been brought up to replace. They watched me strike out, taking my typical lusty rip at Viola's circle change. At that point, as I've heard the story, Clemens said, "Harold, if that cocky rookie takes a hack like that at me, I'm going to flip him."

The next night, facing Boston's Mike Gardiner, I belted my first big-league homer. The day after that, in my fourth game in the majors—August 23, 1992—I stepped in against Clemens. And lined a bullet up the middle for a single. He spent the next minute stomping around the mound, staring at me, yelling, "You little shit! You cocky little fuck!"

"Shut up, you big fuck! You think you scare me? You don't!"

My next time up, he hit me in the head. With a 98-mph fastball. On purpose.

I bounced up, dusted myself off, and laughed all the way to first base. Roger and I were probably not going to be friends.

Unfortunately for us, he was practically unhittable in Game 4. I got my knock and walk, but Clemens held us to three singles through seven innings. My eighth-inning single drove in Atlanta's only run in a 4–1 loss that completed the Yankees' sweep. I finished my first World Series with a batting average of .538, but who cared? Our clubhouse felt like a funeral home. Ted and Jane stayed away.

I barely heard the reporters' postgame questions. Some of them had found out about my little shouting match with the manager during Game 2. "Bret, can you still play for Bobby? Will you demand a deal?" As a player who'd been traded in the middle of a multiyear contract, I could demand to be traded, but it hadn't entered my mind. Bobby Cox wasn't perfect, but who is? I still thought he was one of the four or five best managers in the game. So I mumbled something noncommittal. They turned it into a story: BOONE TO DEMAND DEAL?

A couple of days later I'm cleaning out my locker when the GM stops by. "Bret, I want to ask you a question." I liked that. If John Schuerholz had something on his mind, he said it. "Did you tell the press you want to be traded?"

"No, John. I didn't."

Pretty soon he was asking reporters why I'd even dream of leaving the Braves. "Where would he go?" Schuerholz said. "Heaven? What's better than playing in Atlanta?"

Was he joking? I mean, I like Atlanta, but it's not paradise. I told the writers that I hadn't demanded a trade.

"So you won't demand one?" they asked.

"Well, I didn't say that, either." My contractual right to force a trade was worth a lot of money. I'd earned $2.9 million of Ted Turner's billions in 1999, only $100,000 more than Marge Schott's Reds paid me the year before. I'd be looking for a raise in 2000, and my right to demand a trade was a bargaining chip.

Before long my phone buzzed. It was Tom Reich, my agent. He said, "Schuerholz traded you."

"Whaa-at?"

"You and Ryan Klesko to the Padres for Wally Joyner, Reggie Sanders, and Quilvio Veras."

☆ ☆ ☆

So I was headed back to Southern California—not to the Dodgers with their glittering history, or even the Angels, but to the San Diego Padres, whose loss in the 1998 World Series was an uptick in a long, lousy history. San Diego got swept by the Yankees in the '98 Series, just like we did the next year, then went back to losing in 1999 and looked like they were getting worse. Except for All-Stars Tony Gwynn and Trevor Hoffman, their biggest names would be Phil Nevin, the power-hitting third baseman, and me. Gwynn was forty. And manager Bruce Bochy's no-name rotation had trouble holding leads for closer Hoffman to preserve.

At least they wanted me. That's what Gramps and Dad and Aaron kept saying. *And look at the bright side—you'll play home games an hour from home.*

Mom and Dad's house in Orange County. Hmm. That got me thinking. Dad had a weight room at home, a pro-style gym where he still worked out. At age fifty-two, with his hair going gray, he could still bench-press his weight with ease. He could knock out 500 sit-ups, take a coffee break, and do 500 more. And here I was at thirty years old, switching to a half-ounce-lighter bat every September because the grueling six-month season wore me down.

I decided it was time to get in shape. Dad and I had remade my swing the off-season before. Now I wanted to get fitter than ever. Once again, he was my example. How far past his numbers could I go if I got as fit as Dad was in his prime? How far past *my* numbers?

There was just one thing: no kung fu. Dad could keep all the Jackie Chan dance moves.

In the fall of 1999 I hired Tim Michaels, the trainer who'd helped sculpt Tim "Rock" Raines's physique. It turned out I was born to be a gym rat. Dad was all about flexibility; I was more of a bodybuilder. The weight-room competition to lift ten more pounds, the adrenaline rush of a treadmill sprint or one more set of lifts, the pleasure of a well-earned 1,200-calorie dinner—to me, all that was the best rush this side of a ballgame. It's addictive. By January 2000 I was in the shape of my life, 175 pounds with eight-pack abs and high-caliber guns. I could flip a dime on my biceps by flexing. I *knew* I was on the brink of my best years.

And here's another place to pause the tape.

If you're like 99.9 percent of fans and announcers, you're conditioned to think that strength in the gym means power at the plate. Everybody knows that hitters work out so they can hit more homers.

But everybody's wrong. In real life, it doesn't work that way. To see why, you need to see Walt Weiss, one of the best teammates you'll ever have, in the shower. Nobody was more ripped than Walt. Nobody spent more time in the gym or knocked out more bench-press reps. He was taller than I was. But in fourteen big-league seasons, Walt never hit more than eight home runs. He averaged three homers a year. He used to shake his head and say, "Boonie, I'm stronger than ninety-five percent of the league, and I can't hit the ball out of my shadow."

Power is mysterious. Power is all about keeping your lower half square to the plate while your core muscles twist, generating bat speed. It's a mix of strength, timing, and the torque of those torso muscles uncoiling the instant the ball reaches the hitting zone.

So why get strong? Not to hit homers. You get strong in the off-season and work out all season so you don't get weak in August and September. Because a baseball season is a marathon. No pro athlete plays more games, flies more miles, or gets to more towns at 4 a.m. than a baseball player. The weak fade in August. They go on the disabled list in September. That's when the strong survive.

I wanted to get strong and stay strong all season. Not to prove that Bobby Cox shouldn't have benched me, or that that Braves (or Reds or Mariners) should have kept me. I didn't have to prove anything to anybody. I was an established major leaguer. But what if I could do better?

You want to hear about a gym rat? I became such a gym rat that Tony Gwynn tagged along, hoping I could help him improve.

Tony and I hit it off from the start. He was practically the patron saint of San Diego. I loved his quick-wristed swing, as well as his squeaky voice, infectious laugh, and sunny attitude. One of the purest hitters who ever lived, he told me he could actually guide the ball to particular spots on the field. He could "hit 'em where they ain't." But by the time I got to San Diego, his forty-year-old knees were shot. He had to ice them before and after games, even between innings. I said, "Tony, you could hit .300 for another ten years, but who's going to run for you?" Tony could have played till he was forty-five, maybe fifty, if he'd been willing to go to the American League as a DH, but he was loyal to the Padres. He was determined to retire as a Padre even if it cost him five years, millions of dollars, and hundreds of hits. He knew he was on his last legs, but he just wanted to hang on as long as he could.

By then I'd paired my workout routine with a serious commitment to nutrition. Tony said, "Boonie, put me on a diet. I gotta lighten the load on my knees."

Working with the clubhouse chef, I came up with a menu Tony swore he could live with. The Tony Gwynn Diet featured grilled chicken and fish, steamed vegetables, brown rice, egg whites, avocado, and almonds. And he gobbled it up. This went on for days.

Actually, it went on for day. On the second day, I rolled into the clubhouse to find Tony sitting at his locker, eating nachos with both hands. "Sorry, Boonie," he said. "I couldn't do it! But let's both get three knocks today, what do you say?"

All he did was hit .323 that season, his second-to-last.

12

THE BOONE GOES BOOM

Nobody who lived through 2001 would forget it.

It started as a year of reunions. Aaron was in his fourth season as the Cincinnati Reds' everyday third baseman, playing beside Barry Larkin for a club that had my old teammate Ken Griffey Jr. in center field and my old dad in the dugout. After three years of managing the Royals, Dad took over the 2001 Reds and wrote Aaron in at third base, batting sixth. They became the seventh father-son duo to manage and play for the same team. (The others were the Philadelphia Athletics' Connie and Earle Mack in 1910; the Yankees' Yogi and Dale Berra in 1985; Baltimore's Cal Ripken Sr. and Jr., also in 1985; the Orioles' Cal Sr. and Billy Ripken in 1987; the Royals' Hal and Brian McRae in 1991; and the Montreal Expos' Felipe and Moises Alou in 1992.)

I was coming off a 19-homer year in San Diego. My 74 RBIs had been the most ever by a Padres second baseman, but my 2000 season ended on a down note. I'd hit 16 homers by the All-Star break, but then I banged up my right knee and missed the last six weeks. The injury depressed my numbers. It depressed my agent and me, too, because the Padres didn't want me back. I felt betrayed by Kevin Towers, their general manager. Towers could have picked up my option—the club's contractual right to keep me in 2001—for $4 million. He'd promised me he would. "Don't worry, just get better," he'd said. "We want you back next year. You can consider your option picked up." So I'd shut my season down and started rehabbing my knee. Turns out I had blood and fragments of kneecap floating in there. The knee had started to atrophy. It may have been the same problem Gramps and Dad had with their knees. When your legs go, your hitting, fielding, and baserunning all suffer, but six months in the gym would get me back on my feet.

Then, as soon as the season ended, Towers called to say they *didn't* want me back. Suddenly I was radioactive. Seeing the Padres dump me, other GMs thought, *His knee must be wrecked.* Half a dozen clubs made modest one-year offers, including Lou's crew in Seattle.

I was on the fence about the Mariners. Safeco Field, where they play their home games, is a tough yard for hitters. In those days, before they brought the fences closer to the plate in 2013, it was a longish 405 feet to dead center field and a damn-longish 390 to the power alley in left-center. Even though I made a lot of my money to right and right-center, there was no doubt I'd lose homers in Seattle, and not just homers. How many doubles would the park turn into long outs? As my pal John Olerud used to say about Safeco, "When in doubt, you're out."

It wasn't just the dimensions, either. At some parks, summer heat and wind currents make the ball jump; 390 feet plays like 350. Safeco was the opposite—mostly due to the air. Fans know the thin air at Colorado's mile-high Coors Field helps balls go far—and makes breaking pitches break a little less than at lower altitudes—but they forget that Arizona's Chase Field (1,082 feet above sea level) and Atlanta's Turner Field (1,050 feet) aid hitters, too. Meanwhile, thicker air in coastal cities like Seattle (elevation: 10 feet) slows the ball down and adds bite to breaking balls. Sliders slide more, sinkers sink more, and would-be dingers die on the warning track. Hitting in Seattle felt like swinging a slightly heavier, softer bat.

Then there's the fact that it's one of the majors' smaller media markets, a West Coast town where the home games end after midnight eastern time. Those late games limit your *SportsCenter* appearances. How many of my Web Gems might go unnoticed in Seattle? If that sounds like my ego talking, remember that highlights can turn into endorsements, Gold Gloves, and millions of dollars. The Gold Glove Awards are voted on by managers and coaches, who watch *SportsCenter* just like fans do. Players' contracts feature bonuses for Gold Gloves and other awards. The more famous you get, the more you'll be worth the next time your contract comes up.

So why even think about Seattle's offer?

For one thing, I had friends there—guys like Jay Buhner and Norm Charlton. The city's gorgeous, too, and Seattle fans really love their M's when their M's win.

For another thing, I was still kind of sweet on Lou.

Back in 1993, when the Mariners traded me to Cincinnati, Seattle reporters wrote that Piniella wanted me gone. As usual, the press got the story wrong. Maybe Lou and I were too alike to get along at first, but that changed before the trade. We feuded until the day he told me I'd proved myself to him: "You're going to be my second baseman for the next fifteen years." Then Woodward, the general manager, sent me to the Reds for Dan Wilson. I wasn't mad—Wilson was the catcher they were dying to get. Still, that deal left me feeling I might have some unfinished business in Seattle.

Now it was seven years later. I'd led National League second basemen in fielding three years in a row, including my record-setting .997 fielding percentage in 1997. I'd averaged 21 homers and 77 RBIs from 1998 to 2000, but everybody was bitching and moaning about my knee.

"Nobody wants to go three years," Tom Reich said. As my agent, Reich laid out my options: I could settle for a two-year deal for $4.5 million to $5 million or a risky one-year contract for a lot less, with performance bonuses I might not reach.

"Screw it," I said. "I'll sign for a year and play like hell."

Pat Gillick, Woodward's successor as the Mariners' GM, came up with 3,250,001 reasons for me to choose Seattle: $3.25 million and another chance to play for Piniella. Gillick threw in another $1 million in incentive bonuses he doubted I'd cash in.

"Bret's a nice fit for our ball club, a proven run producer who will add a little pop to our lineup," he announced

I couldn't help thinking, *Whaddya mean, "a little"?*

It turned out he was wrong about the incentives, but right about the pop.

☆ ☆ ☆

In the modern game, three factors are crucial to a manager. He needs to deal effectively with the front office—the owner, GM, and other higher-ups. He needs to deal effectively with the media. And he needs to treat players as individuals. The old "my way or the highway" hard-ass days ended when players started making two or three or ten times as much as the manager. Today the game's superstars are closer in status to the *owners*. The manager's more like a corporate middle manager, trying to churn out the product while juggling demands from above and below. He keeps the troops producing, while taking orders from the general manager and the IT (analytics) department, until profits (wins) decline and he gets fired.

Piniella was a throwback. As he saw it, managers have expiration dates. He was sure to get canned eventually, so he might as well be his own ornery self until his number came up.

In 2001 it looked like that day might be soon, because Seattle was going to hell. In 1998, Woodward had traded Randy Johnson, the towering, intimidating six-foot-eleven Big Unit—the best pitcher they ever had—and they finished the year 76-85. After another losing season in 1999, they traded Griffey, the second-best player in franchise history, to Cincinnati. In 2000 they let the best player in franchise history, Alex Rodriguez, go to Texas as a free agent. According to one account, "The Mariners will try to stay afloat with Boone instead of A-Rod."

No pressure there.

Piniella hoped I could help lead the ball club on the field and in the clubhouse. At the age of thirty-two I was up for the challenge, ready to make my second go-round in Seattle better than my first. I was smarter and more experienced. Also fitter than ever. During the off-season and through spring training in Peoria, Arizona, I took my weight training and nutrition to new levels. I could now match eight-pack abs with my new buddy Mike Cameron.

Cam was naturally lean like a leather belt. We competed to see who could stay strongest with the least body fat. My method was to pump iron for an hour, do half an hour of cardio, eat two dinners, and work out again. He'd do a few bench presses, test at 8 percent body fat, and laugh at me for killing myself. Finally I edged him by testing at 7.7 percent. That's about half the body fat of a runway model. For comparison's sake, the average American man's body is about 22 percent fat. That means he's carrying about 40 pounds of pure fat; I was carrying about 13 pounds. Scarlett Johansson's body fat is about 20 percent, which is low for a woman. Channing Tatum's listed at 10 percent to my 7.7. Just sayin'.

Entering my tenth big-league season, I was leaner and hungrier than ever. Stronger in the middle, too—in the core muscles that power the swing. I felt supercharged, and in April 2001 the Mariners and I took off like a couple of rockets. The team won 20 games and lost only 5 all month, while the Boone batted .344.

The Boone?

Blame Mark McLemore for the nickname. Mack was our super-sub. He played six positions that year, seven if you count DH, hitting .286 and stealing 39 bases at the age of thirty-six. The funny thing is, he'd broken in as a twenty-one-year-old rookie with the 1986 Angels, a club that had Reggie Jackson at DH and my dad behind the plate. To McLemore and the other Angels, Dad was "Boonie." Mack wasn't sure what to call me till I started blistering the ball in 2001.

One day he was doing an interview in the clubhouse when I walked by. "There's the man," he said, explaining that Dad was "Boonie" so I needed a different nickname. "He's rolling, he's the man. He's the Boone!"

I waved and kept going. Later that day, a fan ran up with a cap for me to sign, saying, "My girlfriend's crazy about you." There was a catchphrase in the air at the time—"Chicks dig the long ball"—from a Nike commercial with Greg Maddux and Tom Glavine. Thinking back to McLemore's line, I told the fan, "I guess chicks dig the Boone." He called a Seattle radio station, and the next thing you know there were banners at Safeco: CHICKS DIG THE BOONE.

My wife didn't dig the banners, but that's a story for another time.

I'll admit I liked the attention. I had worked my ass off, even changed my swing, to prepare for this. Why not get a kick out of it? The experts said it couldn't last—the Mariners weren't as good as we looked, they said, and neither was I. How far could a team go with me batting third or fourth instead of A-Rod?

To the top, that's how far. But we were still adjusting to our front-runner status.

Early in the season, with runners at first and second in a tie game, Piniella had third-base coach Dave Myers give me the bunt sign. There I was, batting fifth, striding to the plate to my hard-rockin' walk-up music, Crazy Town's "Butterfly," and he wanted me to bunt! In the words of Crazy Town, *Time is passing, I'm asking, Could this be real?*

Now, you don't have to like bunting to know how: square up with
your chest to the pitcher and the bat flat; don't jab, just let the pitch
kiss the bat, pulling back slightly at impact to deaden the ball. I laid
down a beauty and we won the game with a sacrifice fly.

A night later, the same situation came up. This was getting old. I
called time to discuss my views with Myers. I said, "Are you rumdums
sure you want the best second baseman in the league to bunt?"

He shrugged. "Lou looks pretty sure."

Two foul balls later, I struck out. Piniella looked miffed. I know
I was. Passing him on my way into the dugout, I said in a loud voice,
"The Boone don't get paid to bunt." Lou didn't answer except to spit,
but that was the last time he gave me the bunt sign.

Lou and I always had our differences, but we liked and respected
each other. "A couple of hardheaded individuals, that's us," he said.
Beyond bunting, we disagreed about off days. I hated 'em, especially
when I was hitting. Why screw with a hot streak? Lou, for his part,
liked to rest his regulars from time to time to keep us "fresh."

"I'm gonna give you a day," he'd say.

"Forget it. I don't like to sit." I played through injuries and slumps,
always sure I was going to get three hits and help us win, until one
night, when I popped up and hit a dribbler and struck out twice.

"Boone hasn't got it," Piniella announced to the team. "He needs
a day off."

"Okay, fine!" I said. So after eighty-some games in a row, I sat one
night in Cleveland. Lou told me there was absolutely, positively no
chance I'd get into the game, not even to pinch-hit. That became a
sure thing when we took a 14–2 lead into the seventh inning. By then
I was about as relaxed as I've ever been during a game. In fact I was
sipping a beer in the dugout. That's something I would never do if
there was a chance I'd play, but this was a night off. I moseyed into the
clubhouse, poured a cold beer into a Pepsi can, and went back to my
spot on the bench. I was on my second or third beer when the Indians

cut our lead to 14–9. No worries, we were still up by five runs with two out in the ninth.

Einar Diaz singled in two runs. Piniella brought in our closer, Kazuhiro "Kaz" Sasaki, to get the final out.

Buhner, sitting next to me, said, "You may have to go in."

"No way. Lou promised."

Kenny Lofton singled. Omar Vizquel cleared the bases with a triple and the game was tied. In the bottom of the ninth, Lou started looking my way. I tried to hide behind Buhner, but Lou found me. I cussed him all the way to the plate, where I stepped in against my old teammate, John Rocker, and fanned on three fastballs. We lost 15–14 in the biggest comeback (or worst blown lead) ever seen on ESPN's *Sunday Night Baseball*.

We were still 80-31 that August, leading the AL West by 19 games. Soft-tossing Jamie Moyer was already a 16-game winner. Sinker-slider specialist Freddy Garcia was 13-3. Edgar Martinez and first baseman John Olerud were hitting over .300. Our new right fielder, Ichiro Suzuki, was batting .332, proving a Japanese import could rake in the majors, while I was at .329. Ichiro made our club an international sensation, too. When the Mariners played, thousands of fans gathered around Jumbotrons in Tokyo to yell for Japan's hero and the player they sometimes called B-Boom.

Ichiro was a terrific contact hitter and a pretty interesting character. He knew more English than he let on. Griffey and some of the others had entertained him on a visit to Seattle a couple of years before, giving him some helpful tips, like telling reporters how to pronounce his name: "Itch-y-balls." He thought that was funny. Ichiro loved trying out phrases he heard other players use. We were jogging out to our positions one night when he recognized Ed Montague, the umpire. Ichiro pointed at Montague and asked, "What's up, homeslice?"

What a year. That season was magic by definition—the only year I ever went without a slump.

I'd barreled into the break with a .324 average, 22 homers, 84 RBIs, and my first *Sports Illustrated* cover.

The 2001 All-Star Game at Safeco was a home game. Ichiro batted leadoff for Joe Torre's American League All-Stars. I was honored and humbled—yes, it's possible—to find out that I was batting fourth, between Manny Ramirez and Juan Gonzalez. I went straight to Torre. "Joe," I said, "I just saw the lineup. I don't know what to say except . . . it means a lot." Torre shrugged. He gave me that fatherly grin of his and said, "The year you're having? Who else? You earned it."

Olerud batted sixth and Edgar seventh, giving the Mariners four starters in the AL lineup. The cleanup man got the longest ovation— the biggest, best, loudest, warmest ovation I ever got. That's a sound that stays with you, a capacity crowd sending love your way from all directions. Fifteen years later, I can still hear it. A couple thousand of the 47,000 at Safeco sounded like they were booing, but this time they really were yelling *Booo-ooone.*

I popped up against Randy Johnson (just missed it!) and grounded out to Chipper Jones, but we won the game. Our man Garcia got the victory. Afterward, and for weeks to come, I signed hundreds of copies of that week's *Sports Illustrated*. The cover showed me homering under the words SHOCK WAVE and BRET BOONE: RBI MACHINE. Inside, Richard Hoffer's story said that a certain second baseman was "leading the Mariners to the best record in baseball. Boone's RBI total is one of the season's more astonishing numbers. . . . Fans at Safeco Field are hardly lamenting the defection of Alex Rodriguez, whose 41 homers and 132 RBIs last year landed him the richest contract in baseball history."

Hoffer said I was loving every minute of my career year, especially after a decade of answering questions about Gramps and my dad: *"It's not that I'm not proud of my family,"* Boone says. *"I am. But this is better."*

What was my secret? *SI* credited my work with Dad and my off-season workouts. Piniella said I looked "like Tarzan" when I reported to spring training. Hoffer went on to describe my "huge guns and rolling shoulders—a home run build." He was wrong about that. What I had was an iron man build. I was built to last, to stay strong all season. But I had no gripes about how the story ended: "It couldn't have happened at a better time, not for the Mariners, who figured to lurch through the season without Rodriguez. And certainly not for Boone, struggling against the pressure of pedigree all these years, who's finally made a name—for himself."

A name or two, if you count "the Boone." Seems only fair for a guy who had more than one locker. I had three that year. I'd stroll into our clubhouse at Safeco, slap hands all around, and announce, "I'm here. We can start the game." The Mariners were cruising and my bats, gloves, and fan mail filled three cubicles. One was labeled BOONE, one BOONE'S FRIEND, and one BOONE'S OTHER FRIEND.

Talk about a charmed season: that was also the year our radio audience helped me find my glove.

As you can imagine, I was as fussy about my gloves as about my bats. Some players break in a new glove by tying it shut with a ball stuck in the webbing. Gramps's generation rubbed gloves with shaving cream or something called neat's-foot oil. Many of today's players dunk a new glove in a sink full of water, and then stick it in the microwave for twenty or thirty seconds. Softens it right up. (Torii Hunter punished a glove for making an error by microwaving it to a crisp.) I liked to keep things simple. Each season I'd use one glove in games and a new one during batting practice. Over the summer the BP glove got nice and soft. It became my "gamer" the following year.

My pregame ritual was just as consistent. After batting practice I'd have a bite to eat in the clubhouse, then take a shower, then watch video of the other team's starting pitcher. Twenty minutes before game time, I'd gather up my gear and lug it from the clubhouse to the dugout. Well, that year the Mariners added a step to my routine. They couldn't keep up with the autograph requests, so once every home stand I'd climb on top of the dugout after BP and sign as many as I could. We all had a fine time. Kids lined up, hooting and hollering, throwing stuff down to me. I'd sign their caps and gloves and toss them back.

One time I had my game glove in my armpit. Without thinking, I tossed it into the crowd. Pretty soon it's twenty minutes to game time and I'm searching the clubhouse, having a panic attack. *Where's my gamer?* I wore my backup glove that night, hoping they wouldn't hit anything my way. After the game I went to the broadcast booth. "Tell 'em my glove's gone. Boone must have tossed it to a fan, and he needs it!" The word went out, and the next day a young fan shows up with my precious gamer. I gave him some bats, an autographed jersey, and a hug. It wasn't till later that I looked in the glove's palm and saw a signature. *David Bell.* David was our third baseman, a buddy of mine. He was the grandson of Gus Bell and the son of Buddy Bell, both of them big-league stars. If not for me, David would have been the first third-generation major leaguer, but he never mentioned it. The Boones and Bells got along.

Of course I gave him hell about the glove. "You knew my gamer was missing and you scrawled all over it!"

"Somebody handed it to me, I signed it," he said.

These days David's the bench coach for Mike Matheny's St. Louis Cardinals. We don't see each other much, but when we cross paths I resume giving him shit. I played the rest of my best season with a David Bell autograph glove.

☆ ☆ ☆

In August we smoked the Tigers 16–1 to run our record to 91-36. For you history buffs, that's a slightly better winning percentage than the 1927 Yankees. I hit my 28th home run that day. Olerud smacked his 16th and 17th while lifting his average to .304. Edgar drove in 5 runs to bring his RBI count to 96. We were 18 games ahead of Oakland with a shot at the major-league record of 116 wins in a season.

Announcers like to talk about "team chemistry." I think that's shorthand for "I have no idea why they're winning or losing." I've always thought that chemistry has nothing much to do with leadership, character, or any other cliché. It has to do with talent. The Braves team I played on won because it was *good*. As Bobby Cox told me the day I joined them, "We *roll over* people here." Nobody had more character than Tony Gwynn, but the Padres finished last.

In my experience, chemistry is a by-product of winning, not a cause. When you win, you have a "harmonious" clubhouse. Players hug. They smile. Everybody's happy. Reporters pick up on the vibe. They say the vibe made the wins happen, when it's really the other way around.

Except in 2001. After thumping Detroit we won three in a row to go to 94-36, the best record in fifty years—from a club that was supposed to be reeling after losing A-Rod, Griffey, and Randy Johnson. How do you explain that? Maybe it *was* chemistry. There were no jerks in the home clubhouse at Safeco. Edgar was our elder sage, Olerud the quiet line-drive machine. Cameron and I kept things loose. Piniella was mellowing—at the age of fifty-eight he could cuss an ump without pulling first base from the ground and throwing it. Lou told me, "Son, I don't know how you're doing what you're doing, but don't stop doing it." We all busted our butts for him, finding ways to score one more run or prevent one. No team ever got more out of the talent on its roster.

McLemore, for instance, had to check the lineup every night to see where, or if, he'd be playing. And he couldn't care less. All he cared about was finding a way to get us an edge or a sliver of an edge on every play. For one thing, he was an expert at stealing signs. Mike Cameron and utility man Stan Javier were good at it, too, but Mack might have been the best. If he was on second base he'd study the catcher and crack the other team's signals at a glance. Catchers use one set of signs with nobody on base and another, trickier set with a runner on second, but he was too smart for them. Early that season he came to me and said, "The Boone, my man, do you want to know? If I'm on second, do you want a sign?"

Some hitters don't want the distraction. I said, "Hell yes." So we worked out our own signs. Nothing as obvious as pulling your ear or scratching your nose. Our signs were subtle—if Mack turned his head to the right while he was leading off second, that could mean *fastball inside*. Turning his head to the left might mean *fastball away*. He might clench one hand for a slider, adjust his belt or his package for a changeup.

With his help I sat on some pitches I would have taken or missed. Not many, maybe 15 or 20 all season. But those swings meant a lot. A homer or two, a double instead of a strikeout, a base hit here and there—it adds up.

Were we cheating?

No. Here's where the code comes in again—the game inside the game. There's an unwritten rule about stealing signs. If the other team realizes you're doing it, they'll retaliate. Their pitcher will throw at you. That's the acceptable risk of trying to gain an advantage. If McLemore and I are working our game and the other team catches on, I might wear the next fastball—take it in the neck. Ow. Fine, no problem. I'd bounce up and give the pitcher a nod. *We're even.*

The code works both ways. In the field, I'd keep a sharp eye on any veteran runner who reached second base. The stakes rise when there's a man in scoring position—both teams kick their focus into a higher gear. You can't always be sure if a runner's stealing signs, but if you suspect he is, you start by warning him between pitches. "Keep it up if you want to get drilled." He might be a friend. He might even be my brother, but my job is to protect my team's interests.

Sometimes retaliation gets out of hand, but in most cases it's a simple matter of enforcing the code. Steal signs, get drilled. Peek at the catcher's setup while the pitcher's in his windup, get drilled. Wear wraparound shades to the plate, get drilled—because wraparound shades keep the catcher from telling if you're peeking. Throw at our best hitter and we'll throw at yours. Throw at our pitcher when he's at the plate and we'll throw at yours. (Want a reason to hate the DH? American League headhunters like Pedro and Clemens could hunt heads without getting hit when they bat.)

Of course all these purpose pitches call for a little mind-reading. How do I know someone's stealing signs or intentionally throwing at my head?

Answer: circumstantial evidence.

A veteran learns to read the game. He knows that no pitcher wants to drill anybody in a close game, especially late in the game. The pitcher wants a W for his team and himself. If somebody deserves a drilling, whether it's for stealing signs, peeking at the catcher, showboating after a home run, or bunting to break up a no-hitter, payback can wait. But we're taking notes. We might postpone payback, but it's coming eventually. We might retaliate the next time your team comes to town, or six months from now, or maybe even next year. Meanwhile, Job No. 1 is always to win the game. That's a simple fact that fans, writers, announcers, and even some players often miss.

When I was with the Reds, San Diego's Sterling Hitchcock threw one under our leadoff man's chin. I knew instantly that Hitchcock didn't mean it. How did I know? It was a tie game, nobody out. The last thing he wants to do is put a runner on base—especially a guy who specialized in stealing bases.

Maybe I should mention that our leadoff man didn't lack confidence. But then it wasn't his ego that bothered me. I've got one of those, too. My problem with the guy was that he didn't understand baseball's code.

He jumped up, shaking his fist at Hitchcock. He wanted us to run out on the field and fight the Padres.

"Easy," I said. "He didn't mean it. Think about it—he doesn't want to hit the fastest guy in the game. You'll just steal second."

He didn't believe me. He was sure the Padres were throwing at him because he was a *superstar*.

The next inning, Mike Morgan took the mound for the Reds. Morgan was a great teammate, always willing to protect one of his own, even if the guy was kind of an ass and it would hurt Morgan's shot at a win.

Mike and I stood behind the mound, listening to our leadoff man yell from center field: *"Somebody's got to go down!"*

I told Morgan, "Forget it. If he really thinks they're after him, we can deal with it down the line. You've got a tie game to win."

Another shout from center: *"Down! They're going down!"*

Morgan said, "Well, he's on our side." He felt he had to do the honorable thing. So he plunked the next batter. The run scored and we lost.

I was seething after the game. But our leadoff man still didn't get it. "Boone don't want to protect me!" he said.

I had two aching shoulders wrapped in icepacks. I was tired and sore and pissed-off. I said, "You're a clown. You haven't done shit for our team, and you've got a lot to learn. You were wrong, so shut up." I turned away. That's when he slugged me as hard as he could, right in the back of the neck. I saw stars for a couple of seconds, then I went after him, fists first. It took three other Reds to break up the fight.

☆ ☆ ☆

By 2001 I was doing my part for Seattle with a .331 average, Gold Glove–caliber defense, and the sort of know-how a veteran can contribute. Like handing your pitcher a ball he'll really like.

Down through the years, some pitchers have scratched baseballs with thumbtacks or bits of sandpaper hidden in their gloves or caps. If they gripped and released the ball just right, the rough spot made it dive or veer sideways. There's less of that now—today's TV cameras can zoom in on the smallest detail, making it tough for a pitcher to customize the ball. But a veteran infielder can help. After the last warm-up pitch our catcher would fire the ball to me at second, purposely short-hopping the throw. That way I could flip our pitcher a baseball with a nice scuff on it.

On September 10 we beat the Angels to run our record to 104-40. Seven and a half hours later, in New York, Islamic terrorists flew an American Airlines jumbo jet into the North Tower at the World Trade Center. That day's events put baseball in perspective. Two thousand nine hundred and seventy-seven innocent people lost their lives on September 11, 2001. Selig suspended the season—correctly, I think—with eighteen games left on the schedule.

During a week of national mourning, we held team meetings. "Are we gonna play? *Should* we play?" I thought we should. We'd endured an attack on our country, an event that dwarfed sports. Americans were in disarray. We were looking for something to unify us, even if it was only a distraction like the kids' game we loved.

After seven days the Show went on. The Mariners picked up where we'd left off, stretching our latest winning streak to seven. We won ten of twelve to finish with a record of 116-46, tying a 105-year-old record for the most wins in major-league history, but the cheers weren't as loud now.

I hit a couple of homers in the American League Championship Series, but the Yankees beat us on the way to their fourth straight World Series. It mattered but it didn't. Here we were, the team with the most wins ever, falling short in the playoffs. That hurt. But when we visited Ground Zero that month, with the smoke still rising out of the rubble, the ALCS seemed a lot less important.

I was clearing out my locker at Safeco when John McLaren, Piniella's bench coach, stopped by. "What a year you had," he said.

I said thanks.

"You're the MVP," he said.

I wasn't so sure. It was hard to focus on awards after all we'd been through. I couldn't care less about the American League's Most Valuable Player award.

And that, of course, is a lie. The truth is, I didn't care any more than actors care about Oscars or singers care about Grammys. Not just for me, either. How much would my wife and kids love it if I was the league's MVP? How much would it mean to Mom and Dad, Gramps, Aaron, and everybody else I loved? That shit lasts forever. If I won the award I could sign baseballs *Bret Boone MVP 2001* for the rest of my life. And plenty of stat geeks had me winning. Ichiro, the rookie sensation, had batted .350 with 8 home runs and 69 RBIs to my .331 with 37 homers and a league-leading 141 RBIs. Ichiro had 56 steals to my 5, but my WAR (wins above replacement, a stat measuring how many extra victories you're worth) was 9.2 to his 7.

In the end, the Baseball Writers of America preferred Ichiro. He was the American League's MVP for 2001. I finished third in the voting.

But that long, strange, historic season closed on a note that still chokes me up.

After Ichiro won the AL MVP, I got a little glass trophy in the mail. The Mariners had taken a vote and named me the team's most valuable player.

13

A BLAST IN THE BRONX

I went on to a strong 2002 season—racking up 24 homers and 107 RBIs, slashing .278/.339/.462, and earning my second Gold Glove, while the Mariners won 93 games. Now I was in the money at last. My bet on myself paid off with a three-year, $25 million deal to re-up with the M's. That's nothing like today's money, but thinking back on how hard Dad and Gramps had worked to make a good living at the game, I knew how fortunate my generation was. I remember when Willie Bloomquist got the locker next to me in 2003. He was a rookie infielder making $300,000, the minimum salary, and asked to see my pay stub one day. Major leaguers get paid every two weeks during the season, and my biweekly pay, before taxes, was $641,025.62. His eyes bugged out. I gave Willy my best advice: "You want a check like this one? Play better!" He laughed and said he'd try that.

Every season's a roller coaster. For me, 2003 was like a rocket to the moon, with a minor fender bender in the middle. The Mariners were one of baseball's best teams. Again. Two years after our record-setting 116-win season of 2001, we figured we were the class of the division. Okay, we were a little older. Our DH was forty, and so was our number one starter. But they weren't ordinary graybeards. Everyone knew that Edgar Martinez, a consummate pro, was going to hit around .300. Talk about a thinking man's hitter—there were pitchers who'd tell you Edgar was reading their minds. And if Jamie Moyer didn't have much of a fastball at forty, so what? He didn't have one at thirty, either. Or twenty-five. In fact, our ace had the slowest fastball in the big leagues. His heater topped out at 82. That's ten miles an hour slower than Aroldis Chapman's slider. It's slower than some guys' *changeups*. Moyer got hitters out with more savvy than any pitcher this side of Greg Maddux. Every fifth day he put on a clinic, and I had a great view. He pitched backward, throwing offspeed pitches when he was behind in the count, fastballs on 0-2. He'd tantalize a cleanup hitter with a meatball outside, then slip a sneaky fastball under his hands for strike three.

Like Maddux, Moyer was a master of the psych. If a hitter fouled one of his "fast" balls straight back, Jamie would walk toward the plate while he rubbed the next ball up. He'd say, "Damn, how'd I get away with that one?" Just loud enough for the hitter to hear. "I'd be crazy to throw one of those again." Just screwing with the guy's head. And then strike him out with another one!

That's the kind of club we were. Resourceful. Unpredictable. With help from a great defensive outfield featuring Ichiro, Cameron, and Randy Winn, we could beat you on both sides of the ball. And I was hitting everything hard, feeling stronger than in my 37-homer year in 2001.

We took over first place in April and held it through June and July. I'd roll into the clubhouse and say, "Boys, jump on my back and I'll carry y'all to the promised land." This was the fiery role my teammates expected me to play. By the All-Star break I had a .313 average, 24 homers, 76 RBIs. MVP numbers. I made my third All-Star team, and got a call from the league office.

"Bret, would you like to represent the American League in the All-Star Home Run Derby?"

I had to think it over for about zero seconds. "I'll be there."

It was cool to be one of four AL sluggers—Jason Giambi, Carlos Delgado, and Garret Anderson were the others—taking on the NL's Albert Pujols, Gary Sheffield, Richie Sexson, and Jim Edmonds at U.S. Cellular Field in Chicago. After a decent performance in the 2001 derby (including one in the upper deck), I was flattered to be invited back. It makes you feel pretty damn virile to be one of eight sluggers in the derby, even if you're the squirt in the bunch. The broad-shouldered six-three Pujols and six-six Sexson made me look like an overgrown batboy. I'd been a first-round derby washout two years before, along with Sosa and A-Rod. It was time to step up and do some thumping this time around.

So I prepped. Even for a sort of glorified batting practice, it pays to work the angles. First, you want to win. Second, you don't want to look lame on national TV. Everything's stacked in your favor. The fans are jacked and so are the baseballs. I'd never come right out and say Home Run Derby balls are juiced, but if you ask me if they're livelier than regulation, I'd ask you if the pope wears a big hat. Does a bear relieve himself in the woods? If you stuck a derby ball in the humidor at Coors Field, it might still jump out. Unfortunately for me, you've got to make decent contact or it doesn't jump far.

Derby prep starts with finding the right pitcher. Some guys ask their fathers or drinking buddies to do the job. That might get Dad or Jimmy from the corner bar a few minutes on TV, but those guys probably lack the control to deliver one 60-mph straightball after another over the middle of the plate. The last thing you want is to get fooled, and the next-to-last thing you want is to stand there taking balls out of the strike zone. My favorite BP hurler, the Mariners' bench coach John McLaren, couldn't make it to Chicago, so I turned to former catcher Dave Valle, who was now a color man on Mariners broadcasts.

Watching Valle warm up, I was as nervous as on the first day of spring training. I wasn't thinking, *Win this thing*. I was thinking, *Don't screw up. Just save face—hit one and go from there*. Then I stepped to the plate and got a bad surprise. Valle threw cutters! He couldn't help it—his natural meatball ducked away at the last instant. I couldn't get the hang of hitting it, especially after I started pressing, overswinging, and . . .

Missing.

Let me tell you, it's a sinking feeling to hit grounders and low liners in the Home Run derby. It's worse when your longest fly ball's one of those "Back, back, back . . . *awww*" near misses. But it's *really* bad to swing and miss. Which I did. While tying a record that will last forever—zero homers in the derby—I whiffed on one of Valle's lazy cutters.

You have to laugh at yourself when that happens. Some pitchers and hitters don't mesh, that's all. It wasn't Valle's fault that I couldn't hit his slowballs. I thought back to the 2001 All-Star Game in Seattle, when Troy Glaus went oh-fer in the derby. Troy hung his head and I said, "Who cares? It's an exhibition." Walking back to the dugout two years later, with cameras all around, sending pictures of the homerless Boone to 5.4 million households, I knew how he'd felt in 2001. Giambi tried to buck me up—"No biggie, Boonie" and "Who cares?"—but the other guys couldn't quite look me in the eye. They didn't want to get too close. Ballplayers are superstitious; your oh-ferness might be contagious.

The day after my oh-fer in the 2003 derby, we had a family reunion on the field—two-time All-Star Gramps, four-time All-Star Dad, three-time All-Star me, and new All-Star Aaron, posing for a photo op. That's one of my favorite moments.

I went 0-for-2 in the All-Star Game. My one highlight was getting a note from another AL All-Star, Roger Clemens. Considering our history, I was surprised when my old nemesis asked me to sign some caps and balls for one of his sons. *You're his favorite player,* Clemens's note read. *How ironic is that?* Of course I signed. What's a beanball or two between old buddies like us?

On the road, fans gave me hell for the rest of the season. "Mr. Home Run Derby!" And that was one of the printable lines. Every town seems to have one loudmouth drunk who can somehow afford a ticket near the home dugout, a guy who knows all about the visiting team.

"Yo Boone, nice derby! Maybe you should be in the Singles Derby! The Grounder Derby! But no, you'd strike out!"

I just smiled. A guy who can't handle failure has no business playing baseball for a living. When a couple of teammates needled me, I told them to get back to me after they qualified for their second Home Run Derby.

That July the payroll-slashing Reds fired GM Jim Bowden and manager Bob Boone. Four days later they finished de-Booning their team by trading Aaron and his $3.7 million salary to the Yankees. Aaron cried that day, but when sportswriters pressed him to rip the Reds, he refused. "Hopefully," he said, "I'll go to New York and be part of a winner."

I had my own problems with the press that year. They started at the All-Star Game, where a New York reporter pressed me for a quote. I said how happy I was to be an All-Star and how proud I was of my family, and this writer kept pushing. "What's *wrong* with baseball? It's not perfect, is it?" He kept after me. "What would you change if you could? What's *wrong* with the game?"

Finally I gave the guy an answer. "Well, the commissioner of baseball is also one of the owners. Wouldn't you call that a conflict of interest?"

Next thing I know it's a tabloid headline. BOONE BLASTS COMMISH.

Pretty soon the Mariners' CEO, Howard Lincoln, phoned me. He was hot. "Who do you think you are? You can't criticize Bud Selig!"

That got my back up. "Nobody tells me what I can and can't say."

"You need to call Bud. Tell him you apologize."

"Like hell I will!"

But I made the call. The next day I phoned Selig's office on Park Avenue in New York, not to apologize but to explain. I told the commissioner I'd been pestered for a quote till I expressed an honest opinion. It *was* a conflict of interest for an owner to be commissioner.

Selig heard me out. "There are other people who feel the way you do," he said. He suggested a meeting the next time we were in the same town. We met in Seattle. I didn't give an inch, and neither did he. We shook hands and went our separate ways.

I still think he was wrong. The owners shouldn't run the commissioner's office—as they still do under Selig's old lieutenant, the former union-buster Rob Manfred. At the same time, I've developed real respect for Selig. That day in Seattle he looked me in the eye and told me he had the game's best interests at heart. Today, more than twenty years later, he deserves a lot of credit for presiding over Major League Baseball's recent boom. The game is bigger, more popular and profitable than ever, thanks to twenty-plus years of labor peace on Bud Selig's watch.

☆ ☆ ☆

The Mariners led the AL West in August 2003. Moyer was 16-6 at that point. Ichiro was hitting .330, Edgar .307. I was at .299, batting cleanup, closing in on 30 homers. We were five games up on Oakland and nobody else was close. That was the season I got thrown out of a game for the only time in my fourteen-year career. Want to hear the whole R-rated story? First, a little background: I got along with umpires. You know me—I'm a talker. Not a chatterbox, which is a player who runs his mouth before he earns the right. By 2003 I was a veteran, a three-time All-Star with a right to my opinion as long as I said it the right way.

For instance: me and umpire Ed Montague. Eddie was a veteran, too. By 2003 he'd been umping in the majors for thirty years. A true pro, he was my favorite ump—not because he favored hitters (he didn't) but because he called a fair, consistent strike zone. And he could take a joke. I used to tap him on the ass on my way to the plate and say, in my most endearing voice, "What's going on, fuckhead?"

You've probably heard about the so-called magic words you're not allowed to say to an umpire. Well, to put it in on-field terms, that's fucking bullshit. It's a myth. Like just about everything else in baseball, what you can and can't say to an umpire boils down to two words: *it depends*. If a rookie curses an ump, he's sure to get tossed. But I'd earned the right. Montague knew I was ribbing him. I'd also been in the league long enough to debate him about balls and strikes, as long as I followed the unwritten rules.

Montague was one of the good umpires whose zone was the same in a tie game as in a 12–1 laugher on getaway day when his crew had a plane to catch. But like Bobby Cox, or me, or anybody else I know, he wasn't perfect. Sometimes he missed one, and I let him know it.

But not to his face.

"Outside," I'd yell at the ground in front of home plate. Because you *can* argue balls and strikes as long as you don't face the ump when you do it. Turning to face him would show him up in front of thousands of fans and millions of TV viewers, and that's the real no-no. You also need to remember where the TV cameras are. These days there's one in dead center, so you'd better not make a face and say "Fuckin' outside" if you're facing the mound.

"Eddie, it was a foot outside!" I'd yell at the ground, exaggerating by ten or eleven inches.

"That's enough," he'd say.

"You might have a better view if you got your head out of your ass."

"Boonie, you're pushin' it—"

"Just do your fuckin' job. I'll do mine, and mine's harder!"

None of which got me thrown out of the game. I was near the edge of getting tossed, but I always knew where the line was. With umps I said "fuckin'" without saying "fuck you"—a shade of difference that could keep me from getting tossed.

After the game, I'd see Montague in the hotel bar and we'd laugh about the pitch I still said he missed.

Paul Nauert was no Montague. Nauert was the plate umpire one day in Kansas City, a bad-shadows afternoon game when the ball went from sunshine into shade right in front of the plate. That sort of light's as hard on umpires as on hitters. I knew I was in for a tough at-bat when a pitch bounced and he said, "Strike!"

I looked at the grass in front of the plate. "Paul, that wasn't fucking close."

"Get back in the box," he said.

In a spot like that, you have to protect the plate. I wound up swinging at a ball in the dirt, striking out. I threw my bat. I spiked my helmet off the plate. Nauert threw me out of the game, and I went after him. "You can't toss me for throwing equipment!"

"You did it because you were mad at the first pitch," he said.

"Yeah, but you can't *presume* that."

Our manager, Bob Melvin, came running out to join our philosophical conversation. Bob was an inch from Nauert's nose, yelling, "You can't toss my three-hole hitter because you read his mind!"

"I just did!"

The good guys lost that one, but we didn't lose many that summer. On August 15 we beat the Red Sox to move our record to 74-48. I hit my 30th home run. Then we started a losing streak that lasted a week, blowing our five-game lead. We went into the season's last week neck and neck with the A's, and they beat us by three. In the end, Ichiro wound up hitting .312. Joel Pineiro won 16 games, and Old Man Moyer went 21-7 without throwing a single pitch faster than 85 mph. I finished with 35 homers, 117 RBIs, and my third Gold Glove, while Edgar Martinez batted .294. That was us in a nutshell. The Mariners and I had now averaged 102 wins in three years and made the playoffs once.

Ordinarily, I wouldn't watch the playoffs. It hurts to watch when you think you ought to be there. If you make the postseason, you've got a shot at forever. You might do something they'll talk about forever. Just ask Bobby Thomson, Don Larsen, or Kirk Gibson. The Mariners were good enough, but Oakland was better that year and we missed out again. Once I cleared out my locker at Safeco on September 29, the day after our season ended, I had no desire to watch other guys play postseason baseball.

Except for one guy.

☆ ☆ ☆

When it came to our personas in the big leagues, Aaron and I were oil and water—opponents always hated me, but everybody loved my little bro. "I was always quieter than you, a little more under the radar," Aaron says today. "Who wasn't?"

He broke in with the 1997 Reds with none of the hype that came with my debut as the first third-generation player. Settling in at third base, Aaron hit between .280 and .294 in three seasons with the Reds, with 12 to 14 homers a year. In 2002 he tried swinging harder, with more of an uppercut, like me. Sacrificing average for power, he socked 26 homers in 2002 and made the 2003 National League All-Star team. Our seventy-nine-year-old Gramps, stricken with cancer by then, made it to Chicago for our photo of that All-Star weekend.

Gramps was jazzed to be there. At a dinner with his gray-haired cronies that week, he asked for a show of hands. "How many of you sons of guns have grandkids?" Most of them raised their hands. Then he grinned and added the capper: "Okay, how many have *two* grandsons playing in the All-Star Game, and a son that played in four of 'em?" He was the only one with his hand up.

Six weeks later, the Reds traded Aaron to the Yankees for a couple of pitching prospects you'd never heard of. Playing third base beside Derek Jeter, Aaron batted .254 with six homers in two months in the Bronx. He wound up with a career season—24 homers, 96 RBIs, and 23 stolen bases for the Reds and Yankees—but struggled so much in the playoffs that Yanks manager Joe Torre benched him and played light-hitting Enrique Wilson instead.

I had an easier time with slumps than Aaron did. My impulse was always *Screw you, watch me tomorrow,* while he was more liable to think *What's wrong with me?* At that point he was as low as he'd ever been.

As it turned out, I was in New York for the ALCS, working for Fox TV. They wanted me for my winning personality, of course, but my numbers didn't hurt. Mom's favorite second baseman thumped 35 homers that year with 117 RBIs, a career-high 16 steals, a slash line of .294/.366/.535, my third Gold Glove, and my second Silver Slugger Award.

I was new to broadcasting, but I'd always thought, *How hard can it be?* Answer: easier than facing Mariano Rivera, but tougher than it looks. The best part of my new gig was covering the ultimate baseball show, Yankees versus Red Sox—even if it meant facing a new set of *it depends* decisions.

For one thing, it's tricky to be a still-active player in the broadcast booth. A retired ballplayer can say what he wants. He can say, "Pedro's a headhunter," without worrying that Pedro might fire one up into the booth at him. Not me—I still had to play against these guys next season. What's more, I knew that players on both teams would be going into the clubhouse during the game. The TVs are always on in there. They'd see the telecast and hear everything I said. Those guys were my peers; I had a hundred reasons not to rip them on national TV.

Early in the series, the Yankees' Alfonso Soriano booted a grounder. Joe Buck and Tim McCarver, my broadcasting partners, turned to me. "What happened there, Bret?" My heart sank. I wanted to be straight with the TV audience. At the same time, I knew I'd be seeing Soriano again in the spring. We'd been teammates in the All-Star Game, when he started ahead of me, playing second for the American League. I *wanted* to say, "He got careless. He took it for granted—didn't get his feet in position—and let the ball play him. It was an easy play but he kicked it, and it's his own fault." But I was a rookie in the booth. I kind of chickened out and said, "Bad hop—it happens to all of us."

Pedro Martinez started Game 3 for the Red Sox. As you know by now, Pedro had a reputation. He threw the occasional beanball. Plunking batters in the butt or the back is a legitimate part of the game, but throwing at a man's head is wrong. It's practically criminal. You could end his career or even his life. (Every fan should see the greenish-black bruise a 95-mph fastball leaves on a thigh or glute. You can see the imprint of the ball's stitches in the bruise.) Pedro and I had a relationship going back to our minor-league days. We respected each other, hitter versus headhunter. Off the field, I liked the guy. He had buzzed me plenty of times and plunked me a few, sometimes on purpose, sometimes not—and players know the difference. As I mentioned earlier, it depends on the game situation. The context.

In Game 3, with the score tied, Pedro gave up a double to Hideki Matsui. Next batter: Karim Garcia. Bang, down goes Garcia. And Joe Buck puts me on the spot. He says, "Bret, did Pedro hit him on purpose?"

That's about as touchy as it gets. The next time I faced Pedro, he'd have a lethal weapon in his hand. The politic answer was to say that it happens, that "sometimes a pitch just gets away." But I was still thinking about the Soriano play. I didn't want to wuss out again.

I said, "Yes, of course he hit him on purpose!"

I was proud of myself for telling the truth. At least until the next day, when I walked into the Red Sox clubhouse and who's standing there, giving me the evil eye? Pedro. Looking seriously pissed. Until he grinned and said, "Hey, Boonie, that was no beanball. I throw him a breaking ball!"

I said, "Pedro, we both know what happened."

We agreed to disagree. Pedro and I always had an understanding— he could throw at me, but I'd get my licks in anyway.

☆ ☆ ☆

Pedro was back on the hill for Game 7 against Roger Clemens. The whole baseball world was buzzing. One more win and the Red Sox would go to the World Series with a chance to beat a hex dating back to 1919, when they sold twenty-four-year-old Babe Ruth to the Yankees. Eighty-four years and a million heartbreaks later, Boston had a chance to reverse the Curse of the Bambino. And my brother was part of it. Sort of.

Aaron was batting .125 in the series. He was miserable. He and his wife, Laura, hadn't settled into New York yet. They were still living in a hotel room. On the night before Game 7, I knocked on their door.

Laura let me in. "Your brother's having a tough time," she said.

"That's why I'm here. I want to talk to him."

I walked in and Aaron looked beat. He told me why. "I'm two for sixteen. I'm scuffling so bad. I lost my swing."

I wanted to shake him. I said, "Are you gonna sit there and act like a little bitch? Wake up!" Then I got brotherly. The first six games were done, I said, but there was one more to play.

"You don't know what I'm going through," he said. "You never struggle like this."

"Oh yeah? Check my bubble gum cards for '96 and '97. I've been humbled big-time." I said, "Arnie, I'll admit it, you stink right now, but all it takes is one game. One swing. Especially in the postseason. You might drive in a run. Or the way you're going, you might go oh-for-four and turn a DP to win the game, and all will be forgiven."

"You think so?"

"I know so."

The next day I got to Yankee Stadium and guess what? He wasn't in the lineup. Torre had Enrique Wilson playing third.

So Aaron and I were both spectators—me in the Fox booth, him on the bench as the Red Sox took a 5–2 lead in the eighth inning. Jason Giambi had kept New York close with a pair of homers, a minor miracle considering Giambi's commute to the game. On his way to the stadium he'd spent an hour in a miles-long traffic jam—until a cop recognized the tattooed dude in the Lamborghini and gave Giambi a lights-and-sirens escort to the ballpark.

Still, it looked like Pedro's game. But the Sox were still cursed in those days, looking for their first world championship since 1918. And the Yankees were still the Yankees. In the home dugout, Jeter leaned over to Aaron and told him not to worry. "The ghosts will show up eventually," Jeter said.

Pedro got Nick Johnson to pop out in the bottom of the eighth. Trailing by three, New York had five outs left. Then Jeter doubled. Bernie Williams singled him home. It was 5–3. Hideki Matsui doubled Williams to third. You could see the sweat on Pedro's forehead and in his curly hair. He was gassed. Sox manager Grady Little let him throw his 123rd pitch to Jorge Posada, who doubled in both runs and the game was tied. In the ninth, Aaron took over at third for Wilson. Game 7 went into extra innings, and the score was still 5–5 when Aaron led off the eleventh.

Boston's Tim Wakefield was looking like the MVP of the Championship Series. Wakefield, a knuckleballer, had won Game 1 and Game 4, allowing only 3 runs in 13 innings. He'd retired the Yankees in order in the tenth, and he pretty much owned Aaron Boone. They'd faced each other five times so far in the ALCS. Aaron was 0-for-5 with three lazy fly balls and two strikeouts. But Joe Torre had an idea.

Torre had watched Aaron getting anxious, swinging too soon, yanking Wakefield's floaters foul. So he pulled Aaron aside as he left the dugout to lead off the bottom of the eleventh.

"Try going to right field," Torre said. "Line one to right. That'll help you keep it fair."

While Wakefield finished his warm-ups, Aaron was thinking, *Keep it simple. It's just an AB. Right field, right field.*

Watching from the Fox booth, I thought, *Wakefield! A knuckleballer screws up your timing. On the other hand, it depends. Aaron's so screwed up right now, it could work the other way. Maybe a knuckler's what he needs to come out of it. . . .*

Wakefield's first-pitch knuckler floated toward Aaron, who forgot all about right field. Torre's advice might have helped him let the ball travel an instant longer, but this pitch wasn't going to the opposite field. It wanted to be pulled, and hard. As the ball hung over the plate, muscle memory took over. Aaron planted his front foot and swung hard.

Our dad, watching on TV in a hunting lodge in Idaho with our brother Matt, jumped out of his chair. They both did. I stood up in the TV booth, watching the ball fly toward the left-field seats while the Yankee Stadium crowd stood and held its breath. There was a moment before we all took in what was happening—and then the ball came down in the left-field seats. Wakefield went to his hands and knees on the mound. Aaron raised his arms as he rounded the bases, then jumped into his teammates' arms at the plate.

Cameras flashed everywhere. Loudspeakers played "New York, New York" fourteen times in a row. The Yankees charged out to mob my brother, the unlikely hero, who had a weird thought as he rounded third. He thought, *What are all these people doing in my dream?*

I was supposed to be describing the moment for millions of viewers, but my mic might as well have been dead. For once I was speechless, just overwhelmingly happy for Aaron. Thinking of him tagging along with me and my friends when we were twelve and he was eight, when we were sixteen and he was twelve, always hustling to keep up. Thinking of all the questions he'd had to answer about his grandpa and his dad and his big brother, as if he should outdo us. Thinking of our talk the night before, when he looked beat. *Awesome, awesome.* That was my analysis. That's the sum total of what was in my head, watching my brother jump into the crowd of Yankees at home plate. *Awesome, awesome, awesome!*

The director was yelling in my earphone, "Bret, say something!" But I couldn't. Not without busting out crying. Buck and McCarver were looking at me, waiting for me to speak. A minute passed. I was breaking out in goose bumps, trying to get a handle on my emotions while "New York, New York" rang out and the fans danced. My lips moved, but nothing came out.

Finally the director said, "Bret, that's genius! Letting the moment speak for itself."

A minute later, I pulled off my headphones and headed downstairs to the Yankees clubhouse. Not as a journalist, as a brother. Ordinarily I would never set foot in the Yankees' locker room. That's enemy turf. It's like going to the wrong church, or buying a drink for a pitcher. But I had to see my brother.

I ran into Billy Crystal waving his arms at the clubhouse door, trying to join the party. He was one of the most famous Yankee fans, but he was still an outsider. The guard ignored him and waved me through. I found Aaron in a scrum of teammates spraying champagne on him. I waited for a minute, feeling awkward. Then he saw me and we had one hell of a hug. We both had tears in our eyes. The best hug of my life wasn't with a groupie or even a wife, as much as I loved my wife. It was hugging my brother after he made baseball history.

Neither one of us could speak. There was nothing to say. I didn't have to say, *Arnie, I love you.* He knew.

That night the Yankees held a victory party in the back room of a Manhattan tavern. I went. Someone grabbed me and said, "Boonie, you've got to make a toast to your bro," so I stood on a rickety table. The room got quiet. I looked around the table at Jeter, Torre, Giambi, Clemens, Mariano, Matsui, Posada, Andy Pettitte, David Wells, Soriano, and the rest, all waiting to hear what I had to say.

Lifting a beer toward the ceiling, I said, "Ladies and gentlemen, for one night, and one night only, I am proud to be known as Aaron Boone's brother!" They all laughed. I hopped off the table and shook a few hands. But this was their party, not mine. They were still cheering for Aaron as I slipped out of the bar.

14

AARON, A-ROD, 'ROID WRONGS, AND GOODBYES

The off-season after Aaron's famous home run brought more drama. For starters, our kid brother Matt retired from pro ball. In parts of seven seasons in the low minors, Matt showed occasional power but never got fully healthy. He needed back surgery just to stand up straight. When he could stand, Matt stood six two and weighed a wiry 180. Dad called him the best physical specimen of us all. I don't know about that, but it hurt to see Matt hang up his spikes at age twenty-three. And yet, as much as I loved my youngest bro, I'd always wondered if he was too nice to make the majors. The pro game's so hard that you need some *fuck you* to survive, and he had no meanness in him. A person like that might be better suited to the business world. Today Matt is president and CEO of Boone Action Turf, Dad's artificial-turf firm, installing soccer pitches, putting greens, and baseball fields all over the country.

Matt has his own view of our family story, the outlook of an insider who wound up on the outside looking in. He remembers that night in 2003 when he and Dad were on a hunting trip, watching Aaron hit his Sox-killing homer, jumping from their chairs. The Boones aren't big leapers—between the two of them, they might have a six-inch vertical—but they made up for that with hugs, hollers, and hours of phone calls and texts to relatives and friends. Later, Matt told me he was busting with pride for both of his big-league brothers. "You were always the first among us, but even you had your ups and downs," he said, "and now Aaron's had a moment that's as big as it gets."

Dad's still competitive enough to think he could have matched Arnie's heroics. "Aaron hit a knuckleball that didn't knuckle," he says. "I mean, come on. *I* could have hit that ball out." To this day we argue about stuff like that, one-upping each other every chance we get. I pull rank in the power department, but Dad lasted longer and won more Gold Gloves. Aaron stepped into the ESPN booth as an expert analyst after his homer provided the biggest Boone moment of all. And Gramps lorded it over us all, naturally, because he played back when men were men and the game was ten times better.

For the record, Dad's wrong about that Wakefield knuckleball. Dad never had Aaron's power. If he swung at the same knuckler he'd hit it to the warning track, *maybe*.

Arnie, full name Aaron John Boone, got more than a place in base-ball history that night in the Bronx. He got a new middle name. In Boston he's been "Aaron Fucking Boone" since 2003. Bostonians fig-ured Aaron was golden—postseason hero of the game's top franchise, tall and handsome, happily married to the former Laura Cover, *Play-boy*'s Miss October 1998. (Laura's become a sister to me. She's hardly what most people would expect from a former Miss October—a strong woman, a wonderful wife and mother, a crucial part of Team Boone.) I wonder if Sox fans would have liked Aaron better if they'd known how hard he worked for everything he had despite the heart condition that scared all of us. Or if they'd seen Aaron's face after he tore up his knee in a pickup basketball game.

It happened in January 2004, three months after his historic home run. He'd just re-upped with the Yankees, a one-year deal for $5.75

million. The fine print said no basketball, so the press gave him hell for violating his contract after his injury. They said Aaron was stupid, when he was actually trying to stay in shape for the next season. Contracts contain all sorts of provisions you never hear about. No motorcycle riding, no skiing. There are clauses about drugs, diet, drinking, and probably flossing your teeth. Most of those provisions go unenforced. I've broken a few myself. To me, what mattered was that Aaron wasn't screwing around, he was being the total pro he's always been, trying to do all he could to stay fit and help the Yankees win another pennant. But now his career was in doubt.

Some guys lie to avoid contract trouble. Aaron could have said he hurt his knee jogging or falling down the stairs, but that never occurred to him. Aaron doesn't lie. He's Mr. Integrity. He called Dad first, then Yankees GM Brian Cashman: "I hurt my knee playing basketball." The second call cost him $5 million. Three months later, the Yankees voided his contract. Cashman called it a business move.

"I know Aaron wanted to come back for us," Derek Jeter said. "You feel bad . . . you don't want to see anyone go through an injury like that." Or a long rehab with no team to go back to.

Weirdly enough, Aaron's pickup hoops game changed baseball history in ways that go on today. After dumping Aaron, Cashman needed a third baseman. He traded Alfonso Soriano to the Rangers for shortstop Alex Rodriguez and his ten-year, $252 million contract. With Jeter at short in New York, Rodriguez moved to third and helped the Yankees win six division titles and a World Series from 2004 to 2014. After serving a year's suspension in 2014 for lying about using steroids, forty-year-old A-Rod bounced back with 33 homers to lead the Yanks to last season's playoffs.

Aaron spent months wondering if he'd ever play again. The 2004 season started without him while I was riding high, coming off a 35-homer, 117-RBI, $8.3 million All-Star season for the Mariners. Six months after the thrill of his life, my brother was as downcast as I'd ever seen him. The only plus for him was getting more time to spend with Gramps.

If you're thinking 2004 wasn't our favorite year, you're right. Not long after Aaron came out of knee surgery, Gramps went into the hospital. Our patriarch was diabetic, with aching knees of his own. He was slowing down, not that he'd ever admit being a step slower than in 1955, when he led the American League in RBIs. Grandma Patsy practically had to tackle her eighty-year-old husband to keep him from taking grounders with their great-grandchildren. Gramps was pleased that he'd gotten to know my kids Savannah and Jake, just like I'd known my great-grandfathers Don Boone and Bud Brown.

My first clue that he wasn't immortal came in the '90s, when Gramps and Grandma came to stay with my wife and me in Orlando. Suzi and I were sleeping one night when I felt someone pulling my toe. Instant déjà vu—that's how I woke Gramps up when I was a toddler.

Grandma said, "Your grandpa needs you."

I ran in and found him on the end of his bed with his hand over his heart. "My chest's real tight," he said. I called 911. Five minutes later an ambulance zoomed into my driveway. A couple of paramedics jumped out and hurried to Gramps, but he wouldn't let them put him on a stretcher. He sat there arguing. "It's going to take more than this to bring a Boone down!"

And I thought Dad was the toughest guy I knew.

Gramps had had a heart attack. "A little one," he said. Two days later I picked him up at the hospital, where the nurses were fawning over him like he was Justin Bieber. They didn't want to let him leave, but forty-eight hours was all the recovery time he said he'd "waste" on a heart attack. One nurse told me that the one good thing about seeing him go would be getting a break from his baseball stories. He would never tell Aaron and Dad and me we were hot stuff, but he'd been wearing the nurses out with tales of our exploits. "I started out as the second-best ballplayer Hoover High ever had," he once said, "and wound up as the patriarch of the first three-generation family of major leaguers. That's a pretty good ride."

Even after retiring as a full-time Red Sox scout, he kept his hand in by scouting part-time. Gramps liked to say his tools were his eye and his gut, "none of that technical baloney. I don't need a machine to tell me a kid throws hard." He might have been the last scout who didn't use a radar gun.

Every spring training, wherever I was, I'd rent an adjoining room for Gramps. We'd get up early and meet for breakfast. He'd scan the baseball news while I did the *USA Today* crossword, and then we'd drive to the ballpark. I'd have workouts, drills, and a ballgame to play, but I never had to worry about Gramps getting bored. He knew everybody. He could spend the day schmoozing with former players, coaches, managers, and other scouts. They'd help him up the steps to his seat in the sunshine, telling him how good he looked and asking questions about the old days, our family, and the young players he had an eye on.

In March 2004 he joined me in Peoria, the Mariners' spring-training home, near Phoenix. Coming off my 35-homer season for the Mariners, entering the third year of my $25 million contract, I had a new Gold Glove in my trophy case to go with my second Silver Slugger Award as the league's best-hitting second baseman. When Gramps held court with writers or other scouts, he called me "the best of us" but reminded them that he was no slouch in his day. "Who are the only grandfather and grandson who ever led a league in RBIs?" Us.

I'll never forget how good he looked in that spring of 2004. I drove him to our spring training complex—me in my shorts and flip-flops, him spiffy as usual in shiny shoes, crisply pressed slacks, and a button-down shirt with a plastic comb in the pocket. Even at eighty he took pride in his full head of hair. It was white by then, slicked back with gel.

One morning he brought a duffel bag. "Bret, I want you to have this."

I looked inside. The bag was full of baseballs, gloves, and other gear. There was a ball autographed by Babe Ruth. The next two I pulled out were signed by Ty Cobb and Connie Mack.

I said, "Gramps, you should keep these. They must be worth—"

"Keep 'em," he said. "You never know how long your old Gramps is going to be around."

I thought he was joking. What could take him down? But he knew something he wasn't saying.

His gut, the one thing he always counted on, was turning against him. His stomach was killing him. An operation helped at first, but a couple of months after he gave me that duffel bag he was back in the hospital for more surgery.

He liked the nurses but hated the pain, the needles and tubes, the bedpan. Aaron, rehabbing his knee, joined Grandma Patsy at Gramps's bedside when he could. Mom and Dad and Matt were there all the time, and I'd visit when the Mariners went to Southern California on road trips.

That summer, Gramps lost his voice. From then on, he used a little chalkboard to communicate. *SCHIL* meant Curt Schilling, the best player he'd ever signed. Schilling was leading Boston, Gramps's team, to the playoffs that year, and with Aaron on the shelf the Red Sox might finally win one. Gramps liked that. I told him my fourth-place Mariners still had a shot at the 2004 playoffs. That was a white lie. We were 12 games out of first in June.

In August, while I was on the road, Aaron signed a free agent deal for 2005. He went straight to the hospital to tell Gramps. "Grandpa couldn't talk at all by then," Aaron remembers. "He knew he was dying. We all knew. But he was still listening, still interested in everything we did. So that day I drove straight over to see him. I said, 'Grandpa, I signed. I'm going to be a Cleveland Indian, like you.' And he got it. He smiled."

On one of my visits, I talked about the slump I was in. Two-for-25, something like that. Gramps wanted to give me advice, so he pulled my hands to his chest, moving them into position on an invisible bat. He was reminding me to stay with the grip Dad and I had worked on.

What I remember most is that chalkboard of his. If I mentioned Randy Johnson he'd write *BOB FELLER*. Meaning that Randy was a Pony League wuss next to Feller. I'd play along. "How hard did Feller throw? Tell me again. Eighty-five miles an hour?" He'd grab his chalk. *100+*.

"He was a grumpy old dude like you," I said. We reminisced about the time Gramps introduced me to Feller, back when I was with the Reds. I stuck out my hand, all polite, saying Mr. Feller this and Mr. Feller that, and Feller looked at me like I was a bug. "Kid," he said, "we could show you how this game should be played."

If Dad was with us, he'd say Steve Carlton was as good as Feller. "Carlton had the best slider ever." If Aaron was there, too, he'd throw in another name to stir the pot. "Smoltz's is better." I'd say there were twenty modern guys who threw as hard as Feller or had sliders as good as Carlton's, and start naming them. Pedro, Clemens, RJ, CC Sabathia . . . It was like our Thanksgiving and Christmas arguments through the years, which Gramps and Dad took more seriously than Aaron and I did. Dad would shake his head at my ignorance while Gramps wrote old-timers' names with exclamation points.

TED WILLIAMS!!

When I was alone with him, Gramps liked for me to tell him about my games and the players I admired. Not admired as in "looked up to as a hero." Admired as in looked up to as a hitter. For instance, you might not think much of Barry Bonds as a person. I didn't. He was a me-first guy with a chip on his shoulder, always convinced he was better than everybody else and got treated unfairly. People believe he was performance-enhanced. That's widely suspected even if nobody proved it about Bonds, just as it's suspected of me and a lot of other home run hitters from our era.

But what talent! As I've said before, however you go about it, hitting a baseball at major-league velocities with major-league deception—curves, slurves, splitters, sinkers, cutters, scuffed balls, and beanballs—is the hardest job in sports. And Bonds made it look easy. Between the lines, he was the best I ever played against. Gramps and I loved watching Giants games on TV. I'd point at Bonds's hands. "He's choking up an inch!" Steroids or no steroids, Bonds was the smartest, quickest hitter I ever saw, so smart that you'd swear he could read a pitch before the pitcher threw it, and so quick he could deliver his black maple bat to the hitting zone in no time. In the three years *after* his 73-homer season in 2001, he averaged more than 45 homers while batting over .350—and got walked at a record-setting pace. All that time, other teams were trying to pitch around him! At one point Diamondbacks manager Buck Showalter, who's no dummy, walked Bonds intentionally *with the bases loaded*. The move paid off when Arizona won 8–7.

Yes, it was the steroids era. Yes, hitting stats were up all over. But dozens of hitters were suspected of enhancing their performance. Bonds was the one who really struck fear into pitchers. In 2004 he walked a record 232 times; Sammy Sosa walked 56 times that season. Bonds walked 70 more times in 2004 than Mark McGwire did in 1998, McGwire's 70-homer season.

Here are the four walking-est seasons in baseball history:

Barry Bonds, 2004: 232 bases on balls
Barry Bonds, 2002: 198
Barry Bonds, 2001: 177
Babe Ruth, 1923: 170

Bonds bopped 45 homers in 2004, the year they walked him 232 times (a record that will stand forever), while slashing a ridiculous .362/.609/.812. I kept telling Gramps that he could write *TED* all he wanted, but I'd bet Ted Williams couldn't hit .290 in 2004. "How much better was Ted than the second-best guy? Was it DiMaggio?" I asked. I argued that Bonds was better because he played in a more athletic, competitive era. For one thing, Williams and DiMaggio were only the best *white guys*. Their best years came before black players like Jackie Robinson, Willie Mays, and Hank Aaron were allowed on the field. Barry competed against a deeper pool of talent. "And he's still *way* better than the rest of us."

Who was the second-best player after him? Ken Griffey Jr.? A-Rod? For a little while in 2001 and again in 2003, it might have been me. But if you went back and asked every big leaguer from 1995 to 2005, "Who's the best hitter of our time?" the answer would be unanimous. Bonds. Nobody else was close.

One night Gramps tried to whistle after Bonds knocked one over the right-field wall in San Francisco. He gave me a thumbs-up. I patted his hand. "He's better than Ted," I said, expecting him to disagree again. Instead he changed the subject. He reached for his chalkboard and praised a young pitcher. *THIS JAKE PEAVY HAS A CHANCE TO BE PRETTY GOOD.*

Then he erased that note and wrote me another: *AND BY THE WAY, BONDS IS BETTER THAN TED WILLIAMS.*

I couldn't believe it. Here was my ailing, opinionated Gramps agreeing with me that baseball had evolved. Agreeing that the game was better now, or at least harder. Today's best player was better than the heroes of the olden days. It hurt him to say it, but he was smiling. Here we were, thirty-plus years after he pitched me Wiffle balls in his yard, still sharing the family business. I was grinning, too, until I told him I loved him and busted out crying.

Yeah, the Boones get emotional. Me most of all, maybe.

That was one of my last days with Gramps.

Raymond Otis Boone died on October 17, 2004. That night his Red Sox, who hadn't won the World Series since 1918, beat the Yankees to turn a three-games-to-none deficit in the American League Championship Series to 3–1. A token victory, it seemed like. A face-saver. Except that the Sox had done all the losing they were going to do that year. They ran off three more wins to shock the Aaron-less Yanks in the ALCS, and then swept St. Louis for their first World Series title in eighty-six years. All thanks to Gramps, who must have been keeping an eye on them.

He left this world with a lifetime batting average of .275, 151 home runs, and 737 RBIs. He never made more than $28,750 in a season. He never complained. He was my first baseball hero.

I spoke at the funeral. Not for long, maybe a minute. As you know, I tend to get emotional.

"All the stories I saw in the papers referred to Gramps as the patriarch of the Boone family," I said, "so I looked up *patriarch* to see exactly what that meant. The dictionary says a patriarch is the father and ruler of a family. That was Gramps."

☆ ☆ ☆

Gramps's last year was a down year for the Mariners and me. We lost 99 games while my batting average dipped from .294 in 2003 to .251. My homers and RBIs fell from 35 and 117 to 24 and 83. I was feeling every minute of my thirty-five years.

Spring training 2005 felt empty without him, but missing Gramps wasn't my only problem. Just before spring training began, Jose Canseco released his book *Juiced*. The book, subtitled *Wild Times, Rampant 'Roids, Smash Hits & How Baseball Got Big,* made steroids the number one issue of the new season. Canseco admitted being a steroid fiend. He threw his so-called friend Mark McGwire under the bus as a fellow juicer, and accused other hitters, including Rafael Palmeiro, Jason Giambi, Juan Gonzalez, Ivan Rodriguez, and me.

I didn't know Canseco. I think he was dying to stay famous and trying to sell as many books as subhumanly possible. About 80 percent of his book sounded accurate to me. The rest was speculation. Everybody knew players who were bulking up, some legally and some not, but it was hard to say who was who unless you were an eyewitness. I think Jose made up about 20 percent of his book to connect the dots between his stories and drum up a few more headlines. That's why he threw me in there. Of course he had no idea that I'd changed my swing before the '98 season. To him I was just a muscly little guy who started hitting more homers that year. A suspect.

In the bit about me, he claimed that he slid into second base during spring training in 2001, and took a look at my muscles:

"Oh my God," I said to him. "What have you been doing?"

"Shhh," Boone said. "Don't tell anybody."

Whispers like that were a sign that you were part of the club—the bond of a secret code or handshake. . . .

That never happened. I was never in—or on—a club with Jose Canseco, and I never shook his hand.

Fortunately, there are people who check facts in books. They may not work for Jose's publisher, but they're out there. During his publicity tour for *Juiced,* Canseco went on the *Today* show with Matt Lauer. Lauer challenged him. "You write in the book that you discussed steroids with Bret Boone during a spring training game," he said. "You were on second base and you noticed how big he'd gotten. You made a comment to him and he said something to the effect of, 'Shhh, don't tell anyone.' Of course, baseball writers have looked at the records. And during spring training in any game between the Angels and Mariners, you never reached second base."

Jose stammered and backtracked. "Um, I was on first base. . . . They may have made a mistake in the actual book, but believe me, this incident did happen."

No, it didn't. But the story stuck. I still get asked about it, and why not? I played in the steroid era and knew guys who juiced. The number was nowhere near the 80 percent of big leaguers he claimed—it was more like 25 percent. Some were the ones you'd expect, but about half the users I suspected were pitchers. Some were skinny middle infielders. Famous skinny middle infielders. And while the whiff of suspicion hangs over guys like me and keeps deserving players out of the Hall of Fame year after year, you can bet that several major users have already been inducted into the Hall. But my guess is as good as anybody's.

And me?

I've got a confession to make about juicing. I thought about it. I was always into gamesmanship, and figured that bending the rules was part of the game. Stealing signs, helping your pitcher doctor the ball, even corking a bat—as long as you get away with it, it's fine. But if you don't get away with it, it can stick to you forever. I was with the Reds in 1996 when Chris Sabo shattered his bat and the cork inside the bat flew all over the infield. Sabo got suspended for a week, but the incident haunted him. Twenty years later, it still does. Check out his Wikipedia page if you don't believe me.

Look, I'm no saint. If you told me I could cork a bat and nobody would ever know, I might have done it. I'm not proud of saying that, but it's true. And to me, performance-enhancing drugs (PEDs) were in the same column. If I knew I could use steroids, and hit better, and help my team, and get away with it, I might have done it. I mean, substances have been part of baseball's culture since the invention of the spitball. In Dad's era some players and teams were famous for using cocaine. I've never tried it or even seen anyone use it except in movies. At the same time, I'm not naïve enough to think there weren't—and aren't—plenty of players smoking marijuana. That wasn't my thing, but I'll admit taking beans. For those who never heard of them, beans were what Gramps's generation called pep pills, or "greenies." They've been a part of baseball since time immemorial. Not everybody took them, but I did now and then. A baseball season wears you down. Nobody thought of beans as "uppers" or "speed." They were basically diet pills, the sort of thing long-haul truckers pop to give them a lift at two in the morning.

Beans? Yes. If that's a crime, my generation was guilty.

But steroids? Not me. Not because I was holier than thou, but because I was scared to get caught.

Getting exposed as a juicer would taint everything I ever did or cared about. My career. My family. My future in the game. I'd changed my swing to get better. I'd gone from a lazy occasional jogger to a fitness-crazed gym rat, and from a junk-food junkie to a nutrition nut, all to get as strong and pure as possible, to play better. Any help I'd get from steroids wasn't worth the health risk, not to mention the embarrassment if I got caught. So I stuck to workouts and supplements.

And I took a ton of supplements. Creatine, andro, Ripped Fuel, and more. As long as they were legal, I was interested. I stopped if they got banned, and even went beyond the rules to make sure I was clean. I never understood players who tested positive for drugs and said, "Oh, I had no idea!" It's your job to know what's in your body. It's your job to stay clean and test clean. That's why I used to send my supplements to MLB for testing. That's not routine—you have to pay for the tests. They cost me $1,200 one year, but the peace of mind was worth it, partly because there's a permanent record of what I was taking.

And so, obviously, I'm a hero of baseball's steroids era.

Well, not exactly. I still had my demons. In fact, I was a substance abuser. My substance was alcohol.

☆ ☆ ☆

On April 6, 2005, my thirty-sixth birthday, I homered against the Twins and limped around the bases. You don't need to hear about the injuries. Let's just say it's almost impossible to hit Clemens and Maddux and Mariano when you're at the top of your game. When your shoulders ache and you can't plant your front foot without getting an electric shock through your knee, you can lose the "almost."

I'd already outlasted hundreds of teammates, thousands of contemporaries. I'd enjoyed the rock star life, shaking hands and signing autographs, kissing pretty girls and taking photos and letting everybody buy me a drink. But that life can go to your head. There were times when I let it distract me. A postgame beer became a six-pack or two. Dinner became a party at the best nightclub in whatever town I was in. Drinking eased the sting of waking up every day to the lousiest season of my life. I was hitting .231 with 7 home runs when the Mariners traded me to Minnesota for a player to be named later. Not exactly a compliment. In a month with the Twins I batted .170 with 9 hits, all singles, in 53 trips to the plate. They released me.

I needed a drink.

So I had one, and then another one. I'd polish off a six-pack of beer and reach for another six-pack. Eventually I made the mistake of switching from beer to clear—from the slow, easy buzz of Bud Light or Miller Lite to the sharper edge of Absolut and Ketel One, a bottle at a time. Sometimes it felt like going off the high dive the way I did as a kid, only this time the pool was full of alcohol. You've got to watch out or you might go under.

Nobody knew how much I was drinking. To the baseball men I loved and trusted, it seemed like the usual late-career crisis. I phoned Dad, Aaron, Edgar Martinez, Mike Blowers, and Walt Weiss, asking if I should retire. After fourteen years in the majors and more than 15,000 big-league innings, I felt spent. "It hurts to swing a bat," I said. "Hell, it hurts to get up in the morning."

Most of them said the same thing. "It's your call. Just be *sure*. You don't want to spend the next twenty years looking back, wondering if you quit too soon."

The next day I drove past the liquor store and kept going to the gym. Three months of steamed vegetables and high-intensity workouts later, I was in my best baseball shape since 2003. The Mets flew me to their 2006 spring camp in Port St. Lucie, Florida, as a nonroster invitee. That's ball talk for a guy nobody expects to make the club but who might be worth a roll of the dice.

I popped a few eyes in the clubhouse. Check out the old geezer with the guns and abs! But I didn't hit. My knees got worse—not just more painful but weaker. I'd see a lamb chop of a fastball, stride, and feel my left knee buckle. Hitting without strong knees is like driving on a flat tire. I might have been the physically strongest infielder in camp that year, but there was no doubt I was one of the weakest hitters. So at the age of thirty-six years and eleven months, I called it quits. The Mets announced my retirement.

Dad called a minute later. "Tell me you're joking," he said.

"No, it's for real." I felt like apologizing to him. "I can't hit anymore." I kept myself together till we hung up, and then cried all the way to the airport.

☆ ☆ ☆

The next couple of years were good ones overall, thanks to my kids. Savannah was a fourth grader, sharp as a tack. Her brother Jake was the Ted Williams of San Diego–area T-ball diamonds, setting an example for the twins. Fraternal twins Isaiah and Judah, born in 2004, were as different as night and day. Isaiah was the dark-haired mischief maker, while Judah was the blond introvert, carefully planning his revenge if his twin stole a toy dinosaur. I had a blast helping Suzi wrangle the kids during the baseball season for once. Meanwhile I played golf three or four times a week, like a pitcher, and watched a few ballgames on TV, pulling for old teammates.

After a while, though, I missed the game so much it felt like I'd lost a limb. Those were the days and nights when it got easier than ever to reach for a drink. My wife said, "You're drinking an awful lot." My mom noticed, too. Then one day I was playing golf, driving the cart toward my ball, when I crashed the cart. That's when you know you're wasted, when you're going about two miles an hour and you still crash. At that point it wasn't funny anymore. It was embarrassing. So I checked myself into Promises, the well-known—and expensive—rehab center in Malibu. I'd often talked with other athletes who treated their stints in rehab as mini-vacations. They'd dry out for a couple of weeks and then go right back to their old ways. Not me. In my view, rehab was as serious as a heart attack. I went to every class. Educated myself on alcohol abuse the way I'd done on baseball's labor issues. I came to believe that alcohol had drained the passion out of the end of my career. I remembered getting sick of the pregame drills I'd been doing for seventeen years, and looking forward to that first postgame beer. The biggest edge I ever had on other guys was a fierce drive to play the game I loved, but I had lost my edge. I had let injuries and alcohol steal it.

Rehab cleared my head. I got clean, got back in shape, and got antsy.

Watching baseball on TV, I couldn't help thinking a pitch or two or three ahead. Sometimes my hands would clench when a fat pitch crossed the plate on TV. But I wasn't a hitter anymore, just a viewer.

That gets old. As the 2007 season went by, I quit watching.

The Mariners finished second in the AL West that year. Bonds passed Hank Aaron on the all-time home run list. My buddy Trevor Hoffman became the first pitcher ever to rack up 500 saves. Schilling went 4-0 in the postseason as the Red Sox swept the Rockies in the World Series to win Boston's second championship in four years, the same four years it took me to go from 24 homers and a Gold Glove to house-husband duties and a golf glove.

I kept thinking, *What if I had twenty more homers in me? Or ten? Or one?*

After two years off, I kicked another off-season into high gear. Running. Pumping iron. Hitting thousands of line drives in local batting cages. Eating perfectly. Drinking water. I'd like to say I never touched a drop of alcohol after my weeks at Promises, but I'm not that strong. I got buzzed a time or two, but nothing like the bad old days. I believe there are millions of people who can drink in moderation; I just don't happen to be one of them.

Jim Bowden, the Reds' general manager who'd hired and fired Dad and traded me, was now running the Washington Nationals, with Dad as one of his executives. Bowden liked Boone-style leadership. The Nats were rebuilding, so he signed thirty-four-year-old Aaron to support youngsters like Ryan Zimmerman. Then Bowden phoned thirty-eight-year-old me. He offered a nonguaranteed contract. If I signed, I'd have to prove myself like a rookie. Me, a three-time All-Star! Of course I said yes.

The oldest kid in camp batted .184 in thirteen spring games for the Nationals. Still it felt great to be a hitter again, slumping or not. But they couldn't take me north with the big club with an average like that.

Late in March, a couple of weeks before my thirty-ninth birthday, Bowden gave me a choice: I could give up on my comeback, or I could report to the Columbus Clippers of the Triple-A International League. If I hit in the minors, he might bring me up in April or May. "No promises," Bowden said, "but it's a chance."

Of course I said yes.

The oldest Columbus Clipper was twelve years older than the typical Triple-A player. I spent the rest of the spring pumping iron and hitting line drives in the Clippers' batting cages. Skipping the cold cuts and potato chips in the clubhouse, making my own food.

Drinking water. Signing autographs for teammates who said I used to be their favorite player. Taking long hot showers to ease the aches in my joints, and loving it all, not because it was glamorous or cool but because it was baseball. Along the way I proved I could still pick it at second and hit enough to help the parent club.

I was batting .261 for Columbus when Bowden called. "You can help the Nationals," he said.

I said, "Jim, I've worked my butt off, but I'm a shell of my old self. I could give you four days a week and hit about .260 with ten or twelve home runs."

He said, "I'll take it."

Last question: How much could I help the Nationals? They were going nowhere. I thought they'd lose 100 games in 2008 (102 as it turned out), and I hated losing even more than I hated striking out. I couldn't help thinking that even in my heyday, when I was healthy, the game was *hard*. Except for my slump-free 2001 season, every year of my career had been a battle. Six or seven days a week, four or five times a game, you fight a do-or-die mental and physical war with the pitcher. You fight to survive—to get a hit or two and field your position—and even if you're Ted Williams or Barry Bonds or Ken Griffey or Greg Maddux or Mike Trout, the game is going to humble you. If you're me, you reach an All-Star level for a while, then come back to earth for another bite of humble pie.

Had I walked away too soon the first time? Maybe. But now, in the spring of 2008, I knew I'd given the game all I had. After a long night weighing Bowden's offer, I called him back. "Jim, I want to thank you for your offer. Let's announce my retirement. This time it's for keeps."

I retired for the second and last time with a .266 career average, 252 home runs, 1,021 RBIs, 3 All-Star appearances, 4 Gold Gloves, 2 Silver Slugger Awards, and a new chapter ahead. For almost forty years I'd been Bret Boone, the ballplayer. That was over.

So who was I now?

15

COMEBACKER

After retiring from baseball for the second and last time, I enjoyed golf with no regrets. Most mornings you could find me with my buddies on my home course, the Bridges at Rancho Santa Fe, half an hour from San Diego. Phil Mickelson's a member there, too. Other guys who play there ooh and aah at Phil's swing and they wince at my grip. It's a baseball grip. I've had purists tell me that the last good golfer with a baseball grip was Old Tom Morris back in the 1870s, but nobody argues with my length off the tee. Distance isn't the problem, since I often knock the ball more than 300 yards on the fly. Counting bounce and roll, I've hit a few 400-yarders.

The Boone boys play together when we can. Dad's long off the tee for a man of sixty-eight, but that's short in our group. He thinks his way around the course, waiting for the rest of us to make mistakes. Aaron does everything pretty well and keeps up an expert running commentary while we play. Matt's a good stick for a businessman. When we play as two-man teams it's usually Matt and me against Dad and Aaron, who are so alike they're basically twins born twenty-five years apart. After twenty years of golf I'm still waiting for one of them to get mad.

They pretend not to notice when I outdrive them. I'm the one giving everybody strokes and strutting like a rooster when I win. Still, I'm just a 5-handicapper—no golfer at all compared to the scratch golfers I play with at the Bridges, and light-years from guys who play the game for a living. I've got a chance in a long-drive contest, but none in the club championship. Maybe I should try working on my short game. . . .

No sports cliché is truer than "Drive for show, putt for dough." Gramps once told me about a round Ted Williams played with golf great Sam Snead. Williams said baseball was tougher: "I have to hit a ball moving ninety miles an hour, while your ball sits on a tee." Snead said, "Yeah, but I have to play my foul balls."

To me, the big difference between the two sports is that baseball rewards the long ball most of all, while golf rewards the best putters. You can reach a par-5 hole in two shots, but if you three-putt you'll lose to a plinker who takes three to reach the green and sinks a putt. When you think about it, golf's mainly about bunting.

I still enjoy my time on the links. Some of my favorite post-retirement days were golf outings with Dad, Aaron, and Matt. We'd spend eighteen holes needling each other, laughing it up, doubling bets until the last putt, which I usually missed, but who cares about a golf bet? I would have paid more to spend a day with the Boone boys.

In 2009 I cared about family more than ever. That was the year Aaron's heart went under the knife.

That off-season Aaron, thirty-six, was coming down an off year with the Nationals. After he signed a one-year, $750,000 contract with the Houston Astros, a team physical showed that the heart condition he'd had since college was getting worse. Aaron had been born with a defect in one of the valves in his heart. Doctors said he'd be risking his life unless they replaced the valve.

In March 2009, the Astros called a press conference, and General Manager Ed Wade announced the news. The room was so quiet you could hear my brother clear his throat. "It definitely hits home, but I'm doing well," Aaron said. "I have a strong faith in God, a great family, friends, and teammates. I'm ready to tackle this thing and get on with life."

A week later he checked into Stanford University Medical Center, at Dad's alma mater. I talked to his doctors, who called the operation "a straightforward aortic valve replacement." One surgeon said it was "like changing a flat tire." But I was still scared. Aaron wasn't a car. He was a husband and father with a career ahead of him, and a long life after that. I told the surgeon that my brother's heart was *nothing* like a flat tire. They were about to open Aaron's ribs and cut into his aorta, the body's main artery, to keep him alive for another twenty or thirty or forty years.

Shaking the surgeon's hand, I winked and said, "Don't screw up."

The night before his open-heart operation, Aaron wrote a letter to his son. Brandon couldn't read yet, but Aaron wanted to make sure he had a note from his dad, saying how much he loved him, in case he never woke up. I'll never tell what Aaron wrote, but I will tell you one thing. That letter was more impressive than the homer he hit to beat Boston.

After the operation he gave Laura a woozy hug. Their son came next. I was fourth or fifth in the hugging order. "You look horrible," I told Aaron. I also said I was proud to be his brother.

Against all odds, he got his knees and his heart back in game shape and played in ten games for the 2009 Astros. Aaron went hitless in 13 at-bats, but put the ball in play 11 times like the gamer he was, and retired after the season with a .263 lifetime average, 126 homers, and 555 RBIs.

His ordeal reminded me to tell my own kids how much I loved them. Savannah was almost thirteen, with a name as beautiful and rare as she is. Before she was born I suggested, with my usual humility, that we should call the baby Bret. "It's a perfectly good name for a boy or girl." Her mom looked at me like I had three eyes. So she was and is Savannah, a dean's list student and volleyball star. I promised her a car on her sixteenth birthday if she got straight A's in high school. She did it, so I leased her a VW Beetle. Her younger brother Jake got the same deal a few years later and cashed in his A's for a Nissan Rogue. They think it's a family tradition. I never had the heart to tell them that I never got straight A's or even B's.

I try to help Jake as a ballplayer. I don't give him technical advice on his grip, stride, weight shift, or anything else. That's my dad's department. If Jake has a technical question I still tell him, "Ask your grandpa." They'll hang on the phone for an hour, talking technique. The way I see it, my job's simple: when it comes to baseball, I'm Jake's support system.

It's the same with Isaiah and Judah. They should enjoy being kids, and part of that—not even the biggest part—is enjoying Little League baseball. They need to know their dad would love them just as much if they played soccer, or played with dolls, for that matter. Their big brother Jake may have spent more time on baseball diamonds, but the twins are just as big-league in my book.

I've never managed one of my kids' teams. You'll find me coaching third base in my Hawaiian shirt and bucket hat while Trevor Hoffman coaches first. Sure, my buddy Trevor and I may have ten All-Star Game rings between us, but we stay in the background while Kevin Carnell, a longtime coach who played college ball, runs Jake's team. He's prepared, upbeat, hardworking, not crazy—just what you want in a youth baseball coach. He fills out lineup cards and argues with umps while Trevor and I clap and yell, "Good cut, Timmy," or "Get 'em next time, Johnny!"

There's one thing that always really bothered me about Little League. Trophies for everybody. Along with rules that let everybody bat and games where nobody keeps score, that's modern PC bullcrap at its worst. In sports, in school, or in the business world, it *matters* whether you win or lose. Kids should want to kick ass every game, every at-bat, every pitch, or why play?

Another thing that chaps my ass is how we accept showboating. This is driven by TV. When a Little Leaguer stands at the plate admiring his homer, it's because he saw his heroes do that on *SportsCenter* or YouTube. Pretty soon we'll probably see home run hitters mooning the pitcher.

Maybe I'm partly to blame. I never forgot the Philly fans' cheers when I caught fly balls behind my back in batting practice. I liked entertaining the crowd. So when I smacked a no-doubter in the big leagues, I'd let the bat fly. *Goodbye!* My trademark move was releasing my Louisville Slugger at the top of my follow-through, flipping it like it was too hot to handle. Today they call me the inventor of the bat flip.

Pitchers didn't always appreciate my stylings. In 2002, I flipped my bat after a homer in Colorado. Next time up, the Rockies' Todd Jones beaned me. "Tell Jones I don't care what he likes," I said after the game. "If he wants to hit me, hit me. I'll go to first and if I hit another one I'll flip it farther. So don't give me this Todd Jones tough-guy act, how about that?"

Have I mentioned that Todd Jones wouldn't scare me if he had a bazooka? As a hitter, you've got to laugh at pitchers who try to intimidate you. You've got to say *You can hit me, but you can't scare me.* And you've got to mean it, because talent and attitude are the only weapons you've got. Pitchers can hit you in the head with a 95-mph missile and that's "part of the game." But if a hitter retaliates with his fists, he gets ejected and suspended.

Baseball has always favored pitchers. Why is there a mound in the first place? To give pitchers an advantage. Hitters aren't supposed to watch their homers or flip their bats—that's showboating—but nobody minds when pitchers celebrate by dancing and punching the air when they strike you out—or when they point at the sky (because God's on their side!). Dennis Eckersley, for instance, is remembered as an elite starter who became the best closer of his time. Nobody mentions what a show-off he was. Eckersley would strike you out and pretend his hand was a gun. He'd blow on his finger like he'd shot you dead. And it didn't piss me off—that's how Eck fired himself up.

Today, Eckersley's in the Hall of Fame. I'm not. I understand that he had a longer career, with more years at the top of his game. At the same time, his job was easier. Getting three outs forty or even fifty times a year is easier than playing nine innings 150 or more times, fielding your position on defense, hitting against elite starters and ever-better relievers like him. As much as I love baseball fans, that's one thing most of them don't understand: baseball gets tougher every year, but it gets *more* tougher for hitters.

☆ ☆ ☆

Watching TV games after I retired, I found myself muting the sound. Aaron's one of the few announcers I like listening to. You wouldn't believe the homework he does before every game, including calling and texting Dad and me. But I can't watch him for long. It's plain old sibling rivalry. Whatever my little brother Arnie says makes me think, *Could I say it better?*

He knows what I mean. I was always his big brother, the top dog. When we're together and his famous homer for the Yankees comes up, as it usually does wherever he goes, Aaron likes to mention my postgame toast—when I said "for one night only" I was proud to be known as Aaron Boone's brother.

"*One night only?*" he says.

"I was joking!"

"And reminding me that you were better."

"Well, maybe a little bit. And anyway, I was."

While sibling rivalry kept me from watching Aaron, plain old baseball intelligence keeps me from listening to most of his TV colleagues, who don't know what they're talking about. They're not dumb, just ignorant. Some announcers, especially the play-by-play guys who were never ballplayers, have a hard time seeing the subtleties of the game going on in front of them. So they fill airtime with numbers, graphics, and clichés. Don't misunderstand me here—there are knowledgeable announcers who know their stuff, guys I enjoy listening to—but too many will say something like, "Clayton Kershaw can match a record set by Cy Young" when there's really no comparison. In Cy Young's day, more than a hundred years ago, there were basically no relief pitchers. The starter stayed in the game until he won, lost, or passed out.

Fifty years later, nothing much had changed. If you watch grainy film of baseball in the 1950s and '60s, you'll see the starter throwing 82 or 83 mph in the first inning. Then he wears down. His idea of fitness was probably skipping hot dogs and whiskey between innings. That was just the culture of the time. I'd like to face that guy in the eighth inning, when he's throwing 75 or 76. Batting-practice velocity.

Now flash forward to 2016. You knock the starter out of the game and who comes in? A six-foot-four seventh-inning specialist throwing 100 mph, followed by an eighth-inning specialist and a shut-down closer who throw just as hard, only their stuff darts down or left or right even more. Hitters used to say, "Let's get into their bullpen!" Today you almost want to go easy on the other team's starter so you *don't* get into their bullpen. My dad loves to talk about the great Steve Carlton, and Carlton was one of the best lefties ever, but I faced half a dozen guys with breaking balls as good as his: Randy Johnson, John Smoltz, Francisco "K-Rod" Rodriguez, Darryl Kile, Brad Lidge, Al Leiter. Leiter's left-handed cutter still gives me nightmares. Carlton had impeccable control (286 strikeouts and 90 walks in 304 innings in 1980), but eight years later Clemens struck out 291 and walked 62. Today there are dozens of pitchers with Carltonesque stuff: Clayton Kershaw, Felix Hernandez, Madison Bumgarner, Zack Greinke, Jake Arrieta, and Cole Hamels, for starters. Aroldis Chapman and Craig Kimbrel, for relievers.

My point isn't that I played in baseball's golden age. It's that *every* age is a new golden age, when baseball's being played at the highest level ever. You may not like the DH, wild-card playoffs, defensive shifts, or other aspects of the modern game, but you can still see that. The challenge teams and players face is how to succeed at a game that keeps getting better—and harder and more international—than ever before. Instead of comparing Clayton Kershaw to Cy Young, which is like comparing Tom Brady to Jim Thorpe, announcers should help fans understand how fast the game is changing.

As baseball evolves, smart fans see through the clichés too many announcers still believe.

For example, you hear guys in the booth say, "He swings at everything." But they have no clue. Even Vladimir Guerrero, the free-swingingest hitter of my time, didn't swing at everything. At least not always, and not the same way. Guerrero, the American League MVP in 2004, was a freak, and I mean that as a compliment. Vlad was gifted with the talent to swing at a ball off his shoetops, or six inches outside, or off the bill of his helmet, and hit it 400 feet. He came from the Dominican Republic, where young hitters learn to swing hard and often. As the saying goes, "Nobody walks off the island." Dominicans *hit* (and sometimes field) their way off the island. But Vlad's approach was deeper than you'd think. He might swing at a 2-0 slider that bounced in front of the plate, but with two strikes he'd change his stance. Not enough for announcers to notice the difference, but I saw it. With two strikes, Guerrero would turn his front foot toward the plate—not much, maybe half an inch—to keep his bat in the hitting zone a split second longer.

In baseball, nothing's what it looks like at first glance.

The globalization of baseball didn't end with Guerrero, Pedro Martinez, and other Dominican players. Today baseball is an international game. You can't rise through the minors without competing with driven, talented kids from Puerto Rico, Mexico, Venezuela, Japan, Canada, Australia, and other countries. We're seeing a new invasion of guys from Cuba, including the White Sox' Jose Abreu, the Mets' Yoenis Cespedes, and the Dodgers' Yasiel Puig. (Gramps had a Cuban teammate, Minnie Minoso. A solid player from 1949 to '61, Minoso went 0-for-2 for the 1980 White Sox at age fifty-four, becoming the only major leaguer ever to play in five decades, but a thumper like Puig could break skinny Minnie over his knee.)

What's funny is how the guys in the press box and TV booth always discount the talent of foreign players. Back in 2001, when Ichiro came to the Mariners fresh off seven straight batting titles in Japan, the "experts" said he'd be lucky to hit .280 for us, because Japanese baseball was comparable to Triple-A ball in America. Ichiro hit .350. When the recent influx of Cuban talent began, they said the Cubans would have a hard time here because Cuban baseball was, you guessed it, comparable to Triple-A ball. I knew that was wrong from personal experience. (I still cringe thinking about the time Cuba's national team destroyed me and my collegiate teammates, while Fidel Castro sat in the front row, clapping.) That's why I rolled my eyes after the Pirates signed shortstop Jung Ho Kang last year. The experts said Kang, who'd hit 40 homers in Korea, would be lucky to win a big-league job. Why? Because Korea's top league was comparable to Double-A baseball. Kang hit .287 with 15 homers before he got hurt in September. He's a key part of the Pirates' near future.

Another of my pet peeves is how announcers describe mound conferences. The starting pitcher's on the ropes, the manager comes out, the catcher and infielders gather on the mound, and the announcer claims to know what they're saying. "No pitcher will tell the manager he's tired," he says. "He'll insist on staying in." Bullshit! Some young pitchers might say they want to stay in because that's what they think they're supposed to say. Smart ones tell the truth. Greg Maddux or Jamie Moyer would look the manager in the eye and say, "I'm done." Or "I've got one hitter left." That's not being a wuss. It's knowing your arm. It's being a teammate. So the next time you hear an announcer say no pitcher will ever admit he's toast, don't believe it.

I also had to shake my head one night when the camera zoomed in on the on-deck hitter, a catcher. He had his shin guards strapped on. "That's because there are two outs," the announcer explained. "If the batter makes the last out, he's ready to grab his mitt and mask go behind the plate." Sound sensible? It's actually an amateur move. It only takes a few seconds for the catcher to strap on his shin guards. By saving those seconds and wearing his gear to the on-deck circle, that dumb-ass catcher is telling his teammate, *I think you'll make an out.*

Watching ballgames on TV made me want to ask the announcers, "Where's Aaron? You guys don't know your butts from second base." But they weren't asking my opinion. Nobody was.

I'd expected TV networks and big-league organizations to knock down my door once I retired. Teammates and managers always respected me. Writers used to flock around, asking for quotes. Dad and Gramps had stayed in the game after they retired; they were baseball lifers. But my phone wasn't ringing with offers, and I knew why. It was my supposedly brash personality. Despite the fact that I respected my teams and the game—never ripped a teammate publicly, played hard, played hurt—that was my rep. Nobody wants a loose cannon rolling around being too honest, especially in today's era of careful corporate management. It didn't matter that I had baseball in my blood. The game's establishment saw me as the Boone, a bat-flipping hotshot with a more respectable father and brother. In my low moments, that was more depressing than a case of vodka.

☆ ☆ ☆

One weekend in 2013 I took my twin sons to Cooperstown. "Road trip!"

I've got my beefs with the Hall of Fame, mostly involving the annual voting by the Baseball Writers of America. Most of the writers never played the game, but they're great at playing favorites. At my position, they made Ryne Sandberg a first-ballot Hall of Famer, but not Roberto Alomar. No offense to Sandberg, who didn't have a vote, but Alomar was every bit as good. Jeff Kent, who got only 15 percent of the writers' votes last year, was every bit as good as Sandberg. At my best, I was too. I'm not saying I belong in the Hall. If I had a vote, I'd think, *That guy Boone had some Hall of Fame–caliber years, but not enough of them,* and vote no. What I'm saying is that the voters should think a little harder before screwing around with players' lives and legacies. And I don't hold other guys' popularity against them; it's not Sandberg's fault that the voters liked him personally. It's just a sign of how slanted the voting is.

Every January, when the Hall announces the results, ex-players exchange a million texts like this:

R they nutz?!

Yes

But there's still something special about the Hall of Fame. Isaiah and Judah loved running around, pointing at the tiny gloves and baggy "pajamas" players wore in their great-grandpa's day. We got a tour of the Hall's climate-controlled vault, where we found their uncle Aaron's home run bat from 2003, plus a Ray Boone bat, some of Dad's catching gear, and a few of my old bats. They put on sterile gloves and waved a couple of Babe Ruth's bats.

That visit got me thinking about my place in the game. After eight years on the sidelines, I was forty-five. My knees still ached, but I was antsier than ever. I told Dad I wanted to get back in. "But not with the Nationals. That's your club," I said. "I want to make my own way."

"Call Adam," he said.

Adam Katz, my current agent, thought I was being hard-nosed as usual. He said, "You've got how many connections in the game? Dozens. Hundreds. And you want me to call I guy you never met?"

"I want you to call Billy Beane. Tell him I played for five teams in fourteen years. His teams always had less money and usually beat us anyway. I was impressed. Say I'd like to meet him, that's all."

Katz took a breath. "I'll make the call, but no promises," he said, sounding like an agent.

A couple of weeks later I flew to Oakland. I rented a car, stopped at Denny's for a Grand Slam breakfast—that sounded like good luck—and showed up at Oakland Coliseum a few minutes early. Beane's secretary walked me through the door to his office and I went in to meet with the A's general manager.

Beane's still kind of boyish in his early fifties, with brown hair falling over his forehead. He might not be as handsome as Brad Pitt, who played him in *Moneyball,* but who is? Beane had his feet up propped on his desk. He was wearing flip-flops.

He smiled when he saw me. "Bret fucking Boone."

I said, "Billy goddamn Beane."

We spent a half hour getting acquainted, and then went to lunch and talked for another hour. Not about baseball as much as life and love and family, and how a guy can only play so much golf in his life. I liked Beane because he's a risk taker, not a worrier. Some executives spend their lives looking over their shoulders, wondering if somebody's coming to take their jobs. Not Beane. He's comfortable in his own skin.

"I came to see you because I'm still into the game," I said. "You always compete and succeed with half the money. I'd like to know how."

Beane said he was flattered. "But you're not here for a seminar. What do you really want?"

"A job," I said.

16

GAME CHANGER

Billy Beane was my kind of guy. As self-confident as a man can be, but in a good way. He asked what sort of job I had in mind.

"I don't know. Something in the minors. I can help young players."

Beane didn't need to take a meeting to know what he thought. "You should go to instructional ball for us," he said. "Put a uni on. See how it feels. We can go from there."

That's how I became a special advisor for the Oakland A's. I got my feet wet that fall at their minor-league complex in Mesa, Arizona. For those who aren't familiar with Instructs, as players call instructional-league ball, it's a monthlong camp where prospects learn the ropes of pro ball and play games against other clubs' kids. It felt good to put on a uni after seven years in golf shirts, even if I looked strange in the mirror. Who's the aging guy in the Oakland A's jersey?

Beane introduced me to the coaches and players. "Men, this is Bret Boone, a three-time All-Star," he said. "He hit two hundred and fifty-two home runs and won four Gold Gloves, so listen to him. And if you're not sure how great a player Bret was, just ask. He'll be glad to tell you."

I spent most of my time working one-on-one with kids who had no memory of my heyday. While my knees kept barking for Advil and a cortisone shot, it was a rush to be back on the field. Some of the kids said, "You could still play."

"Yeah, maybe for an inning."

They kept after me to take batting practice. "You used to hit thirty homers? Show us how it's done."

"Sorry," I said. But I finally fell for that one in Bakersfield, another of Oakland's minor-league stops. The players there dared me to take BP. I stepped into the cage, and the bat felt like it weighed a ton. I cued a couple of balls foul, then squared one up and hit a liner to short center. Somebody yelled, "One more!" I took my stance, saw the next pitch floating to the plate, and something clicked. I was twenty-five again. I knocked the shit out of the next pitch. I was sure it was going halfway up the light pole on the far side of the bleachers. Instead it cleared the left-field fence by about an inch. Good enough.

"Sorry, boys," I told the kids. "I'm officially retired from BP."

The lunch line in the clubhouse at Mesa was fifty guys long. "Get out of the way, kids," I said, cutting in front. The players stepped aside. Then I went to the back of the line. When the kid ahead of me asked why, I told him, "You've got a game today. That's what counts."

At twenty, Daniel Robertson was the best A's prospect I saw. A jug-eared shortstop, Robertson could swing the bat. He had perfect footwork and great instincts on defense. So I left him alone. Don't fix it if it ain't broke. After a couple of days he came to me, saying, "Bret, you don't like me? Am I doing something wrong?" That taught me a lesson: a coach needs to express satisfaction, not just criticism.

I said, "There's a reason I haven't been talking to you. You're doing things right. Keep it up."

He lit up like Christmas. "I will!"

That's when I remembered how much it meant when Mike Blowers, Edgar Martinez, Lou Piniella, and other baseball men supported me.

In January 2015, Beane traded Robertson to the Tampa Bay Rays for Ben Zobrist, a veteran second baseman the parent club needed. I think you'll be seeing Dan Robertson in the majors in a year or two.

☆ ☆ ☆

I went back for spring training 2015, starting my first full season as a roving instructor and special advisor, reporting to Keith Lieppman, the A's director of player development. Once again I was jazzed to be on the field and in the clubhouse, even if it was a clubhouse in Oakland's minor-league complex. Because today's minor leaguers have got it made! When I started out in the low minors, we hung our gear bags on hooks like the boxers in *Rocky*. Now they've got a twenty-thousand-square-foot locker room. The weight room's bigger than locker rooms in the '90s. They've got five or six strength and conditioning coaches, digital video libraries, high-tech whirlpools. They've got chefs!

Coaching minor leaguers, you're constantly racking your brain for ways to communicate. The language barrier's no problem. My Spanish may be rookie level, but the A's and other clubs have Spanish-speaking staffers to help. Japanese interpreters were brand-new in 2001, Ichiro's rookie year, but now they're a regular part of the scene. The challenge is tailoring your coaching to every prospect you meet. It's not just that some of them need a pat on the back and others need a kick in the butt. It's that different guys think differently. Some need technical help: "Try it with your hands a little higher. Close your stance a half inch." Others need to learn to think like a pitcher: "He wants to get ahead of you with his second-best pitch." And the job's not only—or even mainly—about getting players to the majors. It's about helping them max out. If a rookie-league player can reach Double-A, or a Double-A talent can spend a month in Triple-A ball, he's done something important. It might not help the club at the major-league level, but when that kid finally hits his ceiling and gets released, he'll know he wasn't a flop. He'll know he gave the game all he had.

I walked around Hohokam Stadium with Rickey Henderson, Oakland's baserunning instructor. Rickey, of course, was a deserving first-ballot Hall of Famer, the best leadoff man ever. He's great company, too, one of the best guys you'll ever meet. Rickey enjoyed soaking up the attention of A's fans yelling his name. Hardly anybody noticed me. "It's the uni," he said. "If you were in a Mariners uni they'd know you." We agreed that I looked weird in an Oakland A's uniform. He said I looked weird, period.

There's nothing baseball-ier than a well-placed needle. So I thanked Rickey for standing next to me.

"Why?" he said.

"Next to you, my ego looks normal-sized."

We watched A's prospects doing wall drills. That's a fielding exercise, not so different from bouncing balls off a garage door like I did as a boy. You stand facing a wall, three paces away. If you've got a partner, he stands behind you, throwing balls off the wall. You react and field them. If you don't have a partner you fire the balls yourself, fast as you can. Either way, it's like sparring. After three minutes you're puffing for air, then you do it again. Rickey and I were pleased to be old men whose fielding drills and jogs along the warning track were optional.

My son Jake came to Arizona for a travel-team tournament. Kirk McKaskill, an old teammate of Dad's, took him to the Angels' spring training clubhouse and introduced him around. Rick Smith, the Angels' longtime trainer, shook Jake's hand and said, "You're Bret's son? Bob Boone's grandson?"

Jake admitted it. "Yup."

"Ray Boone's great-grandson?"

Jake nodded. "That's right."

Smith said, "No pressure!"

☆ ☆ ☆

Spring training's too long. Fifty or sixty years ago, players might have needed a month to get in shape for a new season, not that they ever got close to what we'd call baseball shape. Today, high school players like Jake are fitter than the major leaguers of Gramps's time. Major leaguers could easily prep for the season in two or three weeks. Why don't they?

Money.

Mesa, Scottsdale, Bradenton, Kissimmee, and other towns in Arizona and Florida rely on the dollars spring training fans spend every March. Players, managers, and team executives may know that the spring training schedule is largely a waste of time, but nobody rocks the boat.

The A's opened their 2015 season with an 8–0 win over the Rangers on April 6, my forty-sixth birthday. I was home by then, driving Jake to baseball practice at San Diego's Torrey Pines High School. He'd made the varsity as a sophomore. We listened to sports talk on the way. Dave Palet, Jake's travel-team coach, was on the radio, talking about Opening Day. I thought back to the butterflies I felt every year, trying not to embarrass myself in the first at-bat of spring training, and then the first at-bat of every regular season. That's one thing I've got going for me as a coach: I remember how hard it is to max out. That's what Jake's up against now, trying to prove himself against high school pitchers two or three years older than he is. That's what Oakland's kids are doing, trying to fight their way up through the minors.

The Mets' chubby Bartolo Colon beat the Nationals on Opening Day. That game turned out to be a preview of the Mets' pennant-winning season. The Nationals, Dad's team, were supposed to dominate the NL East, but forty-one-year-old Colon mystified them with a grab bag of two-seam, four-seam, and sinking fastballs. Bartolo's belly cast a shadow, but so what? I loved watching him throw blooper balls because I remembered Colon as a young Cleveland Indians ace who threw 99. He was doing something special, finding a way to survive.

What's it like watching a game when your brother's in the TV booth? It's interactive. When Aaron or one of his partners says something I disagree with, I text him. *Tell Sutcliffe he's dead wrong.* Aaron checks his phone between innings and texts me back. *Sut sez ur wrong.* We're all still busting each other's balls like we did in our playing days.

It usually ends like this: *Tell Sut I was right as usual lol.*

☆ ☆ ☆

In May I flew to Chicago, rented a car, and drove three hours to Davenport, Iowa, home of the Quad Cities River Bandits. They're the Astros' affiliate in the Class A Midwest League, three steps down from the majors. I was there to join the visiting team, the Beloit (Wisconsin) Snappers, one of Oakland's A-ball clubs. My job was twofold: help the Snappers without getting in the manager's way, and keep my eyes peeled for talent on both teams.

The game was under way when I pulled into the parking lot. Davenport's Modern Woodmen Park is a typical minor-league venue, which means it's terrific. You probably know that a renaissance in ballpark design began with Baltimore's Camden Yards in 1992 and continued in San Francisco, Minneapolis, Pittsburgh, and other cities. What most fans don't know is that the same trend has transformed ratty, leaky old bush-league yards into showplaces where you and your family can have more fun than Six Flags for pennies on the dollar. There's an amusement park next door to Modern Woodmen Park, a Ferris wheel rising up behind the left-field wall, music playing, local beers for two dollars apiece

Hungry and beat after three hours on the road, I was dying for coffee. No coffee. Also no spread in the clubhouse, and by "no spread," I don't mean no grilled fish and prime rib. I'm talking *no spread*. Not a Pringle.

My first night there, the Snappers got beat 8–0. Two nights later we came out swinging, took a big lead, and wound up losing 15–8. I told Fran Riordan, Beloit's manager, "That's the worst professional performance in history." Riordan laughed. He's a little younger than I am, an ex-outfielder who never got within a mile of the majors but paid attention. As a manager in the low minors, his main job isn't to rack up victories. It's to deliver worthy players to the next level without messing them up. He needs to correct any blatant bad habits, weed out any obvious psychos, help kids from Latin America transition to life in the United States, help his twenty-two- and twenty-three-year-old former collegians learn to be leaders to nineteen-year-old teammates who got signed out of high school, and always, *always* be ready for surprises.

I spent three games in Riordan's dugout—not saying much, just watching. Before game time I fielded grounders with Snappers infielders, keeping an eye on their footwork. I wore a Mizuno glove Jake gave me when I left home. He'd written his name in it. Fourteen years after playing most of 2001 with a glove David Bell had signed, I picked grounders in Iowa with a Jake Boone–autograph model.

After infield I talked shop with the Snappers' hitters. These kids were former high school or college phenoms, and by *former* I mean last year. The veterans were twenty-two or twenty-three. They liked hearing war stories of Home Run Derbies and at-bats against Greg Maddux and Roger Clemens. I worked in plenty of tips they could use, like how to turn a pitcher's decency against him.

"Here's how." Stepping to the plate, I took a phantom fastball on the arm. "Oww! Arrr!" Fell down like I'd been shot.

"You wouldn't try this against Clemens or Pedro," I said, "or some other SOB who couldn't care if he kills you. But most pitchers aren't like that. They feel bad. They don't want to hurt you. Especially young pitchers. They'll shy away from the inside corner the next time you come up. That gives you a big edge. You can forget about the fastball in. You've just eliminated one of his pitches."

I sat with Beloit's catchers, talking about how to read a batter's body language. My dad was the best at that. Jason Varitek was a master. Russell Martin's good at it. How does a hitter change his stance from at-bat to at-bat? The position of his hands? His breathing? A great catcher can read hitters' minds. That's as good as giving his pitcher a free strike on every guy who comes up.

After three games in the dugout, I switched from my uni to street clothes and spent the last game of the Beloit–Quad Cities series in the stands. You get a better view of the pitcher and hitter from there. From behind the backstop you can watch the pitcher, catcher, hitter, and plate umpire war over the strike zone, the most valuable 460 square inches in sports. Now I was more of a scout than a roving instructor. If a kid on the other team had an extra-sharp breaking ball, or a quick first step in the field, or raw power he hadn't tapped due to bad technique, I'd text Keith Lieppman in Oakland. If I really loved the kid I might also text Dan Feinstein, our director of pro scouting and player development, assistant GM David Forst, and Grady Fuson, Beane's special assistant. Grady's an old family friend, so I'm straight with him. *The Quad Cities kid you love SUX. Trade for the ss!!*

Fuson would text back seconds later. *Shut up rookie evaluator, what do u know??*

It's not exactly how scouting went in Gramps's day.

Between games I fielded calls from young players I'd met during spring training. Calls, not texts. Texts are fine between friends, but if you're a first-year pro and I text *Get yr head outta yr ass & watch the pitcher's fingers,* you might think I was mad. So it's phone calls for kids in the minors. Some want advice. "How do I hit a guy throwing a hundred?" Some just want to hear a friendly voice. I traded calls with a smart, talented kid who wanted to quit because his dad was calling him ten times a day, saying how his batting average fell the night before, or how many at-bats he'd had since his last homer. I spent an hour talking that youngster off the ledge. I think you're going to see him in the majors someday. He's that good. And he's proof that a ballplayer's challenges can be mental, emotional, familial, financial, and even spiritual, not just physical. It's a miracle that anybody makes it.

After dinner, texts, and phone calls, I sat down to relax at the Davenport Ramada Inn. There I was, alone on the road. It occurred to me that there were rows of beers and bottles of Absolut in the bar downstairs. I've had my relapses down through the years, and it's still a daily battle not to drink. I knew I could bring a bottle up to my room and nobody would ever know. Nobody but me.

Me, forty-six years old, with four children who rely on their dad.

I stayed in my room with my laptop.

You know what I love? Google Earth. I always felt like I'd wasted my time in the classroom at USC. What did I know about the world outside the foul lines? I'd been to Havana for an exhibition. Flew in, played ball, got on a plane, and flew home. I played for the minor-league Calgary Cannons and against the Montreal Expos and Toronto Blue Jays, but what did I know about Canada? They liked Coke without ice and sang two national anthems. I'd been Ichiro's teammate, known in Japan as Ba-Boom, but never set foot in Japan.

I wished I'd expanded my horizons. So I sat in my hotel room Google Earthing places I always wanted to visit. Niagara Falls. Mount

Rushmore. The Grand Canyon. The Great Wall of China. The Taj Mahal. The Internet's a hell of a thing—you can fall asleep watching a live feed from the Taj Mahal and wake up in Iowa, ready to go to the park.

☆ ☆ ☆

Next I flew to Atlanta for the Southeastern Conference college baseball tournament, another step in my scouting education. As I player I had a good eye for talent. I'd see a rookie come up in September and say, "That kid's a big leaguer." There are telltale signs. Upper-deck power in batting practice, obviously. A young pitcher's ability to throw two different pitches for strikes, especially if one of them goes 95. An infielder or outfielder with a knack for turning his back to catch a ball hit over his head—that gets your attention. But there's something that means even more to me. If a kid with some talent looks bad at the plate, I like to watch his next at-bat. Suppose he got fooled the first time up—swung from his heels at a changeup, struck out, looked sick. Looked *embarrassed*. How does he react? If he takes the same approach the next time up, hoping to run into a fastball, I am not impressed. If he cuts down his swing—flicks his bat to put the ball in play—I'm still not impressed. But if he looks for a changeup the next time, *even if he doesn't get one,* then I love that guy. Because he's *thinking*. He knows he looked bad before. He knows the other team knows. He knows or at least suspects that climbing the ladder in pro ball isn't about showing off your strengths as much as it's about fixing your weaknesses. That's the guy I pull for. And if he gets the changeup he's looking for and rips it on a line somewhere, even if he lines into a double play, I'll meet him on the top step of the dugout and tell him what a stud he is.

And now that I'm in management, I can tell Grady Fuson and Billy Beane about him.

It's not like I want to be Mr. Superscout. That was Gramps's dream. I haven't settled on exactly what my future in the game should be, so I've spent two seasons soaking up expertise at every level. That's a process with no end to it.

Scouting college ball, for example, is a crapshoot that keeps getting crappier. In my USC days, 20 homers was a prodigious number. Then the bats went ballistic. The Green Easton and Black Magic bats of my era morphed into 33-inch drop-seven models that weighed in at 26 ounces. (My USC bats were drop-three models, 33 inches and 30 ounces.) College sluggers like Kris Bryant hit 30 or more homers. The NCAA responded by deadening the bats, leading to years when pitchers dominated. So they tweaked the rules again. Last year, the NCAA introduced a baseball with lower seams. The new ball flew farther. Breaking balls broke less. (It's the seams cutting through air that makes a ball curve.) Offense went up again, leading some to say we should lower the seams on major-league baseballs.

I got a few ideas at the SEC tournament. For one, it's clear that college ball ain't what it used to be. That's got nothing to do with the new college rules and everything to do with (wait for it . . .) money. Young players can now make so much that they're less willing to spend three or four years playing for free. As a result, the draft skews more toward high school talent with every year that passes. A kid who goes to college has only a couple years before he's "old for a prospect" at twenty-five. Yet purists still wring their hands when the majors' latest rookie phenom fails to lay down a bunt. *Whatever happened to fundamentals?*

Here's what happened: The pressure to win at the major-league level got so great that the best kids get rushed. Instead of being trained in the game's fine points in the minors, they learn at the highest level. A franchise that can save future millions by sending a Kris Bryant down for two weeks will still do so; beyond that, everybody's in a hurry. Look at Bryant's Cubs teammate Kyle Schwarber last season.

A year after playing for Indiana University, Schwarber started in the major-league playoffs. In left field. And he was a catcher! The Cubs loved his power bat, so they let him bumble around the outfield like a punch-drunk fighter. Fans were hiding their eyes, but you know what? I say good for the Cubs and good for Schwarber. There are exceptions to every rule. Schwarber's bat was so good that it outweighed his defense. Rushed or not, his on-the-job training's going to help him in the long run. He'll be better in 2016, and so will the Cubs.

☆ ☆ ☆

At the end of June I was with Beloit again. Fran Riordan had a few days off, so I returned to Class A ball to make my professional managerial debut. It was a blast—a busy, occasionally bumpy, entirely instructive blast.

As a manager in the low minors, you need to stay on top of everything. For instance, you're coaching third base as well as managing. A-ball teams are understaffed compared to the parent clubs—there's a manager, a pitching coach, a hitting coach, a strength and conditioning coach, and a trainer. The trainer may double as traveling secretary, making bus and motel arrangements for everybody. I leaned on the other coaches for help with everything from remembering our signs and our players' names to printing out our lineup card. I made a point of memorizing the umpires' names, a tactic I've always believed in. There are only two umps at a Class A game, as opposed to three at the Double-A level and four calling a Triple-A or major-league game. While a veteran big-league umpire can earn $400,000 a year, A-ball umps make only $500 a week. They appreciate being called by name, even if you say, "Tyler, try my bifocals!"

During the game you're giving signals to the catcher, thinking about pitching changes and defensive shifts. Who needs the extra duties of a base coach? One of our players actually bench-jockeyed me for forgetting to wear a helmet in the third-base coaching box. "League rule, Skip!" he yelled.

I took the high road. "Zip it, you little shit. It's not my goal to grow up to be a third-base coach."

I made some good decisions as a manager and a bad one as a base coach. One night we were down 9–2 with one out in the bottom of the ninth. At that point the percentages say you've got no chance. Our second baseman, Trent Gilbert, all of twenty-two years old, whacked one into the gap. It's bounding around out there as he rounds second base and I'm thinking, *How cool would it be for him to get an inside-the-park home run?* So I sent him. I'd never do that in a close game, but why not give the kid a moment? Well, they threw him out on a bang-bang play. I was kicking myself until Gilbert trotted by me, saying, "Thanks."

We lost three in a row to the Burlington (Iowa) Bees. I was winless as a manager going into our fourth and last game at Burlington. We scored five in the fifth and held on, 6–4. Our players and coaches danced around the clubhouse after the game, taking selfies. I asked what they were celebrating. Somebody's birthday? "Your first victory!" someone said.

If I weren't such a cool, collected dude, I might have hugged them all.

That night I e-mailed my game report to the front office. A paragraph and a half, singling out Gilbert and a couple of others who excelled that night. A minor-league manager knows that his bosses don't want to read a novel. They get a nightly report from every manager and pitching coach in the farm system. Still, I try to add a little personality to my reports. *Tonight, we actually played the game correctly.*

☆ ☆ ☆

July brought the All-Star Game in Cincinnati. I never watched the ones I didn't make during my playing career. (Eleven of them, if you must know.) It's like the playoffs—you want so bad to be there that watching's like asking for a punch in the face. I've still got my three All-Star rings, though. They're not as diamond-studded as World Series rings, but each one's worth about $20,000. I've also got the World Series ring each member of the 1999 Braves earned. It's less impressive than the one the Yankees got for beating us that year, but I keep it in a safe place. I call it my second-place ring. Aaron got one of those, too, as a member of the Series-losing 2003 Yankees. Gramps and Dad each won a World Series while Aaron and I only came close—a fact that Dad will never let us forget.

These days I watch the big games. It was fun seeing Pete Rose get a standing ovation before the 2015 All-Star Game in Cincinnati. Yes, Pete had his failings, and they're going to keep him out of the Hall of Fame forever. Fair enough, he screwed up. I'm biased, but his 4,256 hits—*six great years'* worth over and above the 3,000 mark that makes anyone else an automatic Hall of Famer—matter to me. Watching him wave to his hometown crowd, I thought back to a Pete Rose moment nobody knows about.

In January 1991, Pete got out of a federal prison in Marion, Illinois, where he'd served five months for tax evasion, working in the prison's welding shop for 11 cents an hour. On the day they let him go, his son Pete Jr., my boyhood buddy, picked him up at the prison. Petey, who told me this story, was twenty-one at the time, a third baseman in the Orioles' minor-league chain. They were on the outskirts of Cincinnati, driving home, when they passed a mini-golf course with batting cages behind the mini-golf windmill. Pete said, "Pull over."

They rented helmets and bats. Pete stepped into the cage and took a couple of practice swings. "Turn it up," he told the attendant. "Fast as it'll go." He was facing an Iron Mike–style pitching machine, the kind with a metal arm that comes straight over the top. This being Cincinnati, everybody recognized him. They crowded around to watch the fifty-year-old Hit King, who hadn't swung a bat in his five months in stir. Here comes the first pitch. *Whack*—he rips a bullet that boings off the arm of the machine, hard enough to bend it. The machine tries again, but can't grip the next ball. *Pete broke it!* The fans hoot and holler. He hands the bat to Petey and says, "Some shit never changes."

That moment meant more to me than last year's trumped-up Midsummer Classic. Who won? Who cares? It is *a joke* that the All-Star Game decides which team gets home-field advantage in the World Series. I'm amazed that players, teams, and fans put up with such a crummy marketing gimmick. How can Major League Baseball let an *exhibition game* play a potentially deciding role in the World Series? I mean, I'm all for marketing the game in a world where MLB competes with the NFL, the NBA, and everything else on TV, but marketing can go too far.

Soon after the All-Star Game, I spoke to Beane, Fuson, and two other execs about a catcher in the Astros' system. "Jacob Nottingham—he's a beast," I said. Nottingham was twenty years old, six-foot-three and 227 pounds. He had the most precious resource of all, big-league power potential. A couple weeks later, the A's traded Scott Kazmir, a veteran starter with a 2.38 ERA, for Nottingham, who looked to be Oakland's catcher of the future—until February 2016, when the front office dealt him to Milwaukee in a trade for Khris Davis. My bosses made both deals, but I like thinking my input may have played a part in their decision to get Nottingham.

By late summer 2015 I was on my way to Vermont to join the Burlington Lake Monsters, Oakland's affiliate in the Class A New York–Penn League. This was short-season ball, where an organization's best new prospects get their feet wet in the pros. The club's first-, second-, and third-round draft picks were all at Burlington. The double-play combination had signed for a total of $1.2 million in bonuses. That's on top of their A-ball salaries of $290 a week. My job was to help twenty- and twenty-one-year-olds like them think like thirty-year-old veterans.

After a couple of days of watching, I met with the position players. At first I just answered their questions.

"What was it like in the big leagues?"

"Better than you can imagine."

"We're going to make it, right?"

"No. One or two of you, maybe. There are more early-round draft picks working at Walmart than playing in the majors."

I wasn't in Burlington to interfere in any way with manager Aaron Nieckula. My role was to promote a big-league approach. "Don't worry about striking out," I told the young hitters, because the modern game is risk-reward. "You want to swing hard and do damage. But situations matter. With a runner on third and less than two outs, *we do not strike out*. Because we are professionals. Do not give the ump a chance to call you out on a ball an inch off the black. Foul it off. Or nub an eight-hopper to short and *that's a run*. What's a run worth? A lot. To the team and to you. Because when you fight to get that run home, I'll notice. The organization will notice."

From Burlington I flew home to follow the end of the season. I've got my Gold Gloves in my den, plus a couple of jerseys, pictures of the Boone in his heyday, and an eighty-inch HDTV, my window into the 2015 postseason.

The Nationals were supposed to be there. With Dad supervising their minor-league system, they'd produced as much young talent as anybody: Bryce Harper, Stephen Strasburg, Ryan Zimmerman, Jordan Zimmermann, Anthony Rendon . . . But the Nats imploded down the stretch. In their ugliest moment, closer Jonathan Papelbon tried to choke Harper. Manager Matt Williams would claim he didn't see what happened, but he *knew* what happened and still sent Papelbon out to pitch the next inning. I would have banished Papelbon on the spot. He'd never throw another pitch for any team I managed.

The Nats fired Williams after the season.

The Cubs, with Schwarber in left field, made the playoffs for the first time since 2008. Under GM Theo Epstein, they look ready to contend for the next five to ten years. Epstein scared me by mentioning a friend named Carmine. Carmine was the database he'd used to rebuild the Boston Red Sox. "Like Carmine, we have one here in Chicago called Ivy," he said. "But that's only half the equation. To get ahead these days, you also have to take a humanistic approach." He was right about that, but c'mon. Who *names* his database?

In the National League playoffs, the Dodgers' Chase Utley, one of the game's most aggressive baserunners, plowed into Mets shortstop Ruben Tejada, breaking up a potential double play. Tejada broke his leg on the play. Aaron texted me. *Utley?* He was about to go on-air.

I happen to love Chase Utley. He's one of the best second basemen of the last decade, a hard-nosed guy who plays to win. But that slide was out of line. *Even dirty,* I told Aaron. Coming from me, no shrinking violet on the bases, that was saying a lot.

A week later, Toronto's Jose Bautista launched a game-winning homer in the American League playoffs. Watching the ball go out, Bautista made a show of flipping his bat. He might as well have yanked out his dick and waved it at the Royals.

Suddenly I was back in the news. Reporters asked what I thought of Bautista's bat flip. I didn't say much because I wasn't there. You can't weigh in on a moment like that without knowing the full history of the player and that pitcher, his team and the other team. (Between you and me, the guy went too far, like Utley. There's a line between legit celebration and acting like an ass. Bautista, a good guy, crossed it, and I'll bet you a C-note to a dime he regrets it.) According to Vice.com, "Bret Boone was the first player to develop a bat-flipping reputation. . . . Pitchers, as Boone pointed out, can showboat with a fist-pump, a celebratory shout, pointing at the sky, or literally falling over with excitement. Meanwhile, batters risk getting hit in the head with a fast object if they so much as smile."

Amen. As I've said before and will keep saying till my last breath, hitting big-league pitching is the toughest job in sports. I'm for giving a break to the batter.

☆ ☆ ☆

Baseball has never been healthier. We've had two sensational post-seasons in a row and I'll bet you there's a third one ahead in 2016. Look at last year's World Champions—the small-market Royals, with a throwback of a manager, Ned Yost, and a slew of slap hitters who get on base and keep rallies going. The Royals are modern *and* old-school. They're built on reasonable salaries, speed, and on-base percentage. They play smart, winning, entertaining baseball. They don't hit the ball over the wall like the 2001 Mariners, but in one crucial way the Royals remind me of that great club we had—they take pride in helping each other. When one of them hits a grounder to the right side to get a runner to third, giving himself up to help the team, they're all over him in the dugout, smacking him and telling him how great he is. If there's one thing I learned in Seattle, it's that team spirit's contagious.

But how long can the Royals keep their best players in Kansas City? That's a question for this year and next.

Baseball is richer than ever, thanks partly to my frenemy Bud Selig. The game is also changing faster than ever, entering an era when the good old national pastime becomes more of a science. The new era is *Moneyball* to the max, as computer nerds armed with ever-better analytics put old-fashioned baseball men out of business.

I see a backlash coming. I think there's still a place in the game for men who don't need an algorithm to tell them what to think. Men like Gramps. And Dad. And Aaron. And me.

Right now, the nerds and the old-school baseball men are at war. But maybe they can work out their differences.

I think that's the Next Big Thing in baseball—blending two seemingly opposite approaches into a winning combination. Analytics and instinct. Harvard IQ and baseball IQ. There's no equation that can bridge that gap. You need horse sense—or horsehide sense, to use an old term from Gramps's day.

I can't tell you how many times I've wanted to tackle the computer nerds before they could hand their stacks of numbers to the real baseball men. Because numbers are tools. They're input. You can't let them tell you what to do or you become *their* tool.

Example: Everyone shifts on defense these days. When a left-handed pull hitter comes up, the shortstop moves to the right side of the infield, leaving the third baseman alone on the left side. That makes sense at the major-league level, where hitters are set in their ways and the analysts have thousands of at-bats to build the charts teams use to set their defense—spray charts showing where every hitter tends to hit the ball. But the same strategy filters down to the minors, where the spray chart may be based on 15 or 20 at-bats and hitters are still learning what sort of hitters they are. That's crazy. The chart's meaningless, and the young hitter should be learning to slap the ball the other way. Or bunt!

Fans and "experts" often say defensive shifts are ruining the game. They'll be proved wrong in the next five years, as hitters adapt. Batters (and teams) who insist on pulling the ball into shifts will lose ground (and games) to those who use the whole field, and by 2020 today's shifts will look antique.

Example: Nerds don't always understand numbers.

A hitter in the A's system was useless against a particular starting pitcher. Zero for seven for a batting average of .000. He was left-handed and so was the pitcher. Obviously he had no business in the lineup. Unless you looked past the numbers.

I was *there*. I watched this particular left-handed hitter for a week. He changed his approach from at-bat to at-bat, reacting to the previous pitch, the one before that, and the one that got him out last week. And it worked. He ripped a line drive to the warning track in left-center. Caught. He pulled a bullet down the first-base line. The first baseman made a diving play. For a week, that hitter did everything right. He still went 1-for-22. His manager benched him. But to anyone willing to watch more closely, that hitter had a hell of a week. With a little luck he would have been 6- or even 7-for-22, with a batting average of .273 or .318. He was unlucky for a week, that's all. But that kind of week can stunt a kid's career.

I wanted to tell that kid he was my hero, but that's not my role. Not yet, anyway. I'm a cog in the Oakland organization—a grateful cog who might still be playing golf if not for Billy Beane, the maverick GM who gave me a chance to get back in the game at a crucial time in baseball history.

Right now.

I want to work with other baseball men to blend the latest tools with my bloodlines, the combined knowledge of almost a century of major-league baseball. I want to bridge the gap between old-school ball and modern analytics, to find a major-league mash-up of data and instinct that shows the way forward.

That's the *next* game changer.

KID IN A CAGE

Jacob Bret Boone is almost seventeen. He'll be a shortstop at Torrey Pines High School in 2016, his second year on the varsity.

Physically he's a late bloomer, like his dad. As a five-foot-three, 135-pound freshman, Jake was on the plump side, slower and softer than he'll be as he grows. Soon he grew to five eight and 180. Then he got serious about his diet and weight training, and now he's starting to build baseball muscle. The last time we looked he weighed 169. I told him, "I'm proud of you, buddy. You've become a young man. If you keep improving, you've got a chance to reach the next level."

That would be college ball. From there, who knows?

I caught him sneaking into my closet the other night. *What the . . . ?*

"What are you doing in there?"

"Nothin'."

Do you know what Jake was after? I had a scale in there. He wanted to see if he was down to 168.

We've made a couple of trips to the batting cages at USC. There's a brass plaque on the wall there:

HOME GAME

Boone Family Batting and Weight-Training Facility

This facility honors the baseball legacy of
Ray, Bob, Bret and Aaron Boone
who were the first family to play in the
major leagues over three generations

Jake has heard the family stories too many times to be impressed. He just wants to get his hacks in the cage. Sometimes he'll ask for advice, but I don't like to get technical with him. For the hundredth time I say, "Cage tips? Call your grandpa."

Last November, we drove over to Mom and Dad's house for Thanksgiving dinner. We were all full of turkey, watching an NFL game on the big screen, but of course the talk turned to baseball. Like any young hitter, Jake wants to hit home runs. Dad sat in his easy chair, talking technique. To hit with power, he said, Jake needs to keep his hips closed as long as possible.

I grabbed a bat and jumped up to demonstrate. Taking dry swings in slow motion, I launched a couple of phantom homers to right-center field. "Look at the knob of the bat," Dad said. "See how close it is to his body? Watch how he keeps the knob toward the pitcher as long as he can."

"That keeps the barrel in the zone," I said. "That's why Jeter was so good. He wasn't a power guy, but he kept the barrel in the zone as long as anybody."

Jake said, "Cool." He took the bat from me and tried a few slo-mo swings. Dad and I critiqued him—"Stay stacked," "Hands closer"—and Jake got it right.

"Oh yeah," I told him. "That one's going four hundred feet."

Then we had some pumpkin pie.

The way I see it, what my son really needs from me is moral support. So I've got it easy, because he's a star. All my kids are. Jake may be a ballplayer now, but I say in all honesty that I won't be surprised if he winds up as a CEO, a leading man in Hollywood, or president of the United States.

But right now, at least, it's the family business that lights Jake's fire. Good for him. But I don't expect him to be a big leaguer. While Jake's baseball IQ is off the charts, the competition's so fierce these days—the talent's so deep—that the odds are against him. But it all starts with passion, and he's got lots of that. Jake likes to *hit*. He'll rip a line drive in a high school game and I know he's thinking about doing the same thing in the majors around 2022. He's thinking about getting his name on that plaque at USC, thinking about being the first fourth-generation player in major-league history.

And wouldn't that be something?

BOONE FAMILY STATS

BRET BOONE

Year	Team	G	AB	H	HR	RBI	SB	AVG	OBP	SLG
1992	Mariners	33	129	25	4	15	1	.194	.224	.318
1993	Mariners	76	271	68	12	38	2	.251	.301	.443
1994	Reds	108	381	122	12	68	3	.320	.368	.491
1995	Reds	138	513	137	15	68	5	.267	.326	.429
1996	Reds	142	520	121	12	69	3	.233	.275	.354
1997	Reds	139	443	99	7	46	5	.223	.298	.332
1998	Reds	157	583	155	24	95	6	.266	.324	.458
1999	Braves	152	608	153	20	63	14	.252	.310	.416
2000	Padres	127	463	116	19	74	8	.251	.326	.421
2001	Mariners	158	623	206	37	141	5	.331	.372	.578
2002	Mariners	155	608	169	24	107	12	.278	.339	.462
2003	Mariners	159	622	183	35	117	16	.294	.366	.535
2004	Mariners	148	593	149	24	83	10	.251	.317	.423
2005	2 teams	88	326	72	7	37	4	.221	.290	.350
14 YEAR TOTALS		**1,780**	**6,683**	**1,775**	**252**	**1,021**	**94**	**.266**	**.325**	**.442**

AARON BOONE

Year	Team	G	AB	H	HR	RBI	SB	AVG	OBP	SLG
1997	Reds	16	49	12	0	5	1	.245	.275	.265
1998	Reds	58	181	51	2	28	6	.282	.35	.409
1999	Reds	139	472	132	14	72	17	.28	.33	.445
2000	Reds	84	291	83	12	43	6	.285	.356	.471
2001	Reds	103	381	112	14	62	6	.294	.351	.483
2002	Reds	162	606	146	26	87	32	.241	.314	.439
2003	2 teams	160	592	158	24	96	23	.267	.327	.453
2004	Did not play—injured									
2005	Indians	143	511	124	16	60	9	.243	.299	.378
2006	Indians	104	354	89	7	46	5	.251	.314	.37
2007	Marlins	69	189	54	5	28	2	.286	.388	.423
2008	Nationals	104	232	56	6	28	0	.241	.299	.384
2009	Astros	10	13	0	0	0	0	.000	.071	.000
12 YEAR TOTALS		**1,152**	**3,871**	**1,017**	**126**	**555**	**107**	**.263**	**.326**	**.425**

BOB BOONE

Year	Team	G	AB	H	HR	RBI	SB	AVG	OBP	SLG
1972	Phillies	16	51	14	1	4	1	.275	.333	.353
1973	Phillies	145	521	136	10	61	3	.261	.311	.365
1974	Phillies	146	488	118	3	52	3	.242	.295	.322
1975	Phillies	97	289	71	2	20	1	.246	.322	.329
1976	Phillies	121	361	98	4	54	2	.271	.348	.366
1977	Phillies	132	440	125	11	66	5	.284	.343	.436
1978	Phillies	132	435	123	12	62	2	.283	.347	.425
1979	Phillies	119	398	114	9	58	1	.286	.367	.422
1980	Phillies	141	480	110	9	55	3	.229	.299	.338
1981	Phillies	76	227	48	4	24	2	.211	.279	.295
1982	Angels	143	472	121	7	58	0	.256	.310	.337
1983	Angels	142	468	120	9	52	4	.256	.289	.353
1984	Angels	139	450	91	3	32	3	.202	.242	.262
1985	Angels	150	460	114	5	55	1	.248	.306	.317
1986	Angels	144	442	98	7	49	1	.222	.287	.305
1987	Angels	128	389	94	3	33	0	.242	.304	.311
1988	Angels	122	352	104	5	39	2	.295	.352	.386
1989	Royals	131	405	111	1	43	3	.274	.351	.323
1990	Royals	40	117	28	0	9	1	.239	.336	.265
19 YEAR TOTALS		**2,264**	**7,245**	**1,838**	**105**	**826**	**38**	**.254**	**.315**	**.346**

RAY BOONE

Year	Team	G	AB	H	HR	RBI	SB	AVG	OBP	SLG
1948	Indians	6	5	2	0	1	0	.400	.400	.600
1949	Indians	86	258	65	4	26	0	.252	.352	.345
1950	Indians	109	365	110	7	58	4	.301	.397	.430
1951	Indians	151	544	127	12	51	5	.233	.302	.329
1952	Indians	103	316	83	7	45	0	.263	.372	.367
1953	2 teams	135	497	147	26	114	5	.296	.390	.519
1954	Tigers	148	543	160	20	85	4	.295	.376	.466
1955	Tigers	135	500	142	20	116	1	.284	.346	.476
1956	Tigers	131	481	148	25	81	0	.308	.403	.518
1957	Tigers	129	462	126	12	65	1	.273	.353	.418
1958	2 teams	116	360	87	13	61	1	.242	.302	.406
1959	2 teams	83	168	44	4	19	2	.262	.394	.369
1960	2 teams	41	90	19	1	15	0	.211	.327	.267
13 YEAR TOTALS		**1,373**	**4,589**	**1,260**	**151**	**737**	**21**	**.275**	**.361**	**.429**

ACKNOWLEDGMENTS

Here's where I express my appreciation to all my teammates, coaches, and managers—too many to mention without making the book twenty pages longer. Thanks, guys! I'm also grateful to all my friends—you know who you are—and especially my mom, dad, brothers, grandpas and grandmas, Suzi Boone, and our children, Savannah, Jacob, Isaiah, and Judah.

I'm glad I met Crown's Matt Inman, an all-star editor, and got to write a book for editorial director Tricia Boczkowski, who believed in this project from the start. Steve Ross at Abrams Artists, one of the best agents in the business, put me together with the folks at Crown, including the terrific Julia Elliott, Ellen Folan, Kelsey Lawrence, Julie Cepler, Elena Giavaldi, and Courtney Snyder.

I had a good time working with Kevin Cook, whose book *The Dad Report* made me want to team up with him. Here's a tip of the cap to his home team: Pamela, Cal, and Lily.

Last, but never least, my thanks go out to the baseball fans of Seattle, Cincinnati, Atlanta, San Diego, Minnesota, and the rest of America, and to the game we all love.

—*Bret Boone, February 2016*

PHOTOGRAPHY CREDITS

FRONTISPIECE
Courtesy of the Boone family

INSERT
Page 1, top: Courtesy of the Boone family
Page 1, bottom: Courtesy of the Boone family
Page 2, top left: Courtesy of the Boone family
Page 2, top right: Courtesy of the Boone family
Page 2, bottom: Icon Sportswire via AP Images
Page 3, top: © The Phillies/Paul Roedig
Page 3, middle: © The Phillies/Paul Roedig
Page 3, bottom: Courtesy of the Boone family
Page 4, top: Courtesy of the Boone family
Page 4, middle: Courtesy of the Boone family
Page 4, bottom: Photo by Marty Orr
Page 5, top: Getty Images/*SI* cover
Page 5, middle: AP Photo/Jim Bryant
Page 5, bottom: AP Photo/Mark J.
Page 6, top left: Courtesy of the Boone family
Page 6, top right: Courtesy of the Boone family
Page 6, middle: Courtesy of the Boone family
Page 6, bottom left: Courtesy of the Boone family
Page 6, bottom right: Courtesy of the Boone family
Page 7, top: AP Photo/Mark Duncan
Page 7, bottom: AP Photo/Al Behrman
Page 8, top: Photo by Bill Mitchell
Page 8, middle left: Courtesy of the Boone family
Page 8, middle right: Courtesy of the Boone family
Page 8, bottom: Courtesy of the Boone family

INDEX

Aaron, Hank, 201
Abreu, Jose, 219
Aikens, Willie Mays, 27–28
Aikman, Troy, 79
All-Star Home Run Derby, 179–81
Alomar, Roberto, 145, 221
Alomar, Sandy, Jr., 145
Alou, Felipe, 159
Alou, Moises, 145, 159
Amaral, Rich, 113
Anderson, Garret, 84, 179
Anderson, George Lee ("Sparky"), 143
Angelos, Pete, 128
Arrieta, Jake, 218
Atlanta Braves, 135, 146–55
Ayala, Bobby, 117

Bagwell, Jeff, 97, 126
Baltimore Orioles, 73, 79, 101–4, 128
Banks, Willie, 73
Barberie, Bret, 79
Barrett, Marty, 70
baseball
    about the golden age, 217–18
    as international sport, 219
    autographs, 15, 38, 46, 90, 136–37, 168–
        69, 198, 206, 229
    bat flip, 216, 239
    bats, size/selection, 91–95, 233
    beanballs, 123, 154, 172, 181, 186–88

breaking in new glove, 168–69
clubhouse spread, 88–89, 96, 133, 229
groupies/hecklers, 90, 133, 136, 181
hitting and pitching, 137–39, 144–46,
    160–61, 174, 217–18, 230, 241–42
optional double play, 121–22
showboating, 215–16
signs, 29–30, 164–65, 170–72, 204
slash line, 96, 146, 149, 177, 186
strength and conditioning, 25–26, 156–58,
    163, 205, 217, 225, 227
switch to cowhide balls, 90–91
team chemistry, 170–73, 240
unwritten code/rules, 122–24, 133, 151,
    153–54, 171–73, 183–84
    See also Major League Baseball (MLB)
Baseball America, 97–99
Bautista, Jose, 239
Beane, Billy, 222–23, 237, 242
Belcher, Kevin, 73
Bell, Albert, 72
Bell, Buddy, 36–37, 61, 145, 169
Bell, David, 36–37, 169, 229
Bell, Derek, 72
Bell, Gus, 169
Bell, Mike, 37
Beloit (Wisconsin) Snappers, 228–30
Bench, Johnny, 23
Berra, Dale, 159
Berra, Yogi, 6, 14, 33, 159

Biggio, Craig, 72, 125–26, 141–42, 146
Bloomquist, Willie, 177
Blowers, Mike, 104, 113, 206
Bochy, Bruce, 143, 156
Bodie, Keith, 99–101, 116
Boggs, Wade, 50
Bonds, Barry, 7, 36, 93–94, 145–46, 199–201, 208, 210
Bonds, Bobby, 7, 36
Boone, Aaron
    2003 AL Championship, 7, 8, 188–92
    birth, 38
    drafted by Cincinnati, 126, 140
    heart problems, 142, 212
    injury and broken contract, 194–95
    marriage, 194
    photograph, *ii*
    playing for teams, 159, 212–13
    playing in All-Star Game, 185–86
    retirement, 213
    statistics, 248
    television broadcasting, 216–17, 228
    traded to Yankees, 181, 186
    USC baseball, 125
Boone, Brandon, 213
Boone, Bret, growing up
    birth and naming, 21
    earning his first car, 68–69
    learning to play baseball, 8–9, 33–37, 49–55, 69–70
    photograph, *ii*
    USC scholarship, 75–85, 90, 231, 233
Boone, Bret, playing career
    1987 MLB draft, 72–73
    called up to majors, 100–104
    drafted by Seattle, 85–86
    Gold Glove Award, 7, 142, 177, 185–86, 197, 210, 223, 262
    hitting breaking ball, 104–7
    injuries, 159–60
    Jose Conseco's accusations against, 202–5
    marriage/children, 133–34, 143, 214
    movie career, 82–83
    MVP award, 27, 84, 175
    player's union activities, 126–31
    playing in minors, 87–100
    return to Seattle, 161–85
    rookie hazing, 108–10
    Silver Slugger Award, 186, 197, 210, 262
    slash line, 96, 146, 177, 186
    statistics, 5, 248
    television broadcasting, 186–92
    traded to Atlanta, 146–55
    traded to Cincinnati, 117–18

    traded to Minnesota, 206
    traded to San Diego, 155–58
Boone, Bret, retired from playing
    alcohol abuse and rehab, 207–9, 231
    attempted comeback, 209–11
    coaching Little League, 1–3, 214–15
    hired as Oakland assistant, 222–34
    manager/coach, minor league, 6, 234–40
    relationship with children, 213–14
Boone, Daniel, 9
Boone, Don, 196
Boone, Ike, 11
Boone, Isaiah and Judah, 207, 214, 221
Boone, Jacob Bret ("Jake")
    autographed ball glove, 229
    continuing family legacy, 243–45
    getting technical advice, 214
    playing high school varsity, 227, 243
    playing Little League ball, 1–3, 207
    visit at spring training camp, 226–27
Boone, Laura Cover, 188, 194, 213
Boone, Matthew ("Matt"), 191
    birth and naming, 45–46
    health, injury and retirement, 142, 193
    playing golf, 211–12
    playing high school ball, 125
    playing Little League ball, 54
    running family business, 7, 193–94
    size matters, 81
Boone, Patsy Brown ("Grandma Patsy"), 12, 17, 20, 34, 57, 68, 70, 134, 196, 198
Boone, Raymond
    birth and childhood, 9–10
    breaking into MLB, 6–7, 22–23
    declining health/death, 185, 196–200
    marriage and children, 12
    photograph, *ii*
    playing for Boston Red Sox, 14–15
    playing for Chicago White Sox, 13
    playing for Detroit Tigers, 11–14
    playing for Kansas City Royals, 13
    playing for Milwaukee Braves, 14
    Rookie of the Year award, 23
    scout for Red Sox, 17, 22, 69–71, 197
    signing with Cleveland Indians, 10–11
    statistics, 7, 15, 249
Boone, Robert ("Bob")
    1980 World Series, 7
    athletic ability, 17–19, 25–26
    birth and childhood, 12–13
    breaking into MLB, 6–7
    Cincinnati coach, 119–20, 125, 133
    hired by Nationals, 7, 42, 209, 221, 228, 238

Index

Boone, Robert ("Bob") (cont'd)
  injuries, 27, 37
  managing KC Royals, 140, 142, 159
  managing Reds, 159
  managing Tacoma Tigers, 119
  marriage/children, 20–21, 38, 45–46
  photograph, ii
  playing in low minors, 87–90
  playing Little League ball, 14
  playing with Phillies, 19–31
  sold to Angels, 56–57
  statistics, 7, 85, 249
Boone, Rod, 12
Boone, Savannah, 143, 196, 213–14
Boone, Sue Brown ("Mom"), 20–21, 33–41,
    43, 45–46, 56, 125
Boone, Suzi Riggins, 133–34, 143, 207
Boone, Terry, 12
Boston Braves, 11, 53
Boston Celtics, 21
Boston Red Sox, 7–8, 14, 60, 153–54, 188,
    190, 194, 198, 208, 213, 239
Bowa, Larry, 46
Bowden, Jim, 117, 146–47, 181, 209–10
Bremigan, Nick, 30
Brett, George, 27, 43–44, 53
Brett, Ken, 23
Brooklyn Dodgers, 10, 42, 47–48. *See also* Los
    Angeles Dodgers
Brown, Betty and Martha, 12
Brown, Bud, 196
Brown, George, 12, 21
Brown, Kevin, 138
Bryant, Kris, 233
Buck, Joe, 187, 191
Buford, Damon, 79
Buford, Don, 79
Buhner, Jay, 103, 109–10, 117, 161, 166
Bull Durham (movie), 8, 82, 90
Bullinger, Jim, 132
Bumgarner, Madison, 218
Burlington (Iowa) Bees, 235
Burlington (VT) Lake Monsters, 237–38
Burnitz, Jeromy, 73, 84

Calgary Cannons, 99–102, 105, 113–16, 231
California Angels, 24, 56–57, 59–62, 65–66,
    76, 80, 82, 84, 155, 164, 174, 203, 226,
    249
Cameron, Mike, 163, 170, 178
Campanis, Al and Jim, Sr., 62–63
Campanis, Jim, Jr., 62–63, 65, 78–80, 83,
    95, 97, 111
Campbell, Nolan, 19

Cano, Robinson, 24
Canseco, Jose, 114, 202–3
Cardenal, Jose, 28
Carew, Rod, 50, 67
Carlton, Steve ("Lefty"), 7–8, 23, 25–27, 40,
    43, 46, 51–53, 56, 199, 217–18
Carnell, Kevin, 214
Carpenter, Chris, 72
Carter, Joe, 94
Cashman, Brian, 195
Cespedes, Yoenis, 219
Chapman, Aroldis, 178, 218
Chicago Cubs, 27, 94, 132, 233–34, 238–39
Chicago White Sox, 13, 72, 79, 85, 128, 219
Cincinnati Reds, 7, 37, 49–50, 103, 114,
    117–26, 132–33, 140–46, 155, 159,
    161, 172–73, 181, 185–86, 248
Cirillo, Jeff, 79
Clark, Tony, 84
Clemens, Roger, 66, 139, 149, 153–54, 172,
    181, 188, 192, 199, 206, 218, 230
Cleveland Indians, 6, 11–12, 18, 36–37, 53,
    65, 164–66, 248–49
Cobb, Ty, 50, 91, 198
Colon, Bartolo, 228
Columbus Clippers, 209–10
Compton, Ken, 85
Coolbaugh, Scott, 73
Costo, Tim, 83
Cox, Bobby, 143, 150–55, 157, 170, 183
Cronin, Joe, 14
Cuba, 81–82, 219
Cy Young Award, 13, 26–27

DeCinces, Doug, 82–83, 128
Delgado, Carlos, 179
DeShields, Delino, 72
Diaz, Bo, 56
Diaz, Einar, 166
Dibble, Rob, 114
DiMaggio, Joe, 53, 91, 201
drugs, 195, 200, 202–5
Duncan, Mariano, 125
Durham, Ray, 85

Easley, Damion, 67
Eckersley, Dennis, 216
Edmonds, Jim, 179
Epstein, Theo, 239
Eugene (Oregon) Emeralds, 22

Fehr, Donald, 127, 129–30
Feinstein, Dan, 230
Feller, Bob, 199

Fernandez, Tony, 120
Field of Dreams (movie), 79
Finley, Steve, 73
Fisk, Carlton, 40, 65
Flood, Curt, 129
Fonda, Jane, 150
Forsch, Ken, 56
Forst, David, 230
Fox, Nellie ("Mighty Mite"), 13
Frederick Keys, 87
Fryman, Travis, 72
Fuson, Grady, 230, 232, 237

Garagiola, Joe, 45
Garcia, Carlos, 125
Garcia, Freddy, 166–67
Garcia, Karim, 187
Garciaparra, Nomar, 126
Gardiner, Mike, 154
Gehrig, Lou, 91
Giambi, Jason, 179, 180, 189, 192, 203
Gibson, Kirk, 185
Gilbert, Trent, 235
Giles, Bill, 47
Gillespie, Mike, 78–80, 83–84, 125
Girardi, Joe, 152–53
Glavine, Tom, 8, 128, 135–37, 146–48, 164
Glenn, John, 11
Gold Glove Award
    Biggio, Craig, 141–42
    Boone family statistics, 7
    Boone, Bob, 25, 40, 56, 85, 119, 194
    Boone, Bret, 142, 177, 185–86, 197, 210, 223, 262
    Larkin, Barry, 122
    Rose, Pete, 50
    Schmidt, Mike, 27
    selection, 161
    Wilson, Dan, 118
golf, comparison to baseball, 211–12
Gonzalez, Juan, 167, 203
Great Depression, 10
Green, Dallas, 25, 46, 48, 51
Greenberg, Hank, 11–12
Greinke, Zack, 218
Griffey, Ken, Jr., 7, 72–73, 103, 110, 117, 120, 145, 159, 163, 166, 170, 201
Guerrero, Pedro, 62
Guerrero, Vladimir, 218
Gullotti (Mrs.), 64
Gullotti, Steve, 67
Gutierrez, Jimmy, 133
Gwynn, Tony, 50, 53, 146, 156–58, 170

Hamels, Cole, 218
Hanson, Erik, 117
Harkins, Brian ("Bubba"), 65–66, 110
Harnisch, Pete, 72
Harper, Bryce, 238
Hegan, Mike, 145
Hemond, Jay, 79
Hemond, Roland, 79
Henderson, Rickey, 66, 114, 121, 126, 226
Hernandez, Felix, 218
Hernandez, Orlando ("El Duque"), 149
Hershiser, Orel, 62
Herzog, Dorrel ("Whitey"), 13, 143
Hoefling, Gus, 26
Hoffer, Richard, 167–68
Hoffman, Trevor, 1, 156, 208, 214
Hollins, Dave, 73
Horn, Sam, 70
Houston Astros, 12, 27, 125–26, 141, 149, 212–13, 228, 237, 248
Hubbard, Glenn, 152
Hudson, Tim, 138–39
Hundley, Todd, 145
Hunter, Brian, 150
Hunter, James ("Catfish"), 129
Hunter, Torii, 168

Jackson, Bo, 96–97
Jackson, Reggie, 23, 66–67, 111, 164
Jacksonville Suns, 96–97, 111
Japan, 166, 219, 225, 231
Javier, Stan, 170
Jeter, Derek, 8, 149–50, 186, 189, 192, 195, 244
John, Thomas, Jr. ("Tommy"), 42
Johnson, Davey, 118–20, 125, 132–33, 149
Johnson, Nick, 189
Johnson, Randy, 163, 167, 170, 199, 217
Jones, Andruw, 148
Jones, Larry ("Chipper"), 84, 97, 146, 148, 167
Jones, Todd, 215
Jongewaard, Roger, 86
Jordan, Brian, 149–50
Joyner, Wally, 66, 155
Juiced (Canseco), 202
juicing/drugs/steroids, 202–5

Kaat, Jim, 25
Kang, Jung Ho, 219
Kansas City Royals, 7, 12, 27–31, 62, 85, 96, 140, 142, 159, 239–40
Katz, Adam, 222
Kazmir, Scott, 237

Index

Kent, Jeff, 71–72, 221
Kershaw, Clayton, 217–18
Keuchel, Dallas, 138
Kimbrel, Craig, 218
Klesko, Ryan, 149, 155
Knoblauch, Chuck, 152
Konerko, Paul, 126
Koufax, Sandy, 53, 62

Landis, Kenesaw Mountain, 128, 131
Lankford, Ray, 73
Larkin, Barry, 118, 120–25, 133–34, 146, 148, 159
Larsen, Don, 185
La Russa, Tony, 143
Lasorda, Tommy, 47–48, 143
Law, Vance, 145
Lawrie, Brett, 94
Lee, Derek, 73
Liepman, Keith, 225, 230
Linares, Omar, 81
Little, Grady, 189
Lockhart, Keith, 150–51
Lofton, Kenny, 166
Lonborg, Jim, 23, 25
Los Angeles Dodgers, 62, 125, 134, 155, 219, 239. *See also* Brooklyn Dodgers
Los Angeles Times, 79, 84
For Love of the Game (movie), 82
Luzinski, Greg, 27, 37, 40–42, 46, 55
Luzinski, Jean, 40–41, 45
Luzinski, Kim and Ryan, 41–42, 46
Lynn, Fred, 43, 60

Mack, Connie, 198
Mack, Earle, 159
Maddox, Garry, 47
Maddux, Greg, 135, 137, 139, 146, 148–50, 152, 164, 178, 206, 210, 220, 230
Major League Baseball (MLB)
  as Boone family business, 5–8
  draft process, 72–73, 233
  free agency, 23, 113, 117, 128, 163, 198
  getting harder and better, 6, 41–42, 201, 216–18, 240–42
  injury epidemic, 42
  juicing/steroids, 195, 200, 202–5
  MVP, 27, 50, 84, 149, 175, 190, 218
  parks, design/size, 160–61, 228–29
  players' strike, 126–32
  race/racism, 62, 201
  "reserve clause," 23–24, 127
  role of commissioner, 128–31, 181–82
  role of manager, 162–63, 229

Rule 21(d), 49
salaries/salary cap, 24, 126, 129–31, 135, 155, 177, 234
spring training, 227–28
television broadcasting, 216–20
  See also baseball; World Series
Major League Baseball Hall of Fame, 24–25, 49–50, 151, 216, 221, 226
Major League Baseball Players Association (MLBPA), 23–24
Manfred, Rob, 130, 182
Mantle, Mickey, 13
Maris, Roger, 13
Martin, Billy, 65
Martin, Russell, 230
Martinez, Edgar ("Papi"), 93, 106–8, 166–67, 169–70, 178, 182, 185, 206, 225
Martinez, Marty, 123
Martinez, Pedro, 138, 153, 187–88, 219
Martinez, Tino, 149
Matheny, Mike, 143, 169
Matsui, Hideki, 187, 189, 192
Matthews, Gary, 23
Mattingly, Don, 66
Mays, Willie, 50, 201
McCarver, Tim, 187
McDowell, Jack, 72
McGraw, Frank ("Tug"), 25, 28–30, 52, 56
McGraw, Marky, 46
McGwire, Mark, 81, 114, 200, 202–3
McKaskill, Kirk, 226
McKeon, Jack, 146
McLaren, John, 114–15, 175, 179
McLemore, Mark, 164, 170–71
McNally, Dave, 23
McRae, Brian, 36, 159
McRae, Hal, 36, 159
Melvin, Bob, 184
Messersmith, Andy, 23, 129
Michaels, Tim, 156
Mickelson, Phil, 211
Miller, Marvin, 23–24, 38, 54, 127, 129
Milligan, Randy, 104
Millwood, Kevin, 148
Milwaukee Braves, 14
Milwaukee Brewers, 1, 126, 128
Minneapolis Millers, 10
Minnesota Twins, 73, 75, 117, 206
Miñoso, Orestes ("Minnie"), 219
Mitchell, Kevin, 120
Molitor, Paul, 128
Mondesi, Raul, 99
Moneyball (movie), 222, 240
Montague, Ed, 166, 183–84

Montreal Expos, 23, 26–27, 127, 144, 159, 231
Morandini, Mickey, 83
Morgan, Joe, 27, 49–50
Morgan, Mike, 173, 203–5
Morris, Hal, 120, 124, 127
Morris, Tom, 211
Moyer, Jamie, 166, 178, 182, 185, 220
Mr. Baseball (movie), 82–83
Murray, Eddie, 129
Musial, Stan, 10
Mussina, Mike, 73, 84
Myers, Dave, 164–65

Nauert, Paul, 184
Neagle, Denny, 146–48
Nen, Robb, 67
New York Giants, 10
New York Mets, 23, 73, 118, 149, 207, 219, 228, 239
New York Yankees, 7, 10–11, 27, 65, 114, 128, 139, 149–56, 159, 169, 174, 181, 186–92, 194–95, 202, 216, 236
Nieckula, Aaron, 238
Nixon, Otis, 152
Nomo, Hideo, 134
Nottingham, Jacob, 237

Oakland A's, 6, 7, 23, 94, 111, 114, 119–20, 170, 182–85, 222–30, 237, 242
Olerud, John, 160, 166–67, 169–70
Oliver, Joe, 120–21
O'Neill, Paul, 150
Ortiz, David ("Big Papi"), 106
Ortiz Colón, Adalberto ("Junior"), 115
Otis, Amos, 28
Ozark, Danny, 22, 25, 42–43

Palet, Dave, 227
Palmeiro, Rafael, 203
Papelbon, Jonathan, 238
Parrish, Lance, Jr., 103
Peavy, Jake, 201
Peete, Rodney, 79
Peninsula Pilots, 86–90, 102
Perez, Eddie, 150
Perez, Tony, 120
performance-enhancing drugs, 200, 203–5
Pettitte, Andy, 149, 152, 192
Philadelphia Phillies, 7–8, 19–31, 36–39, 42–44, 46, 48, 51–52, 56–57, 94, 249
Phillie Phanatic (mascot), 47–48
Pierzynski, A. J., 126
Pineiro, Joel, 185

Piniella, Lou, 113–17, 161–67, 170, 225
Pittsburgh Pirates, 62, 125, 219, 228
Plantier, Phil, 70
Playboy (magazine), 194
Plummer, Bill, 103, 109
Plunk, Eric, 115
Posada, Jorge, 189, 192
Puerto Rico, 35–36, 106, 219
Puig, Yasiel, 219
Pujols, Albert, 179

Quad City River Bandits, 228

race/racism, 62, 201
Raines, Tim ("Rock"), 156
Raleigh-Durham Phillies, 19–20, 22
Ramirez, Manny, 167
Raymond, Dave, 47–48
Raymond, Tubby, 47
Reading (Pennsylvania) Phillies, 22
Reich, Tom, 155, 162
Reinsdorf, Jerry, 128, 130–31
Rendon, Anthony, 238
Reynolds, Harold, 99, 113, 154
Rhodes, Arthur Lee, 87–88, 103–4
Rice, Jim, 43
Rijo, Jose, 120, 133
Riordan, Fran, 229, 234
Ripken, Billy, 159
Ripken, Cal, Jr., 65–66, 159
Ripken, Cal, Sr., 159
Rivera, Mariano, 139, 150, 152, 186, 192, 206
Roberts, Robin, 13
Robertson, Daniel, 224–25
Robinson, Frank, 35
Robinson, Jackie, 201
Rocker, John, 150, 166
Rodriguez, Alex ("A-Rod"), 163, 167–68, 170, 179, 195, 201
Rodriguez, Francisco ("K-Rod"), 217
Rodriguez, Ivan, 203
Rogers, Steve, 23, 127–28
Roosevelt, Franklin D., 131
Rose, Pete ("Charlie Hustle"), 7, 28–31, 33, 40, 49–50, 52, 67, 236–37
Rose, Pete, Jr. ("Petey"), 31, 46, 49–50, 236–37
Ruel, Herold ("Muddy"), 13–14
Ruth, "Babe," 91, 188, 198, 200
Ryan, Nolan, 27, 43

Sabatha, Carsten ("CC"), 199
Sabo, Chris, 204

Samardzija, Jeff, 139
Samuel, Juan, 117
Sandberg, Ryne, 221
Sanders, Deion, 120–21, 133
Sanders, Reggie, 73, 120, 149, 215
San Diego Padres, 1, 155–58, 170, 173
Santana, Johan, 138
Sasaki, Kazuhiro ("Kaz"), 166
Schepisi, Fred, 82–83
Schilling, Curt, 70–71, 139, 198, 208
Schmidt, Mike, 7, 22, 25, 27, 30, 33, 40, 46, 49, 67
Schott, Marge, 114, 125, 155
Schuerholz, John, 146, 148, 155
Schwarber, Kyle, 233–34, 238–39
Seattle Mariners, 72, 85–86, 93, 96–110, 113–18, 153, 157, 160–68, 174–80, 182, 185, 195, 197–98, 202–3, 206, 208, 219, 226, 240
Seaver, Tom, 40
Segui, David, 73
Selig, Bud, 126–31, 174, 182, 240
Selleck, Tom, 82–83
Sexson, Richie, 179
Sheffield, Gary, 179
Sheppard, Bob, 152
Showalter, Buck, 200
Silver Slugger Award, 121, 186, 197, 210, 262
Silvestri, Dave, 83
Smiley, John, 120
Smith, Lonnie, 56
Smith, Ozzie, 122
Smith, Rick, 226–27
Smoltz, John, 8, 135, 137, 146, 148, 153, 199, 217
Snead, Sam, 212
Snow, J. T., 67
Soriano, Alfonso, 187, 192, 195
Sosa, Sammy, 132, 179, 200
Sotomayor, Sonia, 132
Spahn, Warren, 11–12, 53
Sparks, Steve, 73
SportsCenter, 161, 215
Sports Illustrated, 79, 150, 167
Stanford University, 18–19
Steinbrenner, George, 128
steroids. *See* juicing/drugs/steroids
St. Louis Browns, 10
St. Louis Cardinals, 10, 169
Strasburg, Stephen, 238
Strawberry, Darryl, 150
Sunday Night Baseball, 166
Sutter, Bruce, 139

Sutton, Don, 66
Suzuki, Ichiro, 166–67, 175, 178, 182, 185, 219, 225
Swift, Billy, 138

Tacoma Tigers, 119
Tampa Bay Rays, 225
Tanaka, Masahiro, 139
Tanana, Frank, 59–60
Tejada, Ruben, 239
Texas Rangers, 37, 60, 61, 195, 227
Thomas, Frank, 82
Thomson, Bobby, 185
Thornburgh, Dick, 30
Tiny (clubhouse man), 88–89
"Tommy John" surgery, 42
Toronto Blue Jays, 94, 231, 239
Torre, Joe, 152, 167, 186, 189–90, 192
Turner, Ted, 150

umpires/umpiring, 49, 70, 97, 114, 161, 182–84, 230, 234
University of Southern California, 75–85, 90, 125, 142, 231, 233, 243–44
Utley, Chase, 239

Valenzuela, Fernando, 62
Valle, Dave, 180
Varitek, Jason, 126, 230
Venezuela, 51, 219
Veras, Quilvio, 155
Vincent, Fay, 128
Viola, Frank, 153–54
Vizquel, Omar, 121–22, 166

Wade, Ed, 213
Wakefield, Tim, 190, 194
Walker, Larry, 146
Washington, D.C., 129
Washington Nationals, 7, 42, 209–12, 221, 228, 238, 248
Wathan, John, 28
Wausau (Wisconsin) Timberjacks, 11
Wegian (Boone family dog), 40
Weiss, Walt, 148–50, 157, 206
Wells, David, 192
White, Frank, 28
White, Rondell, 84
Wilkes-Barre Barons, 12
Williams, Bernie, 149, 189
Williams, Esther, 12
Williams, Gerald, 152
Williams, Matt, 238
Williams, Mitch, 94

Williams, Ted, 10–11, 13–15, 25, 53, 91–93, 141, 199, 201, 210, 212
Wilson, Dan, 73, 84, 117–18, 161
Wilson, Enrique, 186, 189
Wilson, Willie, 27, 29–30
Winn, Randy, 178
Witt, Mike, 56
Woodward, Woody, 85–86, 97, 117, 161–63
World Series
    1903 beginnings, 26
    1948 Indians-Boston Braves, 11–12, 53
    1973 Oakland-Mets, 23
    1977-78 Yankees-Dodgers, 114
    1980 Phillies-Royals, 7, 26–31, 37
    1986 Mets-Red Sox, 118
    1990 Reds-A's, 114
    1993 Blue Jays-Phillies, 94
    1994 players' strike, 126–31
    1995 Braves-Indians, 135
    1998 Yankees-Padres, 155–56
    1999 Yankees-Braves, 149–55, 236
    2001 Yankees-Diamondbacks, 174
    2003 Yankees-Red Sox, 188–92
    2004 Red Sox-Cardinals, 202
    2007 Red Sox-Rockies, 208
    2015 Royals-Mets, 240
    Boone family at, 7, 8, 11–12, 21, 27, 37, 53, 85, 119, 149, 151–54, 236
Wynn, Early, Jr., 13

Yastrzemski, Carl, 43–44
Young, Denton ("Cy"), 217–18

Zahn, Geoff, 56
Zimmerman, Ryan, 209, 238
Zimmermann, Jordan, 238
Zobrist, Ben, 225
Zosky, Eddie, 83

ABOUT THE AUTHOR

Born in El Cajon, California, in 1969, **Bret Boone** reached the major leagues in 1992. He hit 252 home runs, drove in more than 1,000 runs, played in three All-Star games, and won four Gold Gloves and two Silver Slugger Awards in a fourteen-year career with the Seattle Mariners, Cincinnati Reds, Atlanta Braves, and San Diego Padres. A *Sports Illustrated* writer called him "perhaps the coolest guy in the majors—and one of the smartest." Boone lives in Southern California.

His collaborator, **Kevin Cook,** is the award-winning author of *Titanic Thompson, Tommy's Honor,* and *Kitty Genovese.* A former senior editor at *Sports Illustrated,* Cook has often appeared on ESPN, CNN, Fox News, and NPR. He lives in New York.